NEWS

Also by Alan Rusbridger

Breaking News
Play It Again

NEWS

AND
HOW TO
USE IT

Alan Rusbridger

CANONGATE

First published in Great Britain, the USA and Canada in 2020
by Canongate Books Ltd, 14 High Street, Edinburgh EH1 1TE

Distributed in the USA by Publishers Group West
and in Canada by Publishers Group Canada

canongate.co.uk

1

British Library Cataloguing-in-Publication Data
A catalogue record for this book is available on
request from the British Library

ISBN 978 1 83885 161 3

Typeset in Bembo Std by
Palimpsest Book Production Ltd, Falkirk, Stirlingshire

Printed and bound in Great Britain by
Clays Ltd, Elcograf S.p.A.

Contents

For the Committee to Protect Journalists,
whose mission is, sadly, ever more necessary

Preface

Who on earth can you believe any more?

I am writing this at the peak – or so I hope – of the most vicious pandemic to have gripped the world in a century or more. The question of what information you can trust is, all of a sudden, a matter of life and death.

As an average citizen you have four choices about where to find information on this new plague.

You can believe the politicians. That might work if you live in, say, New Zealand or Germany – less so if you are in Brazil, Russia, China, Hungary or the United States. And maybe not so much in Britain.

What about the scientists? As politicians have struggled for authority – or even understanding – some leaders thrust scientists and doctors into the limelight. We began to absorb many lessons in epidemiology, immunology, exponential curves, antibody tests, vaccines and the modelling of viral infections. And we learned that scientists disagree with each other. They harbour – and value – doubts. They even change their minds. To some this is reassuring; to others, confusing.

Or we can turn to our peers. As always, there is good and bad on social media; expertise and madness; inspiration and malicious nonsense. New words have been coined – infodemic and infotagion are just two – to describe an environment of viral information chaos which nevertheless has proved massively addictive as people the world over stumble in search of light.

And then there is journalism. There has been much to admire here: some brave reporting from inside hospitals and on the streets; some clear and honest analysis; some tough investigations into governmental advice and inaction; some brilliant visualisation of data and some admirably simple explanations of complex concepts. The best news organisations have performed a real, vital public service.

But – as with social media – there is bad to counter the good. Some were slow to grasp the immensity of what was happening. There will be a special place in journalistic hell for Fox News and its initial torrent of Trump-echoing propaganda. That coverage will have helped contribute to numberless deaths. There was lamentable confusion about how to cover the nightly parade of presidential lies, sulks, boasts and vainglorious irrelevance that flagged itself as public information. There was uncertainty about how to communicate risk.

Some news outlets – initially, at least – seemed unable to imagine the scale of what was happening: it was easier to report on what videos Boris Johnson was watching in his hospital bed than on the hundreds dying every day all around. The newsrooms that had jettisoned their health or science correspondents struggled. The idiots who suggested that 5G phone masts could be spreading the disease encouraged arson and trashed their own brand. So, it was a mixed picture.

Covid-19 could not have announced itself at a worse time in terms of the question about whom to believe. Survey after survey has shown unprecedented confusion over where to place trust. Nearly two-thirds of adults polled by Edelman in 2018 said they could no longer tell a responsible source of news from the opposite.

This was not how it was supposed to be.

The official script for journalism was that once people woke up to the ocean of rubbish and lies all around them they'd come back to the safe harbour of professionally-produced news. You couldn't leave this stuff to amateurs or give it away for free. Sooner or later people would flood back to the haven of proper journalism.

This official narrative was not completely wrong – but nor was it right in the way the optimists hoped it would be. There was a surge of eyeballs to mainstream media sites, but it was too soon to judge if the increased traffic would remotely compensate for the drastic loss of revenues as copy sales plummeted and advertising disappeared. It normally didn't.

At the very moment when the UK government recognised journalists as essential workers, the industry itself looked more fragile than ever.

Surveys of trust showed the public (especially the older public) relying on journalists, but not trusting them. Another Edelman special report in early March 2020 found journalists at the bottom of the trust pile, with only 43 per cent of those surveyed holding the view that you could believe them 'to tell the truth about the virus'. That compared with 63 per cent for 'a person like yourself'.

As the pandemic wore on, so trust in both UK politicians and news organisations slumped. Between April and May 2020, according to Reuters Institute for the Study of Journalism (RISJ), trust in the government plunged a full 19 points – partly, it was thought, as a result of newspaper investigations which appeared to show double standards between what the government was saying and what its top advisers were actually doing. But if reporters expected gratitude for their efforts they were disappointed: the same period saw an 11-point fall in trust in news organisations.

I spent most of my working life in journalism: I would like people to believe the best of it. I like the company of journalists and, as an editor, was frequently lost in admiration for colleagues – on the *Guardian* and beyond – who were clever, brave, resourceful, quick, honest, perceptive, knowledgeable and humane.

But it was impossible to be blind to so much journalism that was none of those things: editorial content that was stupid, corrupt, ignorant, aggressive, bullying, lazy and malign. But it all sailed under the flag of something we called 'journalism'. Somehow we expected the public to be able to distinguish the good from the bad and to recognise it's not all the same, even if we give it the same name.

The official story paints journalists as people who tell 'truth to power'. But 'truth' is a big word, and we seldom like to reflect on our own power.

Now, four years on from being full-time in the newsroom, I want to bring an insider's perspective to the business of journalism, but also look at it from the outside. How can we explain 'journalism' to people who are by and large sceptical – which is broadly what most of us would want our fellow citizens to be? This book aims to touch on some of the things about journalism that might help a reader decide whether it deserves their trust, and offer a glimpse to working journalists of how they are viewed by the world outside.

What follows is in alphabetical form and is, inevitably, quite subjective and a bit random. It deals with some aspects of how journalism – at its best and worst – is practised, thought about, paid for, owned, controlled and influenced. To many insiders these are givens: to many outsiders they are mysteries.

A decade or more ago none of this would have needed spelling out quite as much as it does today, with mainstream news such an easy target for deliberate and concerted denigration. But journalism has, it seems to me, always struggled to describe itself honestly, if at all. As long as the readers were there and the bottom line looked healthy, there didn't seem much need for the public washing of dirty linen. And, anyway, some of it was too complicated really to get into. Mix in the unhealthy omertà which can sometimes provide a shield from the uncomfortable scrutiny editors like to visit on others, and many aspects of journalism go oddly unexamined.

That feels like a strange thing to write in an age in which the sometimes obsessive social media microscope can be focused on the work of newspapers and individual journalists. It is also true that there is a small industry in the academic consideration of media. But – valuable as the best of it is – the harsh truth is that most of that research will never be read by a single working journalist, let alone the average reader.

So, some of what follows may feel terribly basic. What is a journalist? That is, in a way, the most elementary question of all – which doesn't mean it invites a simple answer. You can train to be a journalist, but you don't have to. We who think of ourselves as journalists can't quite decide if we're a craft or a profession, or neither. You can work for the *Daily Star* or the *Sun* and call yourself a journalist – but your conception of what's involved in the job would differ vastly from someone at the BBC or the *Frankfurter Allgemeine Zeitung*. Oh, and Julian Assange calls himself a journalist. So, while 'proper' journalists may despise him, his fate is – in ways we may only glimpse darkly – intertwined with theirs.

Proper journalists do 'journalism', and have done for three hundred years or more. But in those three hundred years no one has settled on an agreed method. Is there a consensus that everyone aspires to 'objectivity' in their work? No, of course not. What's gospel on one side of the Atlantic is mocked on the other. What's taught in one American

J-school is derided in others. Is there a common view of 'impartiality', 'fairness', 'balance' — or any of the other aspirational words bandied around to label what journalists do, or would like to do — or what others (such as the BBC) should do? No, there isn't.

Is there agreement on common procedures about how to correct work in the digital era? No. There are different metrics, differing ambitions; the aims are not inevitably the same. Some want journalism to be a form of public service; others care more about profit. Can we agree on a common concept of 'public interest'? No. We really struggle.

And does it matter? There have always been those who believe in the Big Tent theory of journalism: 'It's a rough old trade and we stand and fall together, always been that way, always will be.' Part of me believes some of that. Part of me embraces the messiness of what journalism is — its untidy edges and its irrepressible knack for reinvention and resilience.

But the problem today is an existential one.

Sometimes British journalism, in particular, feels like a knowing joke. If you're on the inside it's humourless and disloyal to let the side down. And a bit, you know, boring and woke. But professional producers of news are now in a fight for survival and in competition with many others who don't see it all as an in-joke. How can we explain why it deserves to survive — as, obviously, I think the best of journalism does? In an age of information chaos, a good newsroom is, to me, as essential as the police force, the hospital, the fire station or the prison.

How can we expect an outsider to understand all this? I have written in these pages about techniques, about transparency (or lack of it), about the people who own the press and how their influence works. I have written about some of the most celebrated practitioners of journalism and realise that, even after days spent looking into some of their work, I still have no measure of how much they should be trusted.

If that's true of me, having worked in this imperfect trade for forty years or more, how can we possibly expect an average reader to navigate this maze? Should they pick a brand rather than an individual journalist? We have seen all too clearly how institutions change. Titles that were once incorruptible, or at least honestly campaigning — the *Telegraph*, the *Express*, the *News of the World* come to mind — can mutate into organisations that are ethically and editorially challenged. Why, at their worst, would anyone single them out for trust?

And then there are things that, as I've come to write this book, I find myself unable to explain. I can't see why an industry that is fighting for trust and credibility would knowingly employ columnists who, for instance, are ignorant of the truth of climate change. Why would you do that? If journalism is trying to persuade sceptical readers that it is the safe harbour of reality, why would it handsomely reward and celebrate people for writing rubbish?

We have seen in recent years some high-profile failings of journalism, not least the phone-hacking scandal, which rumbles on to this day. Equally, there are heroes and heroines of reporting as glorious as at any time in a century or more. There is now more disinformation put out into the world than ever before, much of it politically motivated. The owner of a media business can raise or corrupt it. And rarely is a paper all good, or all bad.

So, it's hard to write a book with a simple message about journalism and why it should be trusted. Much of it should; quite a lot shouldn't. It is, as they say, complicated. We need to keep our wits about us as we consume all forms of modern messaging. A sceptical reader is a good reader.

And journalists need to look into the mirror a bit more and try to see themselves as others see them. The best of journalism will thrive. Maybe we needed a pandemic to wake us up to its importance.

A

ACCURACY

There is the technically correct attitude towards accuracy, and then there is the sometimes messy reality. The following is roughly what you will be taught in journalism school:

'Accuracy is the essence of journalism. Anyone can – and will – make mistakes but getting basic and easily checkable information wrong is hard to forgive. Names. Numbers. Addresses. These cannot be fudged if they are wrong: they are either correct or incorrect. If a news organisation has to make a correction, the whole piece feels tainted. If there is a mistake in the basics, how can a reporter be relied upon to get right complex and contentious issues addressed elsewhere in a piece?'

The advice will continue in this vein:

'Once a story is finished, re-read it to catch typos or other mistakes, and there invariably will be some. Some reporters will press send in expectation that a news editor, sub-editor or copy editor will pick up errors. Unfair. News editors, sub-editors and copy editors regularly pick up mistakes but the accuracy of a piece remains 100 per cent the responsibility of the writer. A mistake made while writing to a tight deadline is understandable but it is no defence. When there is no pressing deadline, the best journalists read and re-read a piece as much as they can, maybe even leaving it overnight to look at it again fresh in the morning. And then check again. And again.'

All good advice, and yet it feels like only the beginning. Note the 1947 Hutchins Commission into journalism in the US and its warnings about publishing accounts that are 'factually correct but substantially untrue'. Or read the German-American political theorist Hannah Arendt in 1961 asking the question: 'Do facts, independent of opinion and interpretation, exist at all? Have not generations of historians and philosophers of history demonstrated the impossibility of ascertaining facts without interpretation, since they must first be picked out of a chaos of sheer happenings (and the principles of choice are surely not factual data) and then be fitted into a story that can be told only in certain perspective, which has nothing to do with the original occurrence?'

Or note the carefully qualified BBC Academy definition of accuracy – or, as the corporation prefers to term it, 'due accuracy'.

What is 'due'? 'The term "due" means there is no absolute test of accuracy; it can mean different things depending on the subject and nature of the output, and the expectations and understanding of the audience.' The Academy then echoes the Hutchins Commission: 'Accuracy isn't the same as truth – it's possible to give an entirely accurate account of an untruth.'

Accuracy is, you might say, a destination: the journey is what defines journalism. If those who wish to practise journalism aren't striving for accuracy, it isn't journalism. But can even the journalists always – or even mostly – achieve it?

Take something apparently simple, such as the height of Mount Everest. It is a huge lump of rock, not the shifting sands of opinion . . . Isn't it? Actually, it is much more complicated than that and turns on – among other things – who did the measuring, when and how, and the nature of geology. Here is the online Encyclopaedia Britannica: 'Controversy over the exact elevation of the summit developed because of variations in snow level, gravity deviation, and light refraction. The figure 29,028 feet (8,848 metres), plus or minus a fraction, was established by the Survey of India between 1952 and 1954 and became widely accepted. This value was used by most researchers, mapping agencies, and publishers until 1999 . . . [In that year there was] an American survey, sponsored by the (U.S.) National Geographic Society and others, [which] took precise measurements using GPS equipment. Their finding of 29,035 feet (8,850 metres), plus or minus 6.5 feet (2 metres), was accepted by the society and by various specialists in the fields.' The Chinese and the Italians disagree and have their own figures.

So a journalist in a hurry (i.e. most journalists, most of the time) could easily stub their toe even on a relatively innocent-sounding issue such as the height of a mountain.

Now imagine the intricacies of reporting on climate change *(SEE: CLIMATE CHANGE)* – at any point in the chain from publication to subsequent arbitration or regulation – and having to exercise judgement over such bitterly contested territory.

The British press regulator, the Independent Press Standards Organisation (Ipso), regularly finds itself struggling to decide how to reach a view on the accuracy of competing claims about global warming. Typically, one or more distinguished scientists will complain about an article – often a comment piece – and point out what they claim to be significant inaccuracies. The publisher usually responds by arguing that this is merely a disagreement between people with strong views and that, anyway, comment should be free. Accuracy, in other words, is a matter of interpretation.

Ipso, in common with nearly every editor having to evaluate stories about climate change, simply does not have the in-house expertise to make judgements about the science. It therefore tends to consider the processes of checking or verification that were undertaken in advance of publication, as well as the steps to clarify or correct after the event. But on the issue of accuracy itself it is, more often than not, silent.

Transgender issues are another minefield in which Ipso's view of accuracy may turn on disputed use of terminology in an increasingly polarised debate in which different participants insist on 'their' truth.

Then there are foreign policy issues such as Israel–Palestine, in which the two sides can barely agree on anything to do with language, geography, history, religion or ethnicity, and where well-resourced special-interest groups monitor and stand ready to contest every mainstream article or broadcast.

When do you use the word 'assassination' (rather than 'killing')? Is it a wall, or a barrier, or a fence, or a separation barrier? Is it a border, or a boundary, or a green line, or the 1949 Armistice Line? Is there such a thing as a 'cycle of violence'? If so, who started it – or is better not to go there?

Is an outpost the same as a settlement? Are all settlements illegal? If the Israelis dispute that, should you always say so? Do the Occupied

Territories refer to Palestinian land or territories? What is 'Palestine'? Is there such a thing as a 'right' of return, and does it apply equally to Jews and Palestinians? When, if ever, do you use the word 'terrorist'?

All these conundrums are outlined by the BBC editorial guidelines and taught by the BBC Academy. Anyone who has ever had any involvement with reporting on the Middle East (or transgender issues, or climate change) will quickly discover that the term 'accuracy' – apparently so clear-cut and simple when taught in J-school – can, in fact, be a quagmire.

ACTIVE READER

A viewer slouched in front of their TV is the classic passive audience for news. A newspaper reader may make some more positive choices about what to read, and what to ignore, but is essentially in the same role of passively consuming the news.

But what happens when four billion people on the planet become connected and have the ability to respond, react, challenge, contribute? Will more of them become 'active readers'?

Active reading can, in academic terms, simply refer to the art of reading for comprehension – underlining, highlighting, annotating, questioning and so on. But, as social media took root, a few news organisations tested how willing their readers were to become involved in the process of news-gathering and editing. At the heart of this was the early digital age (1999) dictum of Dan Gillmor, then on the San Jose *Mercury News*: 'My readers know more than I do.' Not always true, but true enough to make the active reader an interesting concept.

The Dutch news site De Correspondent was born with the idea of incorporating active readers from the start. Jay Rosen, the NYU professor who became an adviser to the organisation, explained how the journalists were expected to have a radically different relationship with the reader than in traditional media. 'Expectations are that writers will continuously share what they are working on with the people who follow them and read their stuff. They will pose questions and post call-outs as they launch new projects: what they want to find out, the expertise they are going to need to do this right, any sort of help they want from readers. Sometimes readers *are* the project. Writers also manage the discussion threads – which are not called comments but *contributions* – in order to highlight the best additions and pull useful material into the next iteration of an ongoing story.' Some of these crowdsourcing techniques have been used by journalists on more mainstream papers, notably David Fahrenthold of the *Washington Post*.

The *Drum* profiled how De Correspondent works, using health as an example of how the reader can move from passive to active: 'De Correspondent's philosophy is that 100 physician readers know more than one healthcare reporter. So when that healthcare reporter is prepping a story, they announce to readers what they're planning to write and ask those with first-hand knowledge of the issues – from doctors to patients – to volunteer their experiences.' The site's co-founder Ernst-Jan Pfauth is quoted saying: 'By doing this we get better-informed stories because we have more sources from a wider range of people . . . It's not just opinion-makers or spokespersons, we get people from the floor. And, of course, there are business advantages because we turn those readers into more loyal readers. When they participate that leads to a stronger bond between the journalist and the reader.'

The British news website Tortoise, a 'slow news' outlet launched in 2019, adopted a similar principle: 'We want ours to be a newsroom that gives everyone a seat at the table,' wrote the editor James Harding (a former editor of the *Times* and director of BBC News), 'one that has the potential to be smarter than any other newsroom, because it harnesses the vast intelligence network that sits outside it; one that doesn't just add to the cacophony of opinions but prioritises and distils information into a clear point of view.'

With that aim they opened up their editorial conferences for readers to contribute. It was a bold and imaginative idea. Time will tell whether the tortoise eventually wins.

AGGREGATORS

One of the great dilemmas facing publishers since the birth of social media has been whether they should sit back and expect readers to come to their own platforms, or go to where the audiences actually were. The big tech companies smelled this weakness and created news aggregators. Join them, or dare ignore them?

Facebook, a huge driver of traffic to news sites, decided it was better to keep readers within its own proprietary ecosystem. Apple News was launched in 2015 and by 2019 had 'roughly 90 million' regular users. That's a big number – but publishers were unimpressed by the revenues they received from advertising, even if some of them liked the exposure and the ability to drive subscriptions.

Apple News followed in the footsteps of Google News (2002), available in thirty-five languages and said to be scraping more than 50,000 news sources across the world. Again, publishers could not decide if it was, on balance, a good thing (traffic, marketing, visibility) or bad ('theft', 'monetising our intellectual property'). Assorted publishers – even entire countries – resorted to legal action. Google sometimes responded by fighting the claims or sometimes by simply dropping content.

It soon became a crowded field. Feedly offered a personalised experience. AllTop even aggregated other aggregators (such as Reddit). Flipboard tried to win by feeding everything into a magazine-style layout. TweetDeck enables readers to break down their Twitter feeds by writer, issue or location. And so on.

The best aggregators are so expert at content distribution that it appears to make sense for some publishers to regard them as the main, or only, platform of distribution. But – apart from the commercial downsides (cannibalisation, lack of transparency and data, loss of a direct relationship with the reader) – there is also the problem that some readers stop even noticing which news organisation has created the original article: 'I read it on Facebook.' If you're trying to build a news organisation based on trust, but the readers can no longer easily distinguish your brand from any other, then you have a problem.

ATOMISATION

A printed newspaper was an amalgamation of a hundred or more issues, sections or passions. News, foreign news, football, weather, golf, fashion, crime, politics, crosswords, recipes, finance, relationships, human rights, education, sex advice, editorials . . . and much, much more. It was not long into the digital age before the penny dropped that almost every one of those segments or niches could be done better and in more depth on its own. The crossword no longer needed to be bundled up with news from Iraq or the share prices. The football didn't belong with the book reviews or the parliamentary reports. Welcome to the world of atomisation.

Everything has been atomised. Long stories are fragmented into simpler formats and chunks – a shareable tweet, an Instastory. The once-homogenised audience becomes a million individuals, each with their own personal obsessions and interests. Some want to delve, others to snack. Different subjects are targeted at various platforms. We are in an era of infinite choice. One-size-fits-all will, of course, live on so long as newspapers are printed and news bulletins broadcast. But the atomisation of everything else is here to stay.

ATTRIBUTION

Easy citation might be the humble hyperlink's greatest contribution to media.

In 2010, a *New York Times Magazine* article came under fire for heavy overlap with another author's work. In an op-ed, the *NYT*'s public editor (an independent editor tasked with overseeing journalistic integrity – a position the paper eliminated in 2017) responded by declaring that the issue went deeper than intellectual theft: it was a problem with journalism itself. 'Murky' rules for attribution make reporting much less transparent than academic scholarship, which has a strict set of rules *(SEE: FOOTNOTES)*.

So, the public editor prescribed links. A few hyperlinks to the articles of the accusing author, he suggested, could have given due credit, boosted her reputation, and put to good use the 'digital medium's distinct properties'. A win–win–win.

B

BIAS

The US and UK are mirror images of each other. In the UK most broadcasting is pretty strictly regulated, with an expectation that it strives to be impartial *(SEE: IMPARTIALITY)*. The national printed press, by contrast, springs from different roots: a two- or three-hundred-year tradition of political attachment.

In the US the positions are reversed. There, most newspapers attempt to be as balanced as they can, in their reporting at least, and it is the broadcasters – think Fox News and much of talk radio – which many regard as wildly biased. Both printed and broadcast media in the UK and US accuse social media platforms of creating echo chambers *(SEE: ECHO CHAMBERS)* or filter bubbles. This is usually done without irony.

Bias, along with inaccuracy, is one of the main reasons citizens give for no longer trusting mainstream media. But the most biased media outlets are often the most popular. People appear not to like the idea of bias, but in practice they lap it up – provided it confirms their own.

The people with the hardest job are those in the middle: the public service broadcasters required by law not to be biased. The three-year argument over Brexit in Britain ended up with both Remainers and Leavers vehemently convinced that the BBC was biased against them.

Bias can be boring: stories should surprise, upturn conventional thinking and undermine prejudices. But bias also sells.

BOOKER, CHRISTOPHER

Christopher Booker (1937–2019) was a British journalist and author, and one of the original founders of the satirical magazine *Private Eye*. For around thirty years he had a column in the *Daily* or *Sunday Telegraph* in which he railed against the tide of what he considered to be modernism and the arrogance of professional elites.

Booker's degree (from Cambridge) was in history, but this did not inhibit him from challenging the opinion of world-leading scientists on a wide range of subjects. His *Times* obituary in July 2019 recorded: 'Although he had no scientific training, he wrote prolifically in denial of the consensus on issues including the link between passive smoking and cancer (Booker was a 30-a-day man) and the dangers posed by asbestos. We were being "scared to death" by the dire and unsubstantiated warnings of those who wanted to interfere with our life choices, he believed. Such ideas caused enough consternation for the Health and Safety Executive to issue refutations of several of his claims. He was also a passionate denier of man-made climate change *(SEE: CLIMATE CHANGE)*.

'Needless to say, he was widely rebuked by the scientific community and he was sued by the United Nations' Intergovernmental Panel on Climate Change over accusations he made about its chairman. Booker was only encouraged by such skirmishes. If he was getting under their skin that much, he was convinced he must be doing something right. His campaigning was consistent and his message, unlike the climate, never changed . . . His writings in the *Daily Telegraph* on the European Union exasperated the paper's editor Max Hastings, who wrote in his memoir that "Booker's fanatical hostility to Europe increasingly distorted his journalism."'

Booker was, by all accounts, a charming and amusing man. But the fact that he held down a prestigious column in a leading newspaper for nearly thirty years while doubts were frequently raised about the truth of what he was writing is a telling indication of how Fleet Street thinks about opinion writing.

Why did so many editors continue to use him? Is controversy more interesting and readable than truth? Is fact-checking opinion pieces too labour-intensive? Or should readers understand an 'opinion' column in a newspaper to be just that – an expression of sincerely-held beliefs, no matter that they may have slender, or no, basis in fact. To many of his readers Booker was a near-cult figure who told them what they wanted to hear, 'bravely' defying the politically correct consensus. How many editors dare face down the loyal support of readers who are still handing over much-needed cash for their newspapers?

The *Guardian* columnist George Monbiot was one of several writers or organisations – and even judges – to question Booker's writing in his lifetime. In October 2011 Monbiot asserted: 'Much of his journalism consists of the reckless endangerment of the public.' It's difficult to think of a more serious charge. Monbiot cited Booker's false claims that the danger from white asbestos was insignificant, not to mention scores of articles insisting that global warming wasn't caused by humans. In February 2008 he wrongly asserted that 'Arctic ice isn't vanishing after all.' Monbiot also exposed rookie errors in Booker's writings about energy policy.

In April 2011 a judge took the unusual step of critiquing basic errors Booker had made about a child protection case. Judge Bellamy found that his articles contained 'significant factual errors and omissions . . . All of this underlines the dangers inherent in journalists relying on partisan and invariably tendentious reporting by family members and their supporters rather than being present in court to hear the evidence.' He quoted Lord Hobhouse: 'No public interest is served by publishing or communicating misinformation.'

Another judge, Sir Nicolas Bratza, former president of the European Court of Human Rights, complained to the Press Complaints Commission (PCC) that a column by Booker had misreported his statements about same-sex marriage. Four months later, Booker withdrew them and apologised. And then carried on getting the science wrong on CJD and asbestos, and making rather thuggish attacks on climate scientists with whom he didn't agree.

Many of these errors were chronicled in a number of columns by Monbiot, who directly challenged Booker's editors in an article in May 2011: 'While everyone suffers from self-deception, there must surely be a point beyond which editors decide that they have gone too far. If a journalist keeps making the same serious mistakes, across a wide range of subjects, and if his employers fail either to ensure that he improves the rigour of his research and writing or finds employment elsewhere, then they come to co-operate in a deception of the public. That, I believe, is now the position of the editors of the Sunday Telegraph.'

The *Telegraph* appeared to take no notice. When Booker finally retired in March 2019 the paper acclaimed him as a 'Fleet Street giant' and 'titan'. His obituary referred in almost fond terms to what the paper evidently regarded as 'controversies' rather than errors. 'His determinedly contrarian assaults on the scientific consensus, or what he called "groupthink", infuriated as many readers as they delighted, the more so since he continued to defend his opinions even when, as sometimes happened, they were shown to be based on inaccuracies.' The obituary added: 'His journalism carried an air of confident authority and his column was extremely popular among readers, who had the impression that they were at last getting a glimpse of the reality behind the scenes in the corridors of power.'

You might blink at several phrases there. A scientific consensus is equated with 'groupthink'. A leading columnist defended his opinions even when they were shown to be false. Booker carried 'an air' of authority. Readers believed they were 'getting a glimpse of the reality'.

Societies need contrarians and the awkward squad. It's not a bad thing to question a consensus. But a 'post-truth' media – one in which people who don't know what they're talking about are, for decades, given privileged platforms to denigrate people who do – is highly problematic.

Journalism positions itself as a safe harbour in a world of information chaos, a defence against fake news. It is hard to reconcile this self-image with the lionising of a figure who regularly peddled fakery and ignorance.

BOREDOM

When the *Mail on Sunday* was launched in 1982 it was not an immediate success. Within a short period of time its original editor had been moved on and its new editor, Stewart Steven, bounced in with a lavish advertising campaign which boasted: 'We're a newspaper, not a snooze paper.' The promise was simple: 'We won't bore you.' And, to the *MoS*'s credit, it was an entertaining paper that found a healthy readership and – nearly forty years later – is still with us.

Boredom is the editorial kiss of death. Make them laugh, make them angry, make them cry . . . but, whatever you do, don't send them to sleep. One of the journalist's skills is to take the dullest subject and make it feel important, or moving, or fun, or otherwise compelling. But much of life is actually quite boring. For many years the science of climate change was argued about in dry and technical academic papers. Nobody paid much attention to remote warnings of pandemics. The business of quiet, good, efficient government lacks drama or intrigue. The details of how exactly international trade agreements are negotiated could make even the most diligent reader nod off.

So, what's an editor to do? Boredom means fewer sales, which means less revenue and the whiff of failure . . . and, sooner or later, the sack. In an age of metrics *(SEE: METRICS)* anyone can quickly determine the pieces which are too dull for most people to read.

Here's what happens. A newspaper's managers will spot that some stories are read by a tiny number of readers. They are seeking to cut costs and to do less. An instruction goes out that the paper will in future not write the kind of story that was attracting a tiny readership. And so, quietly, the boring stuff vanishes. It may have been important, but this newsroom doesn't have an 'importance' metric. If not enough punters want it, they won't give it to them – and the readers almost certainly won't miss it.

It all makes perfect sense, except that a newspaper is sometimes there to tell its readers to eat their peas. We may end up, in the words of Neil Postman, 'amusing ourselves to death'. As he writes in the book of that title: 'Americans are the best entertained and quite likely the least well-informed people in the Western world.'

But how do you reconcile an 'importance' metric with a business model that relies on purchasers, eyeballs or clicks? The best tabloids were skilled in using what the former *Daily Mail* editor Paul Dacre termed the 'sugar-coated pill'. He knew that many of his readers were more interested in *Celebrity Big Brother* than in affairs of state. So Dacre unashamedly set out to create a paper that was 'sensational, irreverent, gossipy, interested in celebrities and human relationships and, above all, brilliantly entertaining . . . if [it is] to attract huge circulations and devote considerable space to intelligent, thought-provoking journalism, analysis and comment on important issues'.

Dacre was really articulating the recipe for any good tabloid. Any paper that can simultaneously manage to entertain and engage millions of readers while also addressing the great issues of the day can, as he argued, play an important role in democracy.

BREVITY

'I'm sorry I wrote you such a long letter; I didn't have time to write a short one.' This remark is variously attributed to Mark Twain, George Bernard Shaw, Voltaire, Blaise Pascal, Johann Wolfgang von Goethe, Winston Churchill, Pliny the Younger, Cato, Cicero, Bill Clinton, Benjamin Franklin and . . . but I am already going on a bit. Whoever said it, they were acknowledging that it is quite often harder to write something concise and well-structured than it is to ramble on at length.

But how long is right? If you look back at newspapers from the 1940s to the 1970s, when newsprint was either scarce or expensive, even broadsheet journalists wrote tightly. It was not unusual for the front page of the *Times* even in the 1960s to carry up to twenty articles. But as newsprint became more available and affordable, so reporters got used to writing longer and longer articles. And then, as reading switched to small screens and, often, to smaller newspapers, so the trend went into reverse. Numerous studies (backed by newsdesks' own metrics) also seemed to show that readers generally preferred shorter stories.

A few newspapers decided their unique selling point would be to swim in the other direction. The CEO of the *New York Times* (and former BBC director general) Mark Thompson boasted in his 2016 book *Enough Said*: 'Most newspapers, including such bastions as the *Wall Street Journal* and the *FT*, have reduced the average length of their articles, perhaps in the belief that, in the middle of a breathless modern life, even weighty news needs to be served up with what the hospitality industry calls portion control. The *New York Times* has moved in the opposite direction. Articles are longer than they used to be, sometimes much longer.'

But, in general, concision has always been considered a virtue in journalism. One of the greatest editors of the twentieth century, Harold Evans, put it, well, concisely: 'It is not enough to get the news. We must be able to put it across. Meaning must be unmistakable, and it must also be succinct. Readers have not the time and the newspapers have not the space for elaborate reiteration. This imposes decisive requirements. In protecting the reader from incomprehension and boredom, the text editor has to insist on language which is specific, emphatic and concise. Every word must be understood by the ordinary reader, every sentence must be clear at one glance, and every story must say something about people. There must never be a doubt about its relevance to our daily life. There must be no abstractions.'

BREXIT

Where to begin? We might choose, almost at random, the *Daily Mail*'s front page of 1 January 1973, with its joyous splash headline announcing 'EUROPE, HERE WE COME!' accompanied by another heading claiming some credit on behalf of the newspaper for the glad moment of the UK finally becoming part of the Common Market. 'For ten years the Mail has campaigned for this day. We have not wavered in our conviction that Britain's best and brightest future is with Europe.'

That front page might bewilder anyone under the age of, say, thirty-five, whose only experience of the *Daily Mail* is of a paper that grew ever more fervent in its clamour to convince its readers that Europe represented everything that threatened the country's best and brightest future. But likewise, we could skip forward nearly twenty years and meet a young and ambitious *Daily Telegraph* reporter in Brussels. The young Boris Johnson found the business of routine reporting on the European Union a bit, well, routine. He made a name for himself with a style of writing that was provocative, highly subjective and . . . perhaps we could settle for the word 'inventive'.

Take prawn cocktail crisps. Johnson announced in January 1993 that Europe was about to ban them. This wasn't true but, hey, the actual truth (about the drafting of a measure to reconcile the amount of sweeteners and flavourings in different foods) was kind of dull. It was altogether jollier – and fed into a narrative about the UK's loss of sovereignty – to write about crisps.

Johnson appeared not to care very much if his stories were denied. 'Some of my most joyous hours have been spent in a state of semi-incoherence, composing foam-flecked hymns of hate to the latest Euro-infamy,' he reminisced in a *Telegraph* column some nine years later. 'The ban on the prawn cocktail flavour crisp; the billions spent to export unsmokable Greek tobacco to the Third World; the European Commission's plot to scrap our double-decker buses; the tense inter-national row over the dimensions of the Euro-condom; the vicious and unprincipled dumping of French beef in the Sahel region of Africa.'

Johnson was becoming a star – much to the irritation of his colleagues in Brussels, who were instructed to follow up his stories, even if they weren't actually true. Johnson's finest hour, in his own terms, was a story in May 1992 as countries were taking it in turns to ratify the February 1992 Maastricht Treaty, which paved the way for the creation of a single European currency. The headline on Johnson's *Sunday Telegraph* piece read 'Delors plan to rule Europe' and suggested that Jacques Delors, the president of the European Commission, had a stunning plan to create a European government. The story, as Sonia Purnell's biography of Johnson recounts, was based on a casual conversation with the *Guardian*'s man in Brussels, John Palmer, who had written a dull-but-accurate version of Delors' thinking about such things as majority voting on page eight of his own paper two days earlier. In Palmer's telling, Johnson completely distorted his own story to produce the *Sunday Telegraph* version. Even Johnson was surprised when the Sunday paper ended up leading on his highly creative yarn with its punchy headline. '"Cor," I thought,' Johnson later recalled in his sub-Wodehousian style, 'that was a bold way of expressing it . . . That story went down big.'

Indeed it did. Anti-treaty campaigners marched through the streets of Copenhagen and – in the gleeful words of Johnson – 'derailed the project . . . the aftershocks were felt across Europe, and above all in Britain'. In Purnell's view that story lit the fire that would, years later, become the whole UKIP phenomenon.

Johnson would later describe this form of journalism as 'chucking rocks over the garden wall . . . [and] listening to the amazing crash from the greenhouse next door over in England.' In a single sentence Johnson describes a peculiarly British attitude to journalism – winking, not to be taken too seriously, but delighting when it is.

It also tells you that fake news is not a new thing.

It's difficult to put an exact name to what Johnson was up to in Brussels. 'He wasn't making things up necessarily,' remembered one colleague, David Usborne from the *Independent*, 'just over-egging to a degree that was dishonest . . . he played the *Telegraph* game brilliantly. I told Boris in a jokey way – you're writing out of your ass.' Though Johnson was writing for the supposedly upmarket *Telegraph*, the spirit of his style and intent wasn't a million miles away from the *Sun*'s notorious November 1990 front page – 'UP YOURS DELORS' – which invited the paper's readers to stop whatever they were doing at midday to stick two fingers in the air in the general direction of the 'French fool' and to remind him that his country 'gave in to the Nazis during the Second World War when we stood firm'. Wink, wink.

How much cumulative effect did decades of this stuff have on public opinion? Quite a lot. Here is a former editor, Andrew Neil – no great advocate for the European project – on how such influence works: 'Far more important in shaping political attitudes [than editorials] is the regular coverage in the news and feature pages over a prolonged period . . . day in, day out, in a relentless and sustained manner.' If, for twenty years or more, voters are given only one side of any story, it can't help but shape attitudes. That's what these editors were intending to do, and there's little doubt they eventually succeeded. Within twenty-five years of his eye-catchingly dishonest reporting from Brussels, Johnson had (largely) moved on from writing and was trying, through politics, to achieve the same ends as his journalism.

By the time Johnson was campaigning for Britain to part company with Brussels, democracies the world over were loosening their grip on truth. The man who would soon end up in the White House seemed to share Johnson's easy habit of sliding between facts and what his spokesperson would term 'alternative facts'. As the power of the traditional media waned, it dawned on politicians that they had much greater latitude for saying more or less what they wanted without fear of effective contradiction. Even if journalists wanted to hold them to account, most of their efforts could not keep up with the sheer scale and speed of digital transmission, itself cleverly exploited by politicians and their social media teams.

Yes, there were honourable attempts at creating a cottage industry of fact-checkers *(SEE: FACT CHECKERS)*. But this was a niche activity – and a passive one, responding to active lies, howlers, exaggerations and whoppers which could be pointed at but never extinguished. There were also honourable journalists reporting soberly and accurately on Europe – both in mainstream media and on social media platforms – but they were mostly drowned out by the people who shouted loudest.

The Brexit campaign coincided with the devastation of the traditional business model for newspapers. The previous decade had seen newspaper advertising revenues fall by 70 per cent. Circulation revenues had slumped by a further 25 per cent. Six thousand journalists had lost their jobs. As it happens, large sections of the British press had no particular appetite for keeping Johnson in check. They were – as they saw it – on the same side. And they were in the majority. If you added up the total monthly reach of the *Sun*, *Mail*, *Express*, *Telegraph* and *Daily Star*, there was a 30 million gap in readers between the consumers of Brexit papers (110 million) over Remain papers (80 million). The eventual Brexit referendum margin of victory was 1.3 million.

Whose will was being expressed in this campaign to lever Britain out of the European Union, and how did they do it? This becomes an unbridgeable chicken and egg question.

Most pro-Brexit editors would reply that they simply read the public mood right. The country had fallen out of love with Europe. Newspapers divided into those who were in touch with that shift in public opinion and those who weren't.

The counter-argument was that public opinion had been shaped over decades of being starved of any positive reasons to belong in Europe. Any reasonable concept of public service information – particularly at a time of a hugely consequential referendum – would see it as a near-sacred duty to inform voters about both sides of the question. If you only gave one side then you weren't doing journalism, you were doing campaigning. Neither side would give ground to the other – and this gulf between two ideas of what journalism is, or should be, is as good an illustration as you could have of the uphill struggle to convince a layperson that there is a single idea of what journalism seeks to do. Little wonder so many people find it hard to trust something when its own practitioners can't agree on what they are doing.

Of course, there was a third dimension, in addition to 'reading the public mood right' versus 'giving both sides of the story'. Let's call it 'doing what we're told to by the people who pay our wages'.

Richard Desmond, who bought the *Daily Express* and *Daily Star* with the proceeds of soft pornography, got to determine what *Express* readers were told. There was no pretence in his mind that his newspaper would seek to be even-handed. On the eve of the campaign Desmond had himself photographed with the UKIP leader, Nigel Farage, signing a cheque for £1 million towards his campaign. At that point the *Express* stopped being a newspaper in the ordinarily understood sense of the word.

The *Telegraph* – owned by the reclusive Barclay Brothers – had similarly lost its grip on the ability to distinguish between journalism and advocacy, and was notoriously fined £30,000 for an election email the editor sent to readers instructing them to vote Conservative.

The *Sun* – singing the tune of its proprietor Rupert Murdoch *(SEE: MURDOCH, RUPERT)* – was also confused as to why it was deemed to have stepped over a line by publishing a 'BeLEAVE in Britain' poster for readers to stick in their windows.

So there were three newspaper groups undeviatingly aligned with the beliefs of the people who owned them . . . as well as the majority of their readers. Though the owners had passionately-held views about how Britain should be run, none of them experienced the normal lives of the average reader who would be affected by the fate they wished on the country. Murdoch isn't even British, and spends little time in this country. The Barclay Brothers tend to divide their time between the tax haven of Monaco and the bizarre crenellated castle they built on a tiny island off Sark. Their tax arrangements – involving numerous secretive offshore funds and family trusts in order to minimise contributing to the public purse – are eye-wateringly complex. Richard Desmond has been similarly criticised on a number of occasions for his complicated ways of avoiding paying tax. It has been argued by some that all these individuals would prefer, for the sake of their own finances, to be outside any EU tax regime. That is what you call a conflict of interest. These were the people – along with the *Daily Mail* – who presided over the public discourse about the UK's relationship with Europe.

And they presided via tabloids, the breed of paper which thrives on loud, emotive headlines. The Brexit campaign saw three headline themes emerge: immigration, enemies and threats.

Immigration dominated, before, during and after the campaign itself. Day after day the message was hammered home in giant, shouty slabs of text: 'THERE ARE TOO MANY MIGRANTS'. 'BRITAIN'S WIDE OPEN BORDERS'. 'MIGRANTS PAY JUST £100 TO INVADE BRITAIN'. 'THE INVADERS'. 'MIGRANT SEIZED EVERY SIX MINUTES'. 'MIGRANT MOTHERS COST NHS £1.3bn'. 'WE CAN'T STOP MIGRANT SURGE'. 'MIGRANTS SPARK HOUSING CRISIS'. 'FURY OVER PLOT TO LET 1.5m TURKS INTO BRITAIN'. 'WE'RE FROM EUROPE – LET US IN'. And on and on and on.

Enemies came in a number of forms. 'ENEMIES OF THE PEOPLE' was the *Mail*'s notorious denunciation of the UK's '"out of touch" judges' for insisting that Parliament should be given a say in any plans for implementing the result of the referendum. If it wasn't the judges it was the BBC, or the 'loaded foreign elite' (such as the Remain campaigner Gina Miller). MPs whose idea of sovereignty encompassed the idea that they might vote according to their consciences were denounced as 'MUTINEERS'.

The threats did little to lower the temperature – never forgetting that an MP, Jo Cox, was assassinated in broad daylight on the streets of her constituency as she campaigned for Remain. 'CRUSH THE SABOTEURS', screamed the *Mail* at MPs who didn't go along with Theresa May's legislative proposals. 'WHO WILL SPEAK FOR ENGLAND?' 'IGNORE THE WILL OF THE PEOPLE AT YOUR PERIL'. 'GREAT BRITAIN OR GREAT BETRAYAL'. 'PROUD OF YOURSELVES?'

The story worked on two levels. One was political/ideological/emotional/personal – an increasing hardening of instinctive and polarised positions which did not shift much before, during or after the vote. The other was highly detailed and technocratic/economic/pragmatic/regulatory/legal/constitutional – the big picture and the small print regarding the gritty implications of a vote to leave.

The first sold newspapers and drew eyeballs. The second was dry, complicated and too easily dismissed by questioning who the hell were these experts to tell us what to think anyway. When Oxford-educated Michael Gove indicated that people had had enough of experts he wasn't necessarily wrong *(SEE: EXPERTS)*. The new wave of populist politics was premised on turning experts into the enemy: what the *Mail* used to term 'people who think they know what's best for us'. Any evidence that Britain might end up worse off, or less sovereign, once 'proper' Brexit happened was cut short with two words: Project Fear.

The BBC, duty-bound to be 'balanced', found itself caught in the crossfire between the two sides. It was supposed to be all the things that some Fleet Street tabloids were not – sober, serious, factual . . . and impartial *(SEE: IMPARTIALITY)*. Yet what did 'impartial' mean amid the blundering, fragmented, tortured attempts of the political classes to work out how on earth to deliver on a referendum result whose meaning – two years in – even the Cabinet could not agree on?

Did impartiality require BBC reporters merely to report neutrally on the daily 'he said, she said' of a peculiarly odd Westminster debate – including, in effect, two Conservative parties, a not-very-oppositional opposition and a seven-times-not-elected, self-styled political outsider in Nigel Farage?

'Impartiality' was complicated by the way the apparent centre of gravity had been so effectively dragged rightwards by the relentlessly Europhobic newspapers. People who continued to believe that Brexit was likely to be an economic and foreign policy disaster for the UK were in danger of being presented as undemocratic extremists – to be allowed a voice only if repeatedly challenged and balanced by fervent Brexit hardliners. We tended to hear less from what we might term the rational centre, or from the Gove-despised 'experts'. Entire programmes were so obsessed with the splits within one tribe that other voices – including bewildered European allies and colleagues – were pushed to the margins or remained unheard.

When it came to the post-Brexit referendum election of 2019 one or two skilled backroom manipulators (we can guess who) studied Trump's ability to persuade enough people that black is white and, rather than recoil in disgust, came to the opposite conclusion: it works. Coin one unforgettable message and stick to it. 'Get Brexit done' was brilliant, never mind that the meaning of two of those words ('Brexit' and 'done') was far from clear: this was an age of simplicity, not complexity. Even the so-called mainstream media would do far more to amplify that slogan than question it. Try this stunt: slap the words on a JCB digger and drive it through a pile of polystyrene bricks . . . and watch as news editors obligingly clear their front pages for the image. They were making posters, not doing journalism. And remember this: that, in most countries, governments have unusual power over public service broadcast media. So, in the event that television journalists seem to be getting too big for their boots, it is often useful to drop a heavy hint that there will be a price to pay. Maybe C4 has outlived its usefulness? Possibly it's time to privatise the BBC or wreck its funding model? That should do the trick.

If in real trouble, simply make things up. You'll be amazed how readily even the best journalists will repeat unattributable fictions (see the 'row' over the four-year-old boy in Leeds General Infirmary during the general election of 2019 and what 'happened' during the subsequent visit of health secretary Matt Hancock). By the time the journalists had corrected themselves and Twitter had spent twenty-four hours arguing about the truth, the world had moved on *(SEE: POLITICAL JOURNALISM)*.

So, as Donald Trump has discovered, the liars, myth-makers and manipulators are in the ascendancy in this age – and however valiantly individual journalists attempt to hold them to account, the dice are loaded against them. But many newspapers did the cause of journalism no favours by the way they covered Brexit. They simply couldn't help themselves. The cause was all. Any political or economic vindication will be a long time coming. The damage to the craft of journalism, though, was immediate and deeply felt.

BRIBERY

It's probably best not to. There was a time when journalists thought little of bunging a cop or prison guard some cash – untraceable tenners in brown envelopes – in exchange for information. It was considered so routine that the then editor of the *Sun*, Rebekah Wade (later Brooks), thought little of freely admitting to a parliamentary inquiry in 2003 that 'we have paid the police for information in the past'. Her fellow editor, Andy Coulson, jumped in to clarify that it was 'within the law'. But there, in fact, is no law that allows a police officer to accept money from a journalist.

Coulson and Brooks's colleagues and informants would learn this much the hard way in the wake of the phone-hacking scandal at News International. Coulson himself went to prison (albeit for overseeing other forms of criminality), while Brooks was acquitted – innocent, she said, of what was going on under her nose. But the company handed over millions of emails which led to a six-year investigation into the payments their journalists had routinely been making to public officials. It led to the conviction of nine police officers and twenty-nine others.

The journalists were luckier. Of more than twenty charged, only two were convicted. It turned out that juries were willing to be convinced by a public interest defence. That defence would doubtless have been relied on by the *Daily Telegraph* when, in 2009, it handed over a reported £110,000 to a Whitehall mole – believed to be a disaffected civilian worker – in return for details about all the expenses MPs had been claiming. But the 2010 Bribery Act and amendments to the Criminal Justice and Courts Act 2015 allowed journalists to be prosecuted and face up to ten years in prison, with no public interest defence easily available. So bribery may go the way of three-hour lunches, dodgy taxi receipts and newsroom smoking, to become things of the past.

BUY-UPS

If a newspaper has a source who is selling sensational beans – probably about sex – they must be kept out of range of any other newspaper until the story has lost its commercial value. This leads to a trade craft known as 'a buy-up'. In time-honoured Fleet Street fashion, the bean-spiller may typically be temporarily accommodated in a four-star hotel, very often just off the M25, with a minder or two to debrief them, so to speak, and keep at bay the other hacks with their rival bids wrapped round bottles of Prosecco.

The source may find these encounters less glamorous than he/she may have imagined. Within a few days they find themselves back on the streets with a hangover and often nowhere near the cash sum they had expected.

Buy-ups underpinned many of the sex stories that became the heart of the business model for the tabloids from the eighties and into the noughties. But when is a buy-up not a buy-up? When an item of salacious gossip appears in a broadsheet newspaper courtesy of a book serialisation. It is understood, as they say, that in 2002 the *Times* paid £150,000 for the serialisation of Edwina Currie's diaries, in which the former minister exclusively revealed that she had had an affair with the former prime minister John Major. But that was memoir.

BYLINE

Journalism was, for centuries, an anonymous affair. It was not considered necessary, or maybe even interesting, for the reader to know who wrote a particular article. Anonymous journalism (continued to this day in editorial columns and the *Economist*) came with the authority of the newspaper itself. The *Economist*, addressing why it has never identified individual journalists, explained its rationale in 2013: 'It allows many writers to speak with a collective voice . . . articles are often the work of *The Economist*'s hive mind . . . The main reason for anonymity, however, is a belief that what is written is more important than who writes it.'

This view prevailed well into the twentieth century, with the London *Times* resisting attribution into the late 1960s. But by the seventies, bylines on all but the shortest of newspaper-filler stories were routine. Among the arguments for identifying a writer are:

1) Having the author's name above an article means they are likely to be a little more careful about what they write.
2) Authorship confers responsibility. In the American Civil War, General Joseph Hooker insisted that battlefield correspondents should have bylines 'as a means of attributing responsibility and blame for the publication of material he found inaccurate or dangerous to the Army of the Potomac', as the American academic Michael Schudson has written.
3) Newspapers realised they could build 'stars' out of individual writers. Some writers liked that, but it could be a mixed blessing. Less

'starry' writers sometimes resented the attention – and salary – that resulted from public attention. Sub-editors, who often had a considerable hand in the writing, felt unappreciated. And managements trembled when they realised that the 'brand' of individual writers sometimes trumped the brand of the news organisation for whom they were writing.

4) A general reader can make their own judgements about individual writers. They might, for instance, spot hobby-horses or prejudices in specific reporters and make adjustments for trust – even if, as a rule, they are prepared to trust a title.

Knowing who wrote a particular story may, in an age of greater transparency, not be enough. Campaigners for more openness want to know more than just a name. Readers, they say, are entitled to know a great deal more. As Jay Rosen has put it: 'Drop the voice of God, ditch the view from nowhere, and instead tell us where you're coming from. Then we can apply whatever discount rate we want.' A mere byline, in other words, is just the start. 'Transparency', as the internet philosopher David Weinberger wrote in 2009, 'is the new objectivity' *(SEE: TRANSPARENCY)*.

In any newsroom the appropriation of another's work can earn a habitual offender the title of 'byline bandit'. Bylines are also now used regularly to give a misleading impression, for instance that someone rewriting agency copy at a desk in head office is reporting from a war zone. This growing abuse involves platoons of young 'journalists' hired and trained to 'lift' information, rejig it and present it as newly generated material, a practice referred to as 'ripping'. Newsrooms, even in the online manifestations of major legacy news organisations, with honourable exceptions, are now sometimes little more than content factories in which a byline means so much less than General Hooker's intention in General Order No. 48.

C

CAMPAIGNING JOURNALISM

A gruesome photo of tumours growing on an amputated human ear illustrates 'Dying for a Tan', which is the title of one of the *Sun*'s set of campaigns in early 2020. That particular newspaper exercise was about the danger of sunbeds and seems harmless, even public-spirited.

Nearly all the UK papers do campaigns of one kind or another and they often boast about them. The *Daily Mail*'s proprietor, Lord Rothermere, congratulated retiring editor Paul Dacre in 2018 for having made the company a great deal of money and for 'the sheer power of his many campaigns'. The editor himself itemised some of those 'countless successful campaigns'. He said, 'Whether it has been justice for Stephen Lawrence and the Omagh bomb victims, plastic in supermarkets and in the seas, Dignity for the Elderly, thwarting Labour's plans for super casinos, or putting sepsis and prostate cancer on the map, we have shown that newspapers make a difference.'

The 1997 Lawrence case was Dacre's cause célèbre above all. He was praised for righteous courage even by his political opponents on the anti-racist left, running the headline 'MURDERERS' over five photos of those believed to have got away with killing a black teenager. Dacre took this campaign very personally, because Stephen's father had been hired to do some plastering at the editor's house. Dacre told the BBC later: 'I knew the man. He was clearly a very decent, very hard-working man. Would the *Mail* have still done that headline without that knowledge? Probably not.'

Another of Dacre's pet projects was more problematic. In 2012, he used the weapon of his paper to launch an eleven-page tirade against

Sir David Bell, an ultra-respectable former chairman of the *Financial Times* and supporter of improved press standards. His crime? To threaten the income of the *Daily Mail* by supporting a clampdown on cruel and unethical newspaper methods, including phone-hacking and other intrusions. This 'monstering' used terms more appropriate to the exposure of an arch-criminal, purporting to describe a sinister web of 'left-wing' influence. Media commentator and former *Mirror* editor Roy Greenslade described it as 'a farrago of distortion with added vilification'. But it was designed to intimidate and to an extent may have succeeded.

A notoriously intimidatory campaign was also run by the Murdoch-owned *News of the World* in 2000. This involved publishing photos of convicted paedophiles and their whereabouts. Lynch law followed: an innocent man with the same name as a sex offender was mobbed in Manchester, and a young paediatrician in Wales fled her house in fear after the word 'Paedo' was painted on her door. But the mother of Sarah Payne, an eight-year-old girl who was abducted and murdered in July 2000, subsequently claimed the campaign had been a 'force for good' because it brought about 'Sarah's law' – a limited right for parents to find out if convicted sex offenders had access to their children.

As can be seen from Dacre's proud list, newspaper campaigns can be a grab-bag of whims based on the passing preoccupations of the readers, or indeed, on the various fixations of an editor. Sometimes, as with the self-interested onslaught on Sir David Bell, they can appear downright malign. At other times, they can merely be cynical marketing exercises. The common advice given to tabloid editors is 'Never launch a campaign unless you already know you're going to win it'. Therefore, at a point before reader boredom sets in, the editor always has to find a way of claiming some sort of victory and hastily moving on.

One might argue as a matter of principle that campaigns are a bad and impure form of journalism. Campaigners take sides, instead of simply placing all the salient facts before the readers and letting them make up their own minds. At its worst, this can turn newspaper campaigns into perverse crusades, and sometimes into little more than unscrupulous bullying of their chosen target. A more sympathetic view, however, would be that all investigative journalism is a sort of campaigning. The *Guardian* spent years publishing front-page bribery allegations against arms company BAE Systems. The *Financial Times* similarly chose to foreground its exposure of sexual harassment at the Presidents Club by top businessmen. The *Sunday Times* will always be remembered for thalidomide. The *Mirror* has run powerful campaigns over the NHS. These very acts of saying, with prominence, 'here may be concealed wrongdoing' imply that something should be done about it. Exposure journalism is thus always at bottom a call to social action.

Campaigning is often at the heart of powerful local journalism: save the threatened swimming pool, raise money for defibrillators, look after the lonely this Christmas, fight the job cuts, back this charity, stop this playground from being closed, highlight homelessness, and so on. It is noticeable that American journalists tend to shy away from the word 'campaign'. The winning entries for the great Pulitzer Prize for Public Service will be variously labelled 'investigation', 'exposure', 'exploration', 'prolonged coverage', 'probe', 'examination', 'disclosure', 'revelation' . . . but almost never 'campaign' if only because it seems to overstep a professional sense of detachment.

Campaigns can give a voice to a community and amplify the views of people who would otherwise struggle to be heard. They are at their best when there's not much argument about the justness of the cause they articulate (*Daily Mail* and plastic bags). They are more problematic when they take sides on an issue where the rights and wrongs are more evenly distributed. For example, is genetically modified food a menace? A fair-minded observer might say there are good arguments on both sides and that the scientific jury is still out. The hopes and fears over biotechnology and food offer a perfect opportunity for explanatory reporting and commentary, as well as for searching investigations. But what the *Mail* gave us was literally thousands of articles, stretching over years, denouncing 'Frankenfood'. Its mind was made up at the start – and it pursued the myth with all its considerable and remorseless flair.

Or what about Brexit *(SEE: BREXIT)*? After the result, the *Daily Express* editor Hugh Whittow gloried in his paper's five-year 'crusade' to have a referendum, followed by a 123-day campaign to get Britain out. This was followed by another campaign to have a blue cover for British passports *(SEE: CHAFF)* as an 'icon of British identity'.

Knowing when *not* to campaign is an editorial skill. And learning to distinguish between various forms of campaigning journalism is, for the reader, also useful.

C

CAVEAT EMPTOR

What's the solution for the oceans of rubbish information all around? Fact-checkers *(SEE: FACT CHECKERS)* can do their bit – though it will never be enough. Regulation can have a go – though, as social media companies have discovered, it is almost impossible to imagine it working at global scale without trampling on precious rights to free expression. The main responsibility is going to fall on the consumer. Caveat emptor: buyer beware!

The phrase is not to be taken literally, since most of this information floats freely around and costs nothing. But the principle is right: that it's up to all of us, as consumers of news, to be smarter in working out what feels right and what doesn't.

It can be a life-or-death responsibility. Within weeks of the coronavirus making its bitter potency bite, more than a hundred titles offering some sort of survival guide had been posted on the Amazon and Barnes and Noble websites. A *Washington Post* reporter found that most of them had been self-published – part of a new trend for entrepreneurial 'authors' to rush out e-books on the back of big news stories. Some of them were by people with dubious medical qualifications; others offered guides to 'life-saving' herbs, essential oils and natural remedies.

In the end, no amount of regulation will catch up with the proliferation of misleading, lying, opportunistic information swirling around digital channels, whether mainstream or unofficial. So what does caveat emptor look like in this new world? Dan Gillmor, a journalist-turned-academic who is one of the best guides as to how our behaviour as consumers of news has to change, offered five pointers in his 2010 book *Mediactive*:

1) **Be sceptical.**
   Never take it for granted that what we read, see or hear from media sources of any kind is trustworthy. This caution applies to every scrap of news that comes our way, whether from traditional news organisations, blogs, online videos, Facebook updates or any other source *(SEE: SCEPTICISM)*.

2) **Exercise judgement**

Generalised cynicism feeds the problem. If we lazily assume that everyone is pushing lies rather than trying to figure out who's telling the truth and who isn't, we give the worst people even more leeway to make things worse for the rest of us.

3) **Open your mind**

To be well informed, we need to seek out and pay attention to sources of information that will offer new perspectives and challenge our own assumptions, rather than simply reinforcing our current beliefs *(SEE: ECHO CHAMBERS)*.

4) **Keep asking questions**

This principle goes by many names: research, reporting, homework, etc. The more important you consider a topic, the more essential it becomes to follow up on media reports about it.

5) **Learn media techniques**

Solid communications skills are becoming critically important for social and economic participation. It's essential to grasp the ways people use media to persuade and manipulate – that is, how media creators push our logical and emotional buttons. Understanding this also means knowing how to distinguish a marketer from a journalist, and a non-journalistic blogger from one whose work does serve a journalistic purpose: all create media, but they have different goals. This is all part of developing a broader grasp of how journalism works.

If enough of us began to master most of these techniques we could develop a kind of herd immunity to false information. But, like the coronavirus itself, it would require concerted effort by millions taking their own responsibilities as consumers and spreaders of news seriously to have a real effect. What are the chances?

CELEBRITY

'Kerry Katona breaks down, Sky News – Recommended'. The push notification from YouTube flashed up on smartphones just five days after the death of Caroline Flack, the reality TV show presenter who took her own life on 15 February 2020.

Flack had trodden the classic path of celebrity since she became an actress, getting her first break in 2002 in a TV comedy sketch show called *Bo' Selecta!* before going on to present the phenomenally successful reality show *Love Island*. However, it had all gone wrong when she was charged with assaulting her boyfriend, Lewis Burton, in December 2019. After that, media coverage of her – so crucial to her career – became a lot nastier. It was not surprising that Katona, who had herself lived as a celebrity and with all that entails for the last twenty years, would be willing to be called upon to comment.

However, following Flack's tragic death, and the flood tide of accusations that she had been harassed and bullied by the press and social media, one might have expected that YouTube would have thought twice before putting out a drooling exhortation to watch someone breaking down on television as she described the death of another celebrity who couldn't handle all the difficulties in her own life. But that is the essence of celebrity: a sort of perpetual motion in which each act has an equal and opposite reaction – more celebrity.

The death of Flack, who was said to have had many other problems in her life, prompted a wave of further prurient, self-fulfilling guff condemning all those who had tracked/stalked her every move and then revelled in her misfortune. A lot of the coverage on social media went under the #BeKind hashtag, emanating from Flack's own Instagram post from December: 'In a world where you can be anything, be kind.' Large numbers of those doing the condemning were the very journalists from every section of the media, plus commenters on social media, who had made and then tragically unmade her: a 'circular firing squad', according to one *Guardian* commentator.

Katona talked of her relationship with the media in the Sky interview. She said she too had used the media when it suited her: she defined that relationship as a 'push and a pull kind of thing'. She was acknowledging the truth that celebrity and journalists have always walked hand in hand. Journalists enjoy building them up – and take equal pleasure in cutting them down. The whole arc has a natural life cycle.

CHAFF

'Newspaper editors are men who separate the wheat from the chaff, and then print the chaff.' The quotation is attributed to Adlai E. Stevenson II (1900–65), who ran for US president twice and was an ambassador to the UN.

So, what does chaff look like?

- Ed Miliband was leader of the Labour Party between 2010 and 2015. On 21 May 2014, a photographer captured him rather awkwardly eating a bacon sandwich. This was classic chaff: how they eat a sandwich is literally almost the least important thing we want to know about a potential future prime minister. But the picture was reprinted thousands of times, and spread far and wide digitally. Why? Because it made Miliband look silly, out of touch and incompetent. The day before the polls opened in the 2015 election – in which Miliband lost to Tory leader David Cameron – the *Sun* splashed on the picture (by then almost a year old) with the headline 'SAVE OUR BACON' and subheads that read: 'This is the pig's ear Ed made of a helpless sarnie. In 48 hours, he could be doing the same to Britain', and 'Don't swallow his porkies and keep him OUT'.
- Ed's brother David also came to grief over a piece of food – in his case, grinning gauchely while holding a banana at the 2008 Labour conference. Even the *FT* captioned a column about this moment: 'Yes, I do look a nana'.
- Leading a newspaper in April 2020 with what Boris Johnson was watching on his iPad while in hospital with coronavirus on the same day when nearly 1,000 UK citizens died of the virus.
- The *Daily Mail* splash on 28 March 2017 – 'Never mind Brexit, who won Legs-it!' – next to a picture of the British prime minister Theresa May meeting the Scottish first minister Nicola Sturgeon. This was accompanied by a further Sarah Vine column analysing

the non-battle of the legs. 'Finest weapons at their command? Those pins!' Vine also referred to Sturgeon's legs as 'altogether more flirty, tantalisingly crossed . . . a direct attempt at seduction'. The 'wheat' the leaders had met to discuss was Brexit and the chances of a second Scottish referendum.

- The supposed donkey jacket Michael Foot wore at a Remembrance Day ceremony in 1981, which was said to have lacked sartorial dignity. It was in fact 'a short, blue-green overcoat' bought for Mr Foot by his wife, Jill, at considerable expense.

- 'But her emails.' Donald Trump used the Hillary Clinton email story to great effect, whipping crowds into frenzied cries of 'Lock her up!' In the 2016 election, the *New York Times* was not alone in finding itself disproportionately covering the story. A subsequent three-year State Department investigation found no criminal wrongdoing in Clinton's email practices. By which time many members of the Trump administration were using similarly lax email procedures.

- Blue passports. Some newspapers – notably the *Express* – made a campaign to reinstate blue passports a central pillar of their Brexit coverage.

- Labour leader Jeremy Corbyn being unable to recognise a photograph of TV presenters Ant and Dec during a leadership debate in 2016.

- Barack Obama's tan suit. It was a hot day in August 2014. The president wore a lightweight tan suit during a press conference about increasing the US military response against the Islamic State in Syria. That was it.

- Almost anything to do with Meghan Markle *(SEE: ROYAL COVERAGE)*. The wife of the sixth in line to the British throne. Oceans of ink.

- Neil Kinnock stumbling on a beach. The then Labour leader slipped while walking along the seashore at Brighton in October 1983. Reputable historians have speculated at length on how his career might have been different had he not lost his footing.

And so on. All these answer to the description 'chaff', not 'wheat'. With the passage of time, not one of them told you anything lasting or significant about the person at the heart of the story. But chaff can matter. By repeatedly re-using the picture of Ed Miliband's bacon buttie moment, news and picture editors did help define him as something of a misfit – an elitist (laced with maybe just a trace element of anti-semitism) out of touch with ordinary people.

Wheat is good for you, just as chaff is inedible. But sometimes chaff makes for a better business model.

CHINESE WALLS

Newspapers tell the world they are divided into church and state. Church is the newsroom and state (usually on another floor) is the engine which generates the money to pay the journalists. As advertising grew as a way of paying editorial bills, it was felt prudent to quarantine the editors and journalists from the money. That way readers would feel confident that advertisers could not 'buy' favourable coverage.

By and large the Chinese walls worked. As the media academic Clay Shirky described the world in 2008, the dollars earned from Walmart advertising helped subsidise the *New York Times*'s (very expensive) Baghdad bureau. Walmart got no say in the *NYT*'s coverage of Iraq: and conversely, the paper's newsroom could (and did) cover Walmart aggressively. Everyone on newspapers also knew there were areas of coverage where the Chinese walls might be a bit thinner. If the fashion pages failed ever to mention Gucci, for instance, it was likely that Gucci would not so delicately wonder aloud why they bothered advertising.

There were certainly sceptics who refused to believe the narrative about church and state. The left-wing UK website Media Lens repeatedly attacked the *Guardian* and other mainstream news outlets for its dependency on advertising. 'How likely is it that an ad-dependent press will reveal and consistently emphasise the most destructive aspects of the corporate system, made up of the advertisers on which it depends?' demanded a typical post in 2001. 'How likely is it that such a press will emphasise the adverse health effects associated with products massively promoted in its pages, and on which it depends? What chance that it will seriously analyse the role of corporations in bypassing democracy by seeking to influence domestic and foreign policy? What chance that it will reveal the truth of the symbiotic relationship between corporations, state foreign policy, Third World dictators and profits?'

In fact (it seemed to the editors and reporters at the *Guardian* at that time), there were innumerable examples of the paper doing exactly what the critics at Media Lens refused to believe could ever happen. The paper regularly exposed the tax-dodging and environmentally unsustainable practices of large corporations. The food, coal, mining, banking and motor industries – which included major advertisers – were frequently investigated or criticised.

But, as conventional advertising revenues began to drain away from printed newspapers, there have been notable examples where the Chinese walls were, in effect, torn down by commercial managers who wanted to get their hands on the editorial train set. New media players such as BuzzFeed were found in 2015 to be routinely deleting posts that weren't to the taste of advertisers. The best known in the UK came to light when the veteran political commentator Peter Oborne walked out of the *Daily Telegraph* and promptly denounced it for 'a form of fraud' on its readers. In Oborne's telling – later corroborated by numerous journalists within the newspaper – the advertising department was routinely suppressing articles which were critical of particular advertisers.

Further stories emerged of the commercial leadership of the paper demanding that stories were 'spiked' (deleted). Swathes of 'advertorials' written by well-known staff correspondents, at the commercial team's insistence, found their way into the paper. Editorial staff confessed that they became adept at sniffing which way the wind was blowing and making editorial choices to boost or suppress stories accordingly.

That is a textbook way to lose the trust of readers – and, in that respect, it worked. In 2013 the paper had been selling 555,000 copies a day – around half what it had sold a decade earlier. By the end of 2019 that figure had dropped to 309,000. More troubling for the *Telegraph*'s owners, who placed a premium on the financial returns, a newspaper which had made £57 million in 2013 was making barely £900,000 in pre-tax profits by the end of 2019.

Nevertheless, the twenty-first century has brought a persistent chorus of digital innovators who think Chinese walls are a thing of the past. Survival, they argue, is impossible if you have one company with two different cultures – church and state. The use of metrics *(SEE: METRICS)* in newsrooms is one way news organisations have begun to introduce commercial incentives into editorial zones. Reporters can be rewarded for writing stories that attract numerous eyeballs, or lead to subscriptions. More generally, journalists and commercial teams have felt so beleaguered in recent years that they have often bonded in feeling both at war and ready to explore any new paths to profitability, including ways of working that were previously taboo.

It's difficult not to see increasing pressure for church to merge with state in news companies in future. If it can be done in a way that is up front, honest and trusted by readers – as well as allowing journalists complete freedom to write what they want about anyone – then it may be here to stay. But that's a big 'if'.

CHURNALISM

All day, always-on media devours content with the appetite of a municipal waste shredder. A newspaper or broadcast news bulletin used to be finite: a set amount of space or time to fill by an allotted deadline. But the internet is both vast and fast. Breaking news demands breakneck speed – perhaps no more than five minutes between the news coming in and shoving it out. We might unkindly call some of this recycling.

The writer Nick Davies gave it another name, 'churnalism': 'journalists who are no longer out gathering news but who are reduced instead to passive processers of whatever is happening on their patch, churning out stories, whether real event or PR artifice, important or trivial, true or false'.

In his 2008 book *Flat Earth News*, Davies found reporters writing forty-eight stories a week (9.6 per day). Few had time to do much independent checking or to make phone calls, let alone leave the office. He commissioned research to spot the correlation between material coming in and the subsequent output in four 'quality' newspapers and a mid-market tabloid. The researcher found that 60 per cent of stories consisted wholly or mainly of wire copy (supplied by external agencies); a further 20 per cent contained clear elements of wire copy and/or PR. In only 12 per cent of stories could the researcher say that all the material was generated by the reporters themselves.

This is soul-destroying work for reporters. It's also a bit of a fraud on the public, who imagine journalism to involve things like independence, challenge and original research. If we market something as 'journalism' that isn't really then it simply undermines the already uphill task of explaining what journalism is. It's also self-defeating. Readers can smell reprocessed press releases. Why would anyone pay for that? As the saying goes: shit in, shit out.

CIRCULATION

Sales do not necessarily mean quality. George Orwell, writing in 1946, compiled two lists of the British dailies. One column ranked them by intelligence and the other by sales. He defined intelligence as 'a readiness to present news objectively, to give prominence to things that really matter, to discuss serious questions even when they are dull, and to advocate politics which are at least coherent and intelligible.'

INTELLIGENCE	POPULARITY
1. *Manchester Guardian*	1. *Express*
2. *The Times*	2. *Herald*
3. *News Chronicle*	3. *Mirror*
4. *Telegraph*	4. *News Chronicle*
5. *Herald*	5. *Mail*
6. *Mail*	6. *Graphic*
7. *Mirror*	7. *Telegraph*
8. *Express*	8. *The Times*
9. *Graphic*	9. *Manchester Guardian*

Orwell's point was that there was a striking inverse correlation between 'intelligence' and sales. A similar chart today would include the *Sun* and the *FT* and omit the long-defunct *Daily Herald*, *News Chronicle* and *Graphic*. But, in print terms, the picture would not be so different (*Sun* at the 'bottom' and 'top' of respective charts).

Of course, digital — together with the presence or absence of paywalls — threw all the cards up in the air. As the print circulation figures dropped away vertiginously in early 2020, more and more publishers decided it was better to draw a discreet veil over sales. The circulation wars were over.

CLICHÉ

Have you ever read a story about a petite career girl in a mercy dash? Or a High Street banks bonanza (or, alternatively, clampdown)? Did the story have a fairytale ending? Or did it involve a love child, a love rat or a love nest? The late *Daily Mirror* columnist Keith Waterhouse compiled a list of such clichés for his 1989 guide to newspaper style. He believed a popular newspaper didn't have to be riddled with such 'pun-barnacled vocabulary . . . [it could] invest in a good modern supply of plain English . . . It can re-examine the stereotyped news values that encourage stereotyped writing – and the stereotyped writing that encourages stereotyped observation. It can, in sum, stop selling itself, and its readers, short.'

The Irish writer and columnist (and alcoholic and racist) Brian O'Nolan, aka Flann O'Brien, aka Myles na gCopaleen, wrote an entire catechism of cliché:

> Is a man ever hurt in a motor crash?
> *No. He sustains an injury.*
> Does such a man ever die of his injuries?
> *No. He succumbs to them.*

Or:

> From what sort of time does a custom date?
> *Time immemorial.*
> To what serious things does an epidemic sometimes attain?
> *Proportions.*

If Waterhouse or O'Nolan were still in the land of the living they might see red at people reaching out or going forward. They would despise Twitter storms, and would not Keep Calm and Carry On when reading repeated headlines including the word 'fury'. They would refuse to keep an eye on leading innovative initiatives or iconic high-level strategic priorities. They were not ones to have doubled down or suffered fools gladly.

But they were also enough of newspapermen themselves to know that when you have to file five hundred words in five minutes, clichés don't half help.

CLICKBAIT

You won't BELIEVE how this SHOCKING clickbait works! The results will SURPRISE you!

You will be familiar with that sort of lure to click through to an article which will, inevitably, be crushingly disappointing rather than surprising. It works if your business model is to attract an enormous number of eyeballs with which to dazzle gullible advertisers. If your newsroom prizes reach *(SEE: METRICS)*, then clickbait can bring short-term results. Even if at the cost of long-term credibility.

CLIMATE CHANGE

In some ways the Covid-19 crisis in 2020 can be seen as a dress rehearsal for climate change.

It began as a faraway problem of uncertain severity. A few people affected on the other side of the world. As a story, it failed on almost every count. There was no newsroom metric *(SEE: METRICS)* in existence which would convince a busy news editor – under pressure to drive clicks, or subscriptions, or dwell-time – that this was worth paying much attention to.

Add this: many papers have had to cut back on science or health specialists and foreign correspondents. So there was no one internally to raise the alarm. For the first month (beginning early in December 2019), the story barely merited a mention: it was a discussion circulating among scientists. About five weeks in, the first risk assessments in the west began to appear – but not very much in the media. By eight weeks in, the mainstream medical press had begun to take serious notice. And then, as the effects of the disease began to show up in Europe and America, the mainstream media began to prick up its ears.

It was not easy to catch up. The experts disagreed, and very few newsrooms had the scientific authority to choose between them. The predominant message was that there wasn't too much to be alarmed about: this virus was no worse than the flu. Some news outlets were in full denial mode, or parroted the withering scepticism coming out of the White House and elsewhere. Few newsrooms were skilled at communicating risk, which meant the average reader had no clear direction through most of February, just mixed messages.

It was in early March – fully three months into the crisis – that alarm replaced complacency. A story that had hitherto been in the hands of science and medical writers now swamped everything. Within a short period the virus became an emergency that threatened to overwhelm everyone. It was no longer just about health: it was about business, transport, jobs, security, the economy, immigration, communications, defence, food, banking, sport. And it was too late to stop it.

In four months we had a compressed version of how climate change has been playing out in the media over four decades. Ignore; deny; underplay; ghetto-ise; marginalise; question; disparage; balance; shrug; pay attention; pivot; reassess; jump.

The greatest long-term crisis of our time is, naturally, the greatest challenge for the news. How can it be reported accurately? What attitude should a newsroom take? What proportion of the news should be dedicated to it?

It's an equal challenge for the reader. You might be suffering from information overload, or encountering falsehoods you can't identify. You might be trying to resist cynicism and despair from too much bad news *(SEE: SCEPTICISM)*. You might be worried about whether your own community will be ignored or invested in during the crisis, and whether press coverage will lead to action. You might be concerned about possible solutions to climate change, and how to filter the helpful from the harmful.

Journalism is famously supposed to boil down to 'WhoWhatWhenWhereWhyHow?'. So we could do worse than use these questions as a starting point in trying to assess the reliability of information on climate change. Here is a list of questions a reader might ask of the publications they encounter – and of themselves. They are loosely organised by the three themes: accuracy, attitude, proportionality.

Accuracy

How are questions of accuracy in climate-change reporting handled?
It varies. In the UK, the Independent Press Standards Organisation (Ipso) receives and adjudicates accusations of inaccuracy in print news coverage. For telecommunications, it's the government-approved agency Office of Communications (Ofcom). In the US, no independent regulatory body exists for print, and an arm of the national government, the Federal Communications Commission, regulates the televised press.

Take Ipso as a case study. Since its establishment in 2014, it has often decided not to uphold complaints about accuracy in coverage of climate change: twelve out of fifteen times, according to Katrine Petersen at Imperial College London's Grantham Institute – Climate Change and the Environment. (Many more than fifteen complaints were filed but judged to be outside the remit of the regulator.)

Why so few? The obstacles lie in a combination of the regulator's approach to evaluating scientific data and the shady area of what counts as an opinion piece.

In rulings in favour of the *Mail on Sunday*, the *Sunday Telegraph* and the *Times* in relation to pieces questioning human-made climate change, Ipso has emphasised its inability to 'reconcile . . . scientific debate' or 'prevent a newspaper from publishing controversial opinions on topics which continue to be divisive, such as the existence or impact of climate change'. While Ipso has confirmed that op-eds are subject to Clause 1 of the Editors' Code of Practice requiring papers to 'take care not to publish inaccurate, misleading or distorted information', it appears that comment pieces – as long as they are clearly distinguished as such – have much wider rein to make scientific claims. One of the adjudicated comment pieces, published by a non-scientist during the UK's deadly heatwaves of 2018, declared that the influence of climate change was 'hot air', but Ipso's ruling allowed the op-ed writer to define 'heatwave' himself and to select weather data based on his definition.

Bob Ward, the complainant in so many of these Ipso cases, is the Policy and Communications Director at the LSE's Grantham Research Institute on Climate Change and the Environment. He argues that the fundamental flaw in Ipso's approach lies in the fact that it does not consult scientific experts over factual disputes. In other words, what is the use of a newspaper being required to 'take care' to publish accurate information if its attempts at data analysis can be based in falsehoods and the published information is, in fact, false? In response to similar recommendations to increase consultation with experts in its coverage, the BBC appointed a science editor in 2012.

The three rulings about climate-change accuracy that Ipso *has* upheld tend to focus not on the accuracy of published opinions, but on the accuracy with which those opinions were presented. In an adjudication of a 2017 *Mail on Sunday* news report headlined 'Exposed: How world leaders were duped over global warming', Ipso objected to the accuracy of the word 'duped' and not to the claim that scientists at the US National Oceanic and Atmospheric Administration had manipulated any data. The *Mail on Sunday* was forced to publish a 647-word adverse adjudication addressing that report and the two follow-up pieces containing the same false claims – but the admission was published fourteen months after the articles, garnering little attention. Ipso did not launch a wider standards investigation into the paper, despite the fact that the same reporter breached Ipso's Editors' Code of Practice five times in one year. Concerns have been voiced about the body's ability to ensure long-term accountability in a time when accurate climate-change reporting is ever more crucial.

There remains a final frontier for establishing standards of information accuracy on climate change: social media. Unlike news publications, which can exert reasonable control over the information they publish because they know and employ their columnists and have pre-publication editorial processes, social media is fast and furious. Platforms have billions of 'contributors' churning out instantly-published content every second of the day. These platforms, which appear to have outpaced news publications as a key source of news for most American adults, simply weren't built to evaluate information – they were built to be big and chatty. Filtering wheat from chaff *(SEE: CHAFF)* is left to the user rather than an editor.

There is little consensus among social media companies about how to define and handle false information. Facebook has had tumultuous partnerships with third-party fact-checkers, including Check Your Fact, an offshoot of the climate-sceptic news outlet the Daily Caller. Even once a false post is deleted or an account banned for multiple offences, it is easy to circumvent restrictions and create new accounts *(SEE: SOCK PUPPETS)*. A 2020 study at Brown University found that at least 25 per cent of tweets about climate change were posted by bots, creating the impression that there is a higher level of climate denial online than there actually is. Users can, and should, demand that social media corporations take much greater care to identify and flag false information that might influence the trajectory of our lives. But, for now, it remains a user's prerogative.

In that cause, University of Michigan researcher Lauren Lutzke developed four guidelines for social media users to evaluate posts about climate change:

1) Do I recognize the news organization that posted the news story?
2) Does the information in the post seem believable?
3) Is the post written in a style that I expect from a professional news organization?
4) Is the post politically motivated?

How does the publication cover climate-science consensus and debate?
Gone are the days where mainstream publications quote climate deniers for 'balance' in their coverage of anthropogenic climate change. As the BBC put it: 'You do not need to include outright deniers of climate change in BBC coverage, in the same way you would not have someone denying that Manchester United won 2–0 last Saturday. The referee has spoken.' We've reached a new era in which accuracy in news articles has moved on to a more delicate question: how to balance the urgency of climate change, the nuance of scientific inquiry, and an ever faster, metric-driven approach to news.

Climate science, like any other research discipline, is technical, complicated, and in constant debate with itself. Those are not the ingredients for readable (or clickable) headlines and articles. A headline which reports incremental change *(SEE: INCREMENTAL)* to one aspect of one area of coral in the Great Barrier Reef as recorded by one research team will get precious few clicks compared to one announcing the inevitable collapse of the reef by year X as predicted by science as a whole.

Academic reports tend to look a lot more like dry detail than apocalypse. A good reporter, if allowed to do so, will find ways of expressing degrees of doubt about predictions, situate the results within scientific debate or consensus, and explain what future research might or should be done. Stories that focus on the state of debate or consensus on a topic might also be more informative than those which focus on a single scientific paper or research output. This is particularly true for contested topics within the scientific community, such as the probability of staying below 1.5 or 2 degrees of temperature increase, the attribution of particular extreme weather events to climate change, or the details of the viability of ecosystems such as ice caps and coral reefs.

Journalists simplify complex science because it's their job to make information accessible to their readership. But Lucas Zeppetello, a climate scientist at the University of Washington, argues that more nuance in reporting would strengthen, not weaken, public engagement in climate issues. If the press reflected the lack of scientific consensus about attributing extreme weather events to climate change, for example, it could help build public understanding of climate versus weather timescales. When journalists attribute every cyclone to climate change, even with good intentions, he says, it breeds the same confusion that allows climate deniers to use cold weather events as proof that global warming is a hoax.

A more informed public is better equipped to sort the solid science from the phony – even if it leads to slightly more boring headlines *(SEE: HEADLINES)*. The BBC, for example, included in its 2018 editorial policy on climate change the recommendation that reporters use statements like 'climate change makes this kind of [weather] event both more frequent and more severe' instead of 'climate change caused this event'.

But there's a crucial factor determining whether that nuance makes it in: how the publication is built. If the paper's commercial viability depends on getting millions of clicks or eyeballs on the commuter train, the reporting must be grabbier *(SEE: METRICS)*. If, on the other hand, the paper sees itself as a public service vehicle, it can afford less sensational – and usually more accurate – science.

In reporting on the human toll of climate change, who are the sources?
Of course, climate change is not just a scientific issue. Climate change is already having a profound effect on human social, political and economic conditions around the world. So part of the challenge is how to tell the whole story, and not leave the issue in the ghetto of science and/or environmental coverage.

For many papers based in the UK and US, climate-change stories close to their readership are easiest to report and perhaps more likely to generate immediate interest. These stories are crucial to plug readers in to the realities around them and bust the myth that climate change is a faraway problem.

The reality, however, is that the climate crisis affects the world's most vulnerable communities earliest and most harshly, exacerbating pre-existing inequalities and disadvantages. Its victims often include minoritised indigenous communities, small island nations, previously colonised lands, poor urban neighbourhoods and rural areas with delicate ecosystems. These communities are often referred to as 'frontline' in order to reflect their position in the struggle to survive on a changing planet, particularly if they have organised efforts to protect themselves.

For many of them – without powerful connections or social media clout – the press is a lifeline, offering what might be their only opportunity to pressure decision-makers and organise solidarity. From a journalistic perspective, their stories are exactly the underreported crises that journalists normally yearn for. These are the beats that best complete the mission of a free press: to hold authority to account.

But frontline stories and close-to-home stories don't have to be mutually exclusive categories. In the US, Native American reservations within the country's borders often have the toxic combination of a delicate water supply, political disenfranchisement and rampant poverty that makes them extremely vulnerable to climate-change impacts. The story of the Standing Rock Sioux's protests against the Dakota Access oil pipeline in winter 2016 made front-page news when the flood of non-Sioux protesters and police brutality were at their peak. In the

UK, the working-class community of Blackpool organised an impressive fight for years against the country's first fracking project in their back-yard, led by the 'Knitting Nanas' in yellow pinnies. National coverage for them, fairly paltry to begin with, spiked when three activists from outside the community were imprisoned and the fracking operations caused earth tremors so intense the government suspended fracking indefinitely.

In the publications you read, are these stories covered? Do you hear from frontline communities outside of the moments of mass arrests and peak crisis? Do you get a sense, as a reader, of where people are struggling for climate justice now – both close to home and far away?

Attitude

Does the publication have a stated editorial stance on climate-change reporting?
Some papers and networks have decided to make their attitudes towards climate change explicit, to help readers understand what motivates and shapes their reporting. In 2018, the BBC overhauled its climate-change reporting by releasing an internal editorial policy and position on climate change to staff, as well as requiring all BBC reporters to attend a training course on the new material.

The statement began with a mea culpa – 'we get coverage of [climate change] wrong too often' – and affirmed that the BBC accepts the Intergovernmental Panel on Climate Change's (IPCC) position that climate change is happening and is caused by humans. It warned journalists against the 'false balance' provided by including a climate denier in reports on climate change. It also set out the BBC's Greener Broadcasting strategy, including that it uses its platform to 'ensure that we . . . are informing and educating the public, allowing them to make informed choices about their own behaviours around sustainable living'.

The same year, the *Guardian* published an editorial declaring climate change 'an existential threat' requiring political solutions such as less meat consumption and dependence on fossil fuels. The paper followed up in spring 2019 with changes to its style guide that it said would 'accurately describe the environmental crises facing the world'. Those changes include promoting the terms 'climate emergency, crisis, or breakdown' over 'climate change' and 'global heating' over 'global warming'. Other updated terms were 'wildlife' from 'biodiversity' and 'climate science denier' from 'climate sceptic'. The paper also added the global carbon dioxide level to its daily weather pages so as to position climate change as an issue of daily concern.

If a publication has no explicit stance, questions you might like to ask include: Does it have specialist environmental correspondents or editors? How does it handle impartiality in coverage of climate change?

How does the publication cover analysis of possible responses to climate change?

One element of a publication's attitude is how it regards its role in finding solutions and responses to climate change. Does the paper report exclusively in reaction to research findings and events, or does it provide a platform for exploring ideas about the transitions we need?

Chris Saltmarsh, a campaigner on staff with UK network People & Planet and regular contributor to climate-focused publications, has argued that we are seeing a 'total poverty of ideas about how to respond to the climate crisis commensurate with the scale of the problem'.

He indicates that this is why many young people in the climate movement have turned to reading, and writing for, independent media instead of the mainstream press.

Familiar enough with the science, and tired of despair, the post-millennial generation is looking for political, economic and social solutions to support. They have turned to publications such as Bright Green, a UK-based blog dedicated to 'radical, democratic, green movements', and the *Ecologist*, a combined online newspaper and print magazine reporting on environmental issues since 1970. Both publish the commentaries ('Strategies for social-ecological transformation') and cross-cutting policy analyses ('5 Reasons why a Green New Deal and Universal Basic Income go hand in hand') that have their readers looking constantly forward to solutions.

Voices like these are stealing ground from the mainstream press, who could be offering more of a platform for new thinking on how to transition to a livable planet. If the press wants to be thought of as today's equivalent of the public square, then it should place itself at the centre of such debates *(SEE: PUBLIC SPHERE)*.

Who are the journalists?

Are there reporters based in, and with significant links to, frontline communities? Making their voices a consistent presence in climate coverage could shift attitudes away from the myth that climate change is a distant problem that will primarily affect nature rather than people. Are working-class and non-white reporters well represented in the staff covering climate change? They might do better at ensuring that the coverage reflects the ways in which climate change affects marginalised communities sooner and more intensely. Disrupting the inequalities exacerbated by climate change begins with at least being aware of the inequalities embedded into the ways the crisis is told.

Who are the owners?

Most newspapers and news organisations are not full of climate-change sceptics and deniers. Reporters and editors by and large care about the planet and can see for themselves what's happening. Many of them have families and children: they think about future generations. But what if you work for an owner who has different, and strongly held, views? What if your company is engineered to also pay close attention to those beliefs *(SEE: PROPRIETORS, SEE: PROPAGANDA MODEL)*?

Rupert Murdoch *(SEE: MURDOCH, RUPERT)* described himself in a tweet in 2015 as a 'climate change skeptic [sic] but not denier'. To preserve the meaning of 'sceptic' as someone who values evidence and rigour, we might prefer the term 'doubter' for now: Murdoch said in the same tweet that UN climate meetings consist of 'endless alarmist nonsense' and he has also tweeted mockingly from a plane that his bird's-eye view of North Atlantic sea ice disproved global warming. His News Corp media empire – consisting of assets ranging from the *Wall Street Journal* to Foxtel (and, until 2019, Fox News) to the *Australian*, the *Sun* and an astounding swath of print news and television in Australia – is known, among other things, for its similarly doubtful coverage of climate change.

In January 2020, News Corp cracked along its internal fault lines as Australian bushfires burned outside. As thousands of homes and tens of millions of acres were destroyed in the worst season in recorded history, News Corp outlets in Australia continuously expressed disbelief at the fires' connection to climate change and ridiculed suggestions to cut emissions as a response. Murdoch's son, James, publicly criticised his family's company for what one News Corp employee called 'a dangerous misinformation campaign'. That employee's impassioned resignation email to staff was promptly deleted from News Corp inboxes.

The tension between on-the-ground reporters ready to report climate change with urgency and climate-doubtful (or even denialist) owners is not an entirely uncommon dynamic in news media. In many cases, powerful proprietors are not daftly ignoring the science of climate change but rather picking up on its earth-shattering implications: that the economic growth on which their wealth depends is no longer tenable. Sowing doubt, delaying the renewable economy, is a way of protecting their interests.

The press is not always very good at holding its own power to account *(SEE: DOG EAT DOG)* but it does have a responsibility to examine the power and behaviour of proprietors who exert editorial influence.

Proportionality

How does the front page compare to other papers'?
If climate change is the biggest issue of our times, then you would expect the press to reflect that. But it doesn't often work that way.

Consider the big days. On 6 October 2018, only two national newspapers in the UK featured the IPCC report released that day – the one giving the world an ultimatum about not exceeding 1.5 degrees of heating – on their front pages. The pressing question in the minds of some editors is not what matters, but what sells *(SEE: METRICS)*. So, if you can lead instead on two reality TV stars having a drunken snog, complete with pictures, then you probably will. (And they did.) The dire future the planet faces can wait – and is always with us.

Or check out the littler days. Does a headline about climate change make it anywhere near the front page that day? Are there ongoing investigations on topics related to our changing planet, for example into the role of financial institutions or the efficacy of tree-planting? Are there opinion columnists regularly posting about global warming and its implications or possible solutions? On these littler days, do climate articles ever make it into the email briefings the publication sends out? Must a reader navigate to the science section? If climate change progresses in the manner it is predicted to, there will come a time when – like Covid-19 – it will be unthinkable to move the consequences anywhere down the page, or not to report on it constantly. As the great activist and climate communicator Bill McKibben has pointed out, climate change moves – paradoxically – too slow for our news cycle to keep covering it, but too fast in geological time for us to stop it. It is certainly not, however, any less devastating or important.

What is the publication's economic model: commercial entity or public service? (In other words: why does it exist?)
As long as the economics of publishing sort of added up, editors were not forced into such a dichotomy of making choices on the basis of profit or public service *(SEE: CHINESE WALLS)*.

Metrics *(SEE: METRICS)* based on profit – originating from clicks – are less concerned with public benefit or service. But during the Covid-19 pandemic, newspapers have been deemed public service vehicles, even if they hadn't always thought of themselves as such *(SEE: SUBSIDIES)*. In March 2020, the UK government declared journalists essential workers alongside those in healthcare, food retail and utilities. For those without internet, papers on newsstands were lifelines to information about lockdown orders and guidelines for staying safe. For those connected to the web, newspapers were publishing fact-checked content while misinformation swirled around social media and messaging apps.

Papers themselves articulated their necessity as a public service when they petitioned the government for emergency funding and permission to continue delivering to homes during the lockdown. Those with online paywalls found the funding to make content about coronavirus free and accessible to everyone. This was, literally, a public service. The purpose of news media was perhaps never more clear.

Will that moment of clarity change our attitudes permanently about what news could and should be, particularly for the enduring crisis of climate change? Will we find ways to get free, accurate, consistently updated news that reflects the ways climate change engulfs all aspects of our lives? We can't quite afford to wait and see.

C

Outside of mainstream publications, are there other valuable outlets to follow?
This is a question for you, the reader and media consumer. You're
allowed to wish for perfect newspapers who get it all right on climate
change, but you're also allowed to look around and expand what you
read and listen to. Are there particular topics about climate change that
interest you, such as indigenous sovereignty or renewable technology?
Or perhaps topics you know little about? Are there particular properties that you value in a publication, such as editorial independence,
non-profit structure or affinity with political movements? What about
formats – deep-dive essays or podcasts, or bullet-point newsletters?

Consider shopping around in the growing world of climate change
media. Use these guiding questions when you encounter a new one,
or don't. But certainly, as always, keep an open, sceptical mind. (But
maybe not climate-sceptical, whatever that means.)

COMMODITY NEWS

'Do what you do best and link to the rest.' The advice came from the
digital thinker Jeff Jarvis around 2007, just as people started bandying
around the term 'commodity news'. Jarvis was becoming increasingly
frustrated that he could read broadly similar (or even identical) accounts
of events in numerous different outlets. Where, in a digital age, was the
value in that? Wouldn't it be better to link to the best reliable account
of something and instead devote your (generally declining) resources
to something that made you distinctive, or added real value?

Newspapers shrugged. There was an old-fashioned professional pride
in having your reporter on the spot. Surely the readers cared that you
were there, no matter that dozens (or, in the case of large political
conventions, thousands) of other reporters were also there – sometimes
writing or broadcasting virtually the same thing.

And then there was competition. Persuading news editors 'to link to
the rest' seemed sheer madness. Why would you drive people away from
your offering to someone else's? Surely the whole point was to keep
your readers or viewers captive? And yet the penny slowly dropped that
– in an age of news aggregators – there was less and less value in stuff
that everyone else had. By 2013 Google News was scraping around

50,000 news sites every day. With a big news story a search might return 20,000 identical versions. That's commodity news.

Smart reporters – Andrew Sparrow, with his *Guardian* Live Blog, being a conspicuous example – realised Jarvis wasn't wrong. In covering the political news of the day Sparrow would often divert his readers off to a good-enough version of a story elsewhere. That saved him time to concentrate on the things he particularly cared about. Yes, he was driving traffic elsewhere. But his daily summary of UK political news became an essential one-stop shop. It was comprehensive (especially if you followed the links), informative and unique. So people bounced back.

Jarvis called this 'the new architecture of news'. His fellow academic Jay Rosen invited journalists to think more deeply about what commodity news signified. As early as 2004 he mused (on his PressThink blog) about why it took 15,000 reporters to cover a big political convention. It used to be the case, he wrote, that a convention was 'a political event of major consequence, where big news happens. There the parties conduct important business. They set themselves on a course before the eyes of the nation, and a candidate emerges to lead them into the election. That's news.'

In fact, argued Rosen, a convention was 'a *media* event, but with consequence in politics. There the parties try to impress us, and get their message across. Above all they play to the cameras in a manner that is calculated to "work" on the largest number of people. These are the things a disillusioned but savvy news tribe informs us about. For they are, in a sense, news.'

CONSENSUS

Consensus, that magical synchronism of public opinion or values, is the bedrock of democratic political systems. It's about people agreeing on stuff, maybe not unanimously, but just enough to move forward.

Consensus on anything can shift with the arrival of new information, which nowadays comes in a constant flow largely mediated by the media – conventional or social. So, what is journalism's role? Should the press serve to challenge consensus? Or create more of it?

Journalists may, in some circumstances, include dissident voices and take a disinterested stance *(SEE: IMPARTIALITY)*. For topics on which there is at least perceived widespread agreement (e.g. the abolition of slavery or freedom of speech) journalists may invoke shared beliefs and won't bother too much with opposing views. Then there's what the academic Daniel Hallin called the 'sphere of deviance': topics judged to be outside the realm of legitimate debate, and which don't get coverage.

The boundaries between these spheres shift constantly: we saw climate change move into the BBC's sphere of consensus in September 2018, when it issued a briefing note saying that 'balancing' coverage of climate change was akin to balancing coverage of a finished football match. The score is undebatable; 'the referee has spoken', they wrote.

What would it be like if journalists didn't just follow consensus, but took a more active role in shaping it? The American media professor Gilda Parrella has proposed 'consensus-building journalism', wherein the press would highlight common ground in coverage of controversial topics – exploring avenues for agreement 'without changing essential facts'.

Noam Chomsky and Edward Herman, whose 1988 book *Manufacturing Consent* has shaped so much thinking about this issue, would probably set off warning flares at this point. They have argued that consensus is already shaped – or, as they say, the consent of the governed is 'manufactured' – by the press to conform to the elite consensus on a given issue *(SEE: PROPAGANDA MODEL)*. The story goes like this: modern mass-media outlets cater to powerful interests because of their ownership structures and advertising partnerships. News is therefore filtered clean of stories that would seriously challenge ideas too near and dear to the elite to be debated – such as the necessity of the free market. Forget the press helping to identify consensus between sparring parties: the market has already biased it towards particular positions.

But what if, as some say, the crisis of consensus is even deeper? What if we have lost the consensus itself – the fundamental set of shared values that binds a society and breeds trust across social boundaries? In one of Harvard's Nieman Lab predictions for 2019, the young digital entrepreneur An Xiao Mina declared that what looks like the imminent 'death of truth is actually the death of consensus'.

In this dissensus ('n. disagreement, quarrel, dissension'), forged largely online, people are more likely to trust folks they know than journalists or experts *(SEE: EXPERTS)* the sacredness of honesty seems to be crumbling. We can throw up our hands at the dizzying digital landscape or we can recognise, as Mina does, that something more profound must be going awry. The press could adapt by openly studying and writing about why the loss of consensus is happening: after all, encapsulating dissent is what it should do best.

CONSTRUCTIVE JOURNALISM

Most news feels negative – and it's almost certainly a turn-off for many readers or viewers. A number of studies have found audiences for news feeling helpless, anxious, bombarded and disengaged. Their outlook on life can become more negative, cynical and distrustful.

Conversely, researchers have found an inclination for people preferring to share positive news than negative. Two social psychologists at the University of Pennsylvania researched the sharing habits of *New York Times* readers, based on thousands of articles on the *NYT* website. The study, reported on in the paper in 2013, found that: '[Readers] tended to share articles that were exciting or funny, or that inspired negative emotions like anger or anxiety, but not articles that left them merely sad. They needed to be aroused one way or the other, and they preferred good news to bad. The more positive an article, the more likely it was to be shared.'

'If it bleeds, it leads' used to be the maxim for local TV news. But a concentration on the exceptional – 'man bites dog' rather than the more usual 'dog bites man' – can obviously hold up a distorting lens to society. Most people do not get mugged, burgled or murdered during their lives. By and large, most people in modern democracies are healthier, more secure and happier than in the past – but the deliberate use of fear by some news and social media means they don't feel it. By concentrating simply on bad or dramatic news – and by failing to offer any solutions – are journalists alienating audiences as well as giving a misleading impression of their communities?

The academic Michael Schudson cites the example of President Lyndon B. Johnson complaining about the tendency for news to be bad news to Henry Luce, publisher and editor of *Time* magazine. Johnson waved the current copy of *Time* at Luce and exclaimed, 'This week 200,000 blacks registered in the South, thanks to the Voting Rights Act. Three hundred thousand elderly people are going to be covered by Medicare. We have a hundred thousand young unemployed kids working in neighbourhoods. Is any of that in there? No. What's in here?' Luce replied, 'Mr. President, good news isn't news. Bad news is news.'

This was the background that led in the late twentieth century to a movement towards offering constructive news. It started – where else? – in Scandinavia and, in the words of the Dutch journalist Bas Mesters, added 'What now?' to the usual five Ws of reporting: Who, What, Where, Why and When. Next question: What now?

Constructive journalism is one name for this project. It overlaps with ideas variously labelled civic journalism, citizen journalism, community journalism and communitarian journalism. It imagines a huge shift in how news is imagined, conceived, marketed, produced, sold and consumed. So, it's not going to happen tomorrow. But, like all big and worthwhile ideas, it may have stamina.

CRAFT

In most walks of life it's pretty clear what skills are involved. We know what a plumber or a heart surgeon/science teacher/patent lawyer does. We can imagine the training that prepares an electrician for their job. Never mind if it's a skilled manual worker or a professional, we can appreciate the craft behind what they do.

Get half a dozen journalists in a bar and they will not agree on whether journalism is a craft, a profession or a vocation. Just don't get them going on bloggers. Unlike a dentist, a joiner or a vet, a journalist can still hold down a living with no training at all. There are plenty of (often very good) journalists in Fleet Street who just sort of stumbled into the job. It's not routine, but it happens.

The most quotable catalogue of the essential qualifications for being a good journalist was coined in 1969 by Nick Tomalin (1931–73), who himself had no training for the job – although an English degree from Cambridge probably helped to get him his start on the *Daily Express* gossip column. Every British reporter knows the first sentence: 'The only essential qualities for real success in journalism are ratlike cunning, a plausible manner, and a little literary ability.'

In that article – written for the *Sunday Times* at a stage in his career when he was a stylish and much-travelled foreign correspondent – Tomalin elaborated on his triad of qualities. Ratlike cunning was 'needed to ferret out and publish things that people don't want to be known (which is – and always will be – a very serviceable definition of news). The plausible manner [is] useful for surviving while this is going on, helpful with the entertaining presentation of it, and even more useful in later life when the successful journalist may have to become a successful executive on his newspaper.' The literary ability spoke for itself.

Tomalin added some other abilities that were 'helpful, but not diagnostic. These include a knack with telephones, trains and petty officials; a good digestion and a steady head; total recall; enough idealism to inspire indignant prose (but not enough to inhibit detached professionalism); a paranoid temperament; an ability to believe passionately in second-rate projects; well-placed relatives; good luck; the willingness to betray, if not friends, acquaintances; a reluctance to understand too much too well (because *tout comprendre c'est tout pardonner* and *tout pardonner* makes dull copy); an implacable hatred of spokesmen, administrators, lawyers, public relations men and all those who would rather purvey words than policies; and the strength of character to lead a disrupted life without going absolutely haywire. The capacity to steal other people's ideas and phrases . . . is also invaluable.'

It's a quirky, mischievous and enjoyable list, but it goes only so far in describing the reporting skills at which he himself excelled until he was killed by a missile in the Golan Heights barely four years later. Not one of those skills – except possibly a knack with telephones – would make its way onto a curriculum for journalist training today. Which is not to say that they are bad qualities for a journalist to inherit or acquire.

Tomalin's one-time editor Harold Evans was much more methodical in trying to articulate the various crafts involved in putting together a great newspaper. His first book, *Essential English for Journalists, Editors and Writers*, was a primer in how to write clearly, powerfully and crisply. He analysed what made a good sentence or a grabby intro. He knew how to structure a story for clarity and narrative sweep. He had an acute ear for style, an eagle eye for cliché and included a definitive course on how to write the perfect headline.

Evans followed this up with equally detailed and authoritative books on design and layout, on copy editing, on headlines and on the use of photographs and graphics. At the age of eighty he produced yet another book on why writing well matters.

Those arguing for journalism as a craft have one very persuasive reason why journalism can never be regarded as a profession: professions are regulated. The members of any profession will be required to sign up to a set of standards – and can be suspended, or struck off, if they contravene them. Applied to journalism, that implies some form of licensing of the press and the people who work in it. But in the UK we got rid of that in 1695 and it's difficult to imagine who could possibly be trusted to reintroduce any form of 'licence to practice' in the twenty-first century.

There are certainly highly *professional* journalists, as well as journalists who excel at the kind of crafts that Harold Evans described – to which, in our current age, could be added any number of digital skills. There are numerous colleges and universities where the basic elements of journalism – and technology – can be learned *(SEE: TRAINING)*. But 'professional' journalism now co-exists with multiple 'amateur' sources of information – some of them highly 'expert', authoritative and trust-worthy. Quite how people who make a living from the professional exercise of their skills will distinguish their own craft from the efforts of millions of others is a big, wide-open, gaping question.

CRAP DETECTION

'The first thing we all need to know about information online is how to detect crap, a technical term I use for information tainted by ignorance, inept communication, or deliberate deception.'

This was from Howard Rheingold's 2009 essay 'Crap Detection 101', which itself was an homage to Ernest Hemingway's dictum: 'The most essential gift for a good writer is a built-in, shockproof, shit detector.'

'Learning to be a critical consumer of Web info is not rocket science,' continued Rheingold. 'It's not even algebra. Becoming acquainted with the fundamentals of web credibility testing is easier than learning the multiplication tables. The hard part, as always, is the exercise of flabby think-for-yourself muscles.'

The phrase also cropped up in a 1969 lecture by the American media theorist Neil Postman, who advocated fifty years ago that crap-detection ought to be taught in schools: 'As I see it, the best things schools can do for kids is to help them learn how to distinguish useful talk from bullshit. I think almost all serious people understand that about 90% of all that goes on in school is practically useless, so what I am saying would not require the displacement of anything that is especially worthwhile.

'Even if it did, I would still be able to argue that helping kids to activate their crap-detectors should take precedence over any other legitimate educational aim. I won't attempt such arguments here because of the lack of time. Instead, I will ask only that you agree that every day in almost every way people are exposed to more bullshit than it is healthy for them to endure, and that if we can help them to recognize this fact, they might turn away from it and toward language that might do them some earthly good.'

D

DATA

We live in a world where we are creating data nearly all the time. Think about the forms you fill out when you apply for a driving licence or visit the doctor's surgery. Or when you tap your travel card, telephone a loved one, or like a friend's Instagram post. In each of those cases, information is created and stored in a database somewhere. This structured information has become an important source of stories and evidence for journalism, leading to a set of practices that are collectively called data journalism.

Data journalism has been behind some of the most important and effective stories in recent years. Many Pulitzer Prize winners for investigative and public service journalism are these days credited in terms such as: 'impactful reporting, based on sophisticated data analysis' or 'for exhaustive data analysis and haunting storytelling'.

The roots of data journalism go back to the late 1960s and a young reporter and computer programmer by the name of Philip Meyer. He argued that we should apply methods and techniques from the social sciences in what he called 'the search for a verifiable truth'. Data allows us to move beyond mere anecdotes to quantify issues and offer vital context to stories. It allows us to spot trends and answer the question of what is typical and what is not. It can unpick claims by politicians, test the financial health of an industry and reveal systemic societal failings that affect people's lives.

Let's take a simple example. Imagine a very small dataset. It has four rows and four columns.

Donor name	Recipient	Donation value	Donation date
Andy	Carole	20	13 March
Bob	Bridgette	50	20 April
Conor	Alice	2000	7 March

This tiny dataset tells us that something has happened, when it happened, between which actors and how much was given. But it also throws up numerous journalistic questions as well. Who are these people? What is their relationship? Why was the money given? Was it the first and only occasion this happened? Did the donor receive anything in return? Now, imagine this same dataset with hundreds or thousands of rows spanning many weeks, months or even years, and you will see the opportunities to spot trends and stories. The same approach can apply to any dataset, whether it be restaurants failing hygiene inspections, council spending on social care, or export records showing components of weapons being shipped to war zones.

Data is a source like any other. We ask questions of it, interview it, if you will, in the same way you would an expert human – and with the same critical eye and scepticism. Most countries have an official statistics office. More than one hundred have some form of freedom of information law that can be used, with varying effect, to obtain documents and statistics. Some journalists are leaked sensitive but vitally important datasets, and others create their own from scratch, either by surveying readers, 'web scraping' (using a computer to extract information from web pages) or manually inputting figures into a spreadsheet.

Data offers two key things for journalism: a unique additional source of information, and an efficient, often more accurate, mode of reporting. Perhaps the most prominent example in recent years is the Panama Papers exposé from the International Consortium of Investigative Journalists (ICIJ). This year-long project saw hundreds of reporters in dozens of countries examine the biggest data leak in history. This unique database gave journalists an insight into the secretive workings of a leading financial services firm. The data was structured in such a way as to allow reporters methodically to search through troves of documents, emails, details of clientele and complex business structures.

There was a time when powerful computers were prohibitively

expensive and the size of a small city apartment. Nowadays, the hardware of a small laptop and the exponential storage capacity of the cloud has enabled journalists to do things that were unimaginable even a decade ago. Skilled data reporters can now write computer scripts to fetch data for them, analyse trends and even read through thousands of documents at lightning speeds. These techniques have shone a light on some of the most important issues of our times – including the detection of bots trying to influence elections, the tracking of modern slavery or revealing deforestation using satellite images – as well as the mass collection of citizens' data by public and private bodies without knowledge or consent.

Data journalism doesn't just help reporters find stories. It also offers new ways to present them to audiences. Sometimes a chart conveys a situation better than words ever could; maps give the geographic context; interactives can help readers place themselves within a story.

Data literacy is now recognised as a core skill for the modern journalism student. Many universities have introduced compulsory modules on it and hundreds of events and meet-up groups dedicated to sharing these skills have sprung up across the world. The 'open source' mindset of many technologists has also meant tools for interrogating and presenting data are now free or relatively cheap to use.

Whilst data adds much to the practice of journalism, it needs to be treated with caution. Among its pitfalls are the potential to be misunderstood at best, and massaged and manipulated at worst. Reporters and readers alike need to challenge it. Where did the data come from? Who collected it, how and why? This is doubly important when misinformation is rife and trust in media waning. But with due diligence, data and technology offer ways for journalists to fulfil their watchdog function as never before.

DATELINE

The byline tells you who wrote a piece. The dateline tells you when and where the piece was written. If honestly used, it should be an aid to understanding and trust. There is – usually – a world of difference between the eyewitness testimony of a reporter filing first-hand, on the spot, and another who is five hundred miles away in the nearest bureau.

The qualifier 'usually' is needed because there can (or, in wealthier times, used to) be a macho tendency just to get the dateline at all costs. Plane crash? Assassination? Flood? War? Jump on a plane: we need our reporter there in full Kevlar jacket for the byline picture or the piece-to-camera. We were there. Or we were before Covid-19 grounded us.

But if the adrenalinised hunger for the dateline becomes too pumped up in a newsroom, it can tell against understanding. The ten hours it's taken to be there could, in an ever more connected world, sometimes be used to better effect by someone back in the office. All news editors nurse private memories of the piece written on the plane in order to get the dateline on the story. The dateline is sometimes up against the tyranny of the deadline. And there's only ever one winner there.

DEADLINE

Once upon a time a deadline was a simple concept: a single point in the day at which the newspaper was ready to go. Whether you were a reporter or production editor, you understood this was the one undodge-able given in life. Miss that moment and your newspaper (if you worked in Fleet Street) wouldn't be on the trains or vans heading north to Scotland.

Newspapers still have print deadlines. Meanwhile, every minute of every day of every week someone somewhere in the world will fish out their mobile phone to check on your news site for the latest update or breaking news bulletin. So every minute is now a deadline – in addition to the print one at the end of the day.

What does this mean?

- Much more pressure on reporters and editors. To get it right, to get it out. All the time.
- Less time to read, reflect, check, analyse, double-check, discuss, check again.
- It's inevitable that more mistakes will creep in.
- Those mistakes will quickly be spotted and called out on social media . . .

- So you better have swift, responsive mechanisms to correct mistakes . . .
- Otherwise people will think you're taking the mick.

DEATH KNOCKS

Death knocks are a rite of passage for young reporters. The practice sits alongside other kinds of cold-call interviews such as doorsteps and vox pops *(SEE: VOX POPS)*, but approaching a grieving family within hours of a death is the most difficult call of all.

There is a perfectly rational and humane reason for a death knock: it gives the family an opportunity to ensure that any information published is accurate, and that any story gives a well-rounded portrait of the dead person. In some cases, the family may want to co-opt the news organisation into a campaign it believes may prevent a similar death: to reform a hospital treatment, for instance, or to support an aspect of road safety.

These are sound journalistic principles – but the fundamental reason underpinning the death knock, dinned into every young reporter, is that any sudden death that occurs between a few seconds after birth and three score years and ten is a story. It is the human interest element that captures the imagination of readers, whether within a local community or the national one. But the first time a reporter walks up the path to knock on the door – probably hoping that no one is in – he or she is fighting an internal battle against a lifetime's societal norms. It doesn't feel right.

It is also a moment that focuses the reporter on the cognitive dissonance of readers and viewers: the people who criticise a death knock are more than likely to be the very ones who want to read the resulting story. Reporters can only comfort themselves, as the door finally opens, with the fact that it is the job of a journalist to report events, no matter how tragic. The reason for death knocks, therefore, may be legitimate but it has been used to condone some appalling intrusions into grief by reporters and newsdesks that have long since ceased to question the means, so focused are they on the ends.

The UK Editors' Code of Practice lays down some rules. Clause 5, which deals with intrusion into grief or shock, states: 'In cases involving personal grief or shock, enquiries and approaches must be made with sympathy and discretion and publication handled sensitively. This should not restrict the right to report legal proceedings, such as inquests.'

These guidelines, however, are too often not honoured in the breach. Some examples of serious excesses by journalists were documented in a review of the 2017 Manchester Arena bombing by Lord Kerslake, a former head of the UK civil service. Kerslake's team found that most of the families of the twenty-two men, women and children who died in the bombing had negative media experiences, with the honourable exception of the *Manchester Evening News*, which was singled out for praise in its approach. Shocking examples included a child being given condolences by a reporter on the doorstep before the official notification of her mother's death; a sister given condolences by a reporter on the death of her brother, although the family had not been warned that he was likely to be among the fatalities; and two alleged cases of media impersonation, one by someone claiming to be a bereavement nurse. The UK's mainstream press all denied that any member of their staff was involved, blaming foreign freelancers. That made little difference to the families and their attitudes to the press.

Most reporters don't behave badly on the doorstep. It's good to get out of the office and talk to people. As often, the behaviour of a few tells against the interests of the many.

DELINGPOLE, JAMES

James Delingpole (b. 1965) is an Oxford-educated writer who rose without trace to be a 'journalist', columnist, novelist and contrarian. He also describes himself as a satirist and entertainer, a grouse-shooter and as 'a member of probably the most discriminated-against subsection in the whole of British society – the white, middle-aged, public-school-and-Oxbridge-educated middle-class male'. His own website pronounces: 'He is right about everything.'

But not about climate change *(SEE: CLIMATE CHANGE)*. Delingpole, an English graduate with no apparent journalistic or scientific training, believes that human-made global warming is 'evidently and demonstrably not a problem'. The people who pretend otherwise are, he says, 'crooks, liars, idiots or shills . . . CO_2 does far more good than harm. Fossil fuels . . . are the ideal solution to our energy needs. Renewables are a waste of everyone's time – and always will be.' And so on.

Delingpole is the 'climate change correspondent' of the right-wing website Breitbart, much-loved by the Trump administration. So, even though he is clueless on climate change, his words have influence. But surely no self-respecting editor of a mainstream newspaper would hire Delingpole to write nonsense on something he knows nothing about? Journalism has to be better than the internet, or else why would anyone trust it? It's the difference between an approach based on craft *(SEE: CRAFT)* and the Wild West.

Try 'Delingpole' and 'climate change' in any search engine, however, and you'd be amazed how in-demand a literal know-nothing can be. He's been commissioned to write columns on the issue in the *Express*, the *Daily Mail*, the *Telegraph*, the *Spectator*, *Investor's Business Daily*, the *Sun*, the *Australian* and more. A good many trained freelance journalists could only dream of being that in-demand. In these mainstream outlets, Delingpole serves up the same stuff he spouts at Breitbart: wind farms are a waste of time and money. The most knowledgeable scientific specialists alive – one with actual science degrees! – are talking rubbish. Arctic sea-ice is growing, not shrinking. People who argue otherwise are corrupt and greedy. And so on.

Nor does he confine himself to climate change. At the height of the Covid-19 crisis he took to retweeting the claims of quack doctors who claimed to be able to cure coronavirus patients and led a movement to refuse to wear face masks. He has rubbished the organic food movement and dismissed ocean acidification as alarmist and of no danger to marine life ('Almost everything that could be factually wrong, is wrong' – ocean scientist Dr Phil Williamson). He notoriously cheered on his friend, the writer Toby Young, for attacking the *Guardian* columnist Suzanne Moore and '[giving her] such a seeing-to she'll be walking bow-legged for months'.

If these were the witterings of a marginalised blogger we could shrug and ignore Delingpole. But the health of journalism depends on editors making reasoned judgements about whom to commission. If a writer's words appear in, say, the *Telegraph* or *Spectator*, then an average reader might well assume that he/she has some credibility. It is the editorial equivalent of the 1960s advert for tinned salmon: 'It's the fish that John West reject that makes John West the best.'

In any John West-style rational system of knowledge, editors would reject Delingpole – on climate change at least (and probably much else) *(SEE: NEWS AMNESIA)*. So the very act of giving him a 'respectable' platform from which to address an audience of millions lends credence to the view that climate change is, broadly, a hoax. That's obviously very bad for the planet and the species, and it has real consequences, as we saw with all the people without science degrees who said coronavirus wasn't a thing. But it's also really bad for the press. Gradually, the idea takes hold that the criteria for being published in some of the most noted newspapers and magazines is not a respect for truth, knowledge or expertise. It's . . . something else.

Delingpole writes about critically serious issues with a winking titter. His jaunty delight in baiting feminists, environmentalists and social justice warriors of all hues leads to the impression of journalism as a kind of extended in-joke. There will always be a market for that, as there will apparently be editors willing to commission it. But pity the confusion in the general public's mind as they try to understand the word 'journalism'.

DISINFORMATION

It refers to intentionally disseminating mistaken information, sometimes covertly, in order to influence public opinion, obscure the truth, discredit an opponent or spread public cynicism, distrust or apathy. The culprit may mix truth with false conclusions and lies. It can be traced back to the Russian term *dezinformatsiya* (information designed to sow doubt and increase mistrust in institutions). Disinformation may not be a new thing, but the scale and speed at which information can be spread in the digital age is without precedent in history. The French media commentator Frédéric Filloux described the explosion in disinformation thus: 'What we see unfolding right before our eyes is nothing less than Moore's Law applied to the distribution of mis-information: an exponential growth of

spared personal publicity of any kind, even about the fortress they have constructed in the Channel Islands, and even though they have chosen to become newspaper owners. It always seems pretty rich that titles which derive most of their income from laying bare the private lives of others should show no embarrassment about protecting their own proprietors from scrutiny, through what amounts to a system of social nuclear deterrence.'

Such a significant concentration of unexamined power in a few hands could be immensely dangerous, but for two things. One is *Private Eye*, the satirical magazine which is used by disaffected journalists to blow the whistle on their own employers, or on rivals. The Street of Shame column doesn't have a sacred regard for facts – former editor Richard Ingrams used to operate by a 'ring of truth' test ('It has the ring of truth! We'll put it in . . .') – but on a regular basis the magazine sniffs out ethical failings within news organisations and publishes them without fear or favour. Like journalists are supposed to do.

The other safety valve is social media. Twitter and Facebook have no editors, or proprietors to nobble them. There is no hierarchy, respect or order. But out of this anarchy does come a form of scrutiny. No longer can the biters have immunity from being bitten back. It is – literally – out of control. No wonder so many of them hate it.

DUTY OF THE PRESS

The following was published nearly 170 years ago and still stands as one of the most cogent texts on how journalism should work, and how its role in society is, or should be, different from – as well as separate from – all other forms of power.

'The first duty of the press is to obtain the earliest and most correct intelligence of the events of the time, and instantly, by disclosing them, to make them the common property of the nation. The statesman collects his information secretly and by secret means, he keeps back even the current intelligence of the day with ludicrous precautions until diplomacy is beaten in the race with publicity. The press lives by disclosure: whatever passes into its keeping becomes a part of the knowledge and history of our times; it is daily and for ever appealing to the enlightened force of public opinion – anticipating, if possible, the march of events – standing upon the breach between the present and the future, and extending its survey to the horizon of the world. The statesman's duty is precisely the reverse . . .

'The responsibility [the journalist] really shares is more nearly akin to that of the economist or the lawyer, whose province is not to frame a system of convenient application to the exigencies of the day, but to investigate truth and apply it on fixed principles to the affairs of the world . . . The duty of the journalist is the same as that of the historian – to seek out the truth, above all things, and to present to his readers not such things as statecraft would wish them to know but the truth as near as he can attain it.'

The *Times* was responding in February 1852 to a rebuke from Lord Derby, shortly to become prime minister, who had urged the press to 'remember that they are not free from the corresponding responsibility of statesmen'. The rejoinder was penned by John Walter III, the proprietor, along with John Thadeus Delane, the editor, and two leader writers, Henry Reeve and Robert Lowe. It rejected the idea that a newspaper had the same duties or liabilities as politicians.

'The purpose and duties of the two powers are constantly separate, generally independent, sometimes diametrically opposite. The dignity and freedom of the press are trammelled from the moment it accepts an ancillary position . . . [it cannot] surrender its permanent interests to the convenience of the ephemeral power of any Government.'

Walter's statement of principle has worn well in the intervening period. The press should absolutely be independent of all forms of power, but especially of political power. Whether all journalists have lived up to the exhortation is a different thing. And 'appealing to the enlightened force of public opinion' is a noble ambition, although sometimes difficult to sustain either as a business model or in an age of populist politics.

E

ECHO CHAMBERS

Do we now live in filter bubbles, listening only to the pre-selected voices who share our views and prejudices? This is a persistent criticism of the digital age – and it is a myth, at least according to computer and social scientists who have explored how people are behaving online. Two Oxford Internet Institute academics, Elizabeth Dubois and Grant Blank, published research in 2018 arguing that, in fact, we live in a 'high-choice environment' which leads most internet users to more diverse content and perspectives.

'When we look at the entire media environment,' wrote the authors, 'there is little apparent echo chamber. People regularly encounter things that they disagree with. People check multiple sources. People try to confirm information using search. Possibly most important, people discover things that change their political opinions. Looking at the entire multi-media environment, we find little evidence of an echo chamber. This applies even to people who are not interested in politics. Thus, the possibility of being in an echo chamber seems overstated. Of course, there are a small number of individuals with both very low interest in politics and low media diversity for whom being stuck in an echo chamber is more likely.'

Imagine, by contrast, a world in which carefully pre-selected information (based to a large extent on your political leanings) was packaged up and delivered to your doorstep in a format which required you to accept one version of events. The only way of escaping that particular echo chamber was to make a trip out to the newsagent and purchase an alternative viewpoint in a different newspaper.

Now, that really was a filter bubble.

EDITORS

Piers Morgan started freelancing in national newspapers at the age of twenty-three after studying journalism at Harlow College and a period on local newspapers in South London. For a while he wrote a showbiz column, hobnobbing with celebrities, often placing himself at the centre of stories. By the age of twenty-eight – after just five years in the national press – Morgan was promoted by Rupert Murdoch to be editor of the *News of the World*. His period at the helm was not an unblemished success, but within two years he had moved on to become editor of the *Daily Mirror*. He was just over thirty.

The *Mirror* had sold five million copies a day in its prime: when Morgan took over it was still selling 2.4 million copies a day. At the peak of its influence it was a Labour-supporting tabloid for the working classes, though it had long since lost a hefty slice of readership to the Murdoch-owned *Sun*, which had arguably been more in tune with the Thatcher era of populism and self-advancement.

What qualities did Morgan bring to the job? He was an effervescent vortex of energy, controversy, sensation, bellicose campaigns, self-promotion and provocation. If he had no particular political hinterland – far less in Labour politics – he was clever, shrewd and in tune with celebrity culture, including the reporting of royalty as soap opera. He had little experience of news reporting beyond his spell on a South London local paper, though, and that lack of hard news experience, already painfully exposed during his brief tenure on the *News of the World*, would later prove his Achilles heel on the *Mirror*, when he published faked pictures of British soldiers allegedly mistreating prisoners in the Iraq War.

But none of that stood in the way of his becoming a national newspaper editor. Once enthroned he was, *ex officio*, a person of immense influence in the land. His subsequent diaries record how, overnight, he went from being a jobbing journalist to a figure to whom statesmen and royalty paid court. He proudly (if perhaps hyperbolically) records his frequent contact with the prime minister: '22 lunches, six dinners, six interviews, 24 further one-to-one chats over tea and biscuits, and numerous phone calls.'

Even with the declining influence of the mainstream media, editors still have enormous destiny-defining power. They can build people up or break them. They can bully, pursue and persecute people; or they can glorify, praise and promote them. They can influence minds and sway outcomes. If the Piers Morgan *Mirror* had come out in favour of war in Iraq in 2003, it would have made Tony Blair's job of prosecuting that conflict a good deal easier. No wonder the prime minister spent so much time lunching, and generally courting, an editor with a direct line to millions of voters.

Few, if any, roles in public life come with such power and so little oversight or accountability. Of course editors are bound by the law – and by whatever modest form of self-regulation may exist in a particular territory. But otherwise there is – often – little real check on their behaviour.

In Morgan's case he had little effective oversight from the publicly listed company which employed him. Nominally, his boss was the CEO of Trinity Mirror, Sly Bailey, who had come from an advertising background and who was responsible for about 150 newspapers in all. She was part of a board which contained not a single director with journalistic experience. Bailey eventually fired Morgan for what she described as a 'catastrophic editorial error' but appeared to have taken little action to see how much illegal behaviour had been going on under her nose at the Mirror Group titles. The company eventually set aside £70 million to deal with the unexamined criminality of mass-scale phone hacking that was left unexplored.

This is not to point the finger uniquely at Morgan, who has many journalistic strengths as well as significant weaknesses. But his newspaper career does illustrate the singularity of the role. Someone with very little experience is appointed – with no process – by a solitary individual. Then, he is appointed – again with no process – to a job of almost uniquely immense influence in a democratic society, and with little accountability or oversight. If a bank or charity or university ran on such lines Piers Morgan would be first in line to denounce them.

It's not that this power is necessarily undesirable or wrong (though, of course, many would argue that it is). If you are going to have a truly free and independent press, it is notoriously difficult to create structures of scrutiny and control over editors while at the same time preserving their autonomy. But it does highlight the question of who then become the gatekeepers *(SEE: GATEKEEPERS)* to the information and opinions – the two often commingled – we receive from major news outlets.

Dog is generally reluctant to bite dog *(SEE: DOG EAT DOG)*, so the training, background, lives and opinions of editors are rarely held up to scrutiny by other journalists. The contrast with the searchlight glare that is turned on other influential figures in society is striking.

When, in September 2019, the UK Supreme Court – another supposedly independent arm of our unwritten constitutional arrangements – ruled that it had been unlawful for Parliament to have been suspended over Brexit some journalists went into meltdown, arguing that, in future, judges were now fair game for public scrutiny. 'Where do these top lawyers live?' thundered Quentin Letts in the *Sun*. 'Which clubs do they belong to and what are the political views of their spouses? All these – and more – will in future be legitimate fare. Your honours, welcome to the boxing ring. Don't forget to insert your gum shields.'

Letts was making the case for transparency. If people have huge influence over our lives, then we're entitled to know a great deal more about them. Such as, 'Who did you sit next to at your last posh dinner? What charities do you support? Who gave your children their work experience internships? Do you have any overseas investments? Did you pay tax on them?'

It is doubtful whether editors would think the same wish for transparency should be extended to them. How much should we know about editors? How much they're paid? Who they sit next to at posh dinners? Their tax arrangements? Whether they send their children to private school? How they vote? Which clubs they belong to? How they were appointed? How often they speak to leading politicians?

The irony is that some of the most aggressive editors are the most thin-skinned. Even the legendary Harold Evans admitted to not having a thick skin. But for more recent evidence, see Piers Morgan virtually any day of the week on Twitter, or consider his long-lasting feud with the editor of *Private Eye*, Ian Hislop. Dishing it out is one thing, taking it quite another.

The route to being a gatekeeper has changed over the years. There was an age when some editors were public intellectuals – think C.P. Scott of the *Manchester Guardian*, or J.L. Garvin or David Astor of the *Observer*; or Peregrine Worsthorne at the *Sunday Telegraph*. In Scott's famous 1921 essay he speaks of a newspaper having 'a moral as well as a material existence . . . its character and influence are in the main determined by the balance of these two forces. It may make profit or power its first object, or it may conceive itself as fulfilling a higher and more exacting function.' The public intellectual editor placed the greatest value on having a moral influence – chiefly through editorials and commentary.

There are few such figures in charge of newspapers today. People climb to the top because they are excellent at some aspect of the trade: they may be elegant writers or consummate production journalists. Commercial acumen and a flair for marketing will count for more than an understanding of economics or foreign policy. An editor today will need to understand technology and the power of metrics *(SEE: METRICS)*. Ideally, they will be good managers of people.

Once in place, any editor will be exceptionally busy and have little time in their crowded lives to read deeply into a subject. George Bernard Shaw recognised how little editors knew for themselves. 'Lighthouse keepers with wireless sets,' he wrote, 'know more of what is going on in the world than editors.' There are editors who barely, if ever, leave the office except to rest their heads at home.

But the job they step into – at least in some newspaper cultures – hands them a megaphone. Suddenly they can pronounce on things for which nothing in life has prepared them – e.g. a deep understanding of economics or foreign policy – and can back up their views with threats against anyone who dares to disagree. Now, of course, the best editors rely heavily on clever and diligent specialists who do know what they're talking about. But this requires a modicum of self-knowledge and humility, which is not always the hallmark of an executive driven enough to climb to the top.

The big city papers in America do things differently. They recognise that just because an editor is skilled at writing headlines, laying out a page or overseeing an investigation, it doesn't necessarily mean their opinions are worth listening to. Great newspapers such as the *New York Times*, *Washington Post* or *Wall Street Journal* accordingly separate the job of gathering and publishing news from the role of commenting on it. The executive editor does the news. The opinion editor does the rest.

Max Frankel, on becoming executive editor of the *New York Times* in October 1986, sent his staff a memo that began: 'From this moment on, as in my first 25 years at *The Times*, I have no editorial opinions.' It was the very first thing he wanted to impress on the reporting room. Len Downie, who subsequently held the same position at the *Washington Post*, explained his own approach in an online chat on washingtonpost.com in 2004. 'I decided to stop voting when I became the ultimate gate-keeper for what is published in the newspaper. I wanted to keep a completely open mind about everything we covered and not make a decision, even in my own mind or the privacy of the voting booth, about who should be president or mayor, for example.'

The contrast could not be greater with a more modern trend in British newspapers to 'through edit' a paper so that everything is driven by a singular view – the front-page headline, the selection of the news angle, the carefully-picked columnist's spleen, the editorial thundering.

The choice doesn't have to be binary. There have been plenty of great editors who did not seek to impose their own views on every piece of copy and on every reader. Harold Evans of the *Sunday Times*, Peter Preston of the *Guardian*, Max Hastings of the *Telegraph*, Andreas Whittham Smith of the *Independent*, Mike Molloy of the *Mirror* – to name but a few – were all editors who carved out big reputations for fairness and openness, as well as toughness.

In recent times societies have become more polarised – and some newspapers with them. In an age short on trust, the role of gatekeepers is likely to draw the kind of attention some journalists insist on for almost everyone else. But there is, in an age of both information over-load and information chaos, still a need for editors. The best are like orchestral conductors: they make no noise themselves, but they coor-dinate and lead a collection of virtuoso individuals to produce something that can sing, move and even overwhelm.

The best editors have passion as well as calm, breadth as well as focus, nerves of steel as well as powers of empathy. They must have cool judgement and, preferably, a backbone. Most of the time it is the reporters, not the editors, who are most exposed and who are taking the most risks. The editor is there to back them and bring the institutional protection of the organisation to shield them.

Good editors should know a little about a lot, and be honest about what they don't know. They should understand their main job is to give people true information about things that are, or will be, important to their lives – even if a) they don't (yet) understand why they might be important, and b) those stories don't always attract clicks, or eyeballs, or advertising. A much less significant part of their job is telling people what to think. Trying to influence opinion is an entirely different activity than trying to keep people informed.

They should believe in free speech, and the freedom and independence of the press. Some historical knowledge of how those freedoms were won is always an advantage. They will be required to make a ridiculous number of decisions at speed and will get some of them wrong. They should be big enough to correct and apologise when they do. They will never please all their staff at once; many of them may, at any one time, have a different idea of the newspaper's priorities or values. The editor's job is to create a shared sense of those values, the main one being a belief in free expression, open debate and a respect for hard evidence as well as differing views. The impulse to publish should – in general – trump the impulse to withhold. But a good editor also knows when not to publish.

Of course, no editor is that perfect: we all fall short. But – as much as people understandably, and reasonably, question the role of gatekeeper/ editor – we should acknowledge that good editors are needed now as much as ever. If not more.

ELITE

Rage against the elites, besides being a decent name for a rock band, has become somewhat of a unifier. All along the political spectrum, distrust in the mainstream media often boils down to a fear that the news reflects powerful interests more than it does the concerns of the ordinary citizen.

On the left, Chomsky and Herman argue that news challenging the status quo – namely, market capitalism and warmongering – gets filtered out as the mass media caters to elites keen to protect their own power *(SEE: PROPAGANDA MODEL)*. On the right, populists such as Donald Trump, Brazil's Jair Bolsonaro or Turkey's Recep Tayyip Erdoğan blame the media for negative coverage, citing the liberal and elitist bent of their newsrooms.

Crunching the numbers, a 2017 Reuters Institute report found suspicion of powerful agendas to be the single biggest reason for public distrust in the press in the UK. Americans of diverse persuasions were alarmed when the richest person in the world bought the newspaper of their capital city (unduly, as it turned out – at least to date) *(SEE: PROPRIETORS)*. People seem to agree: elites have too large a role in the media. But who are they? Donald Trump offered this definition at a 2018 rally in North Dakota: 'They call them the elite. These people. I look at them, I say, that's elite? We've got more money and more brains and better houses and apartments and nicer boats. We are smarter than they are. They say the elite. We are the elite. They've been stone-cold losers, the elite. Let's keep calling them the elite . . . Let's call ourselves the super elite.'

If your head is spinning and you've forgotten what 'elite' means, then you're on the right track. Jeffrey Bell, scholar of populism, wrote that objection to elite power 'really isn't dependent on education status or income . . . it's a world view.' In other words, as Cathleen Decker formerly of the *LA Times* has written, elites are in the eye of the beholder.

This is certainly not to say that elites are entirely fictitious. The public has picked up on two (true) historical phenomena: one, that those empowered to make decisions and handle knowledge (politicians, officials, lawyers, journalists, 'experts', academics) tend to be a pretty homogeneous demographic. The second is the steady stream of scandals, leaks and cases of fraud which offer evidence that people in power do not always act in the interests of the public. On their own, these truths are alarming: representative democracy depends on an alchemy of selflessness by the officials and trust by the citizens, and inconsistency disrupts the balance. Taken to their extremes, though, those observations point to an even more sinister conclusion for some members of the public: elites are a single body working together to swindle the common folk. America's Trump, Britain's Farage, Hungary's Viktor Orbán and their ilk have recognised this appetite for a rejection of those polished elites who hide things. In their place, they've constructed an alt-elite who purport to hide nothing: not their wealth, not their tweetable disdain for dissidents, not even their bigotry.

Not everyone, thankfully, believes that representative democracy and a free press are total shams. But it is safe to say that the twenty-first century has been marked by an erosion of trust in their facilitators *(SEE: TRUST)*. The press could and should slow the erosion by explicitly addressing the real eliteness of its national newsrooms – the preponderance of upper-class journalists, the preponderance of news from upper-class geographies *(SEE: GRENFELL)*. Data from the US Bureau of Labor Statistics analysed in the *Atlantic* shows 92 per cent of reporters worked from within metropolitan areas in 2011, with about 13 per cent in Manhattan alone. This trend mirrors the hegemony of London's Fleet Street, at the expense of the regions to the east, west and north. The profession itself, once welcoming to those without a university degree, has radically flipped: a 2016 Reuters study found that 86 per cent of UK reporters had a university degree, and among the newbies with three or fewer years on the job the figure is 98 per cent. The same study found UK journalists to be 94 per cent white. On both sides of the pond, for better or for worse, the tradition that aspiring reporters bounce around the *Chronicles* and *Gazettes* of tiny towns before heading to national newsrooms is disappearing as digitally-dependent publications usher young, savvy graduates through the doors of their urban headquarters.

But perhaps the internet could help too, by doing one of the things it does best: decentralisation. Connected remotely to their teams, journalists in and from marginalised communities could contribute news frequently and meaningfully from their bases. National newsrooms could do serious outreach to recruit new reporters from underrepresented demographics and regions, looking far outside the prestigious universities and journalism schools. Journalists can also find new and innovative ways to involve readers in their reporting *(SEE: ACTIVE READER)*.

The growing fear of elite-powered media won't be solved, of course, solely by diversified newsrooms. But it's a start. Transparency *(SEE: TRANSPARENCY)* will help, too. The horizontal world *(SEE: HORIZONTAL)* is not going away. Change will come . . . slowly.

EPISTEMIC CRISIS

Epistemology refers to the theory of knowledge and how we can make distinctions between justified belief and opinion. The Vox writer David Roberts coined the phrase 'epistemic crisis' to describe the American experience of losing any sense of how we come to know things or who we trust. 'The primary source of this breach, to make a long story short, is the US conservative movement's rejection of the mainstream institutions devoted to gathering and disseminating knowledge (journalism, science, the academy) – the ones society has appointed as referees in matters of factual dispute,' Roberts wrote.

'In their place, the right has created its own parallel set of institutions, most notably its own media ecosystem . . . the right did not want better neutral arbiters. The institutions it built scarcely made any pretense of transcending faction; they are of and for the right . . . Indeed, the far right rejects the very idea of neutral, binding arbiters; there is only Us and Them, only a zero-sum contest for resources. That mindset leads to . . . "tribal epistemology" – the systematic conflation of what is true with what is good for the tribe.'

EXPERTS

Experts go in and out of fashion. When Michael Gove, one of the leading British MPs spearheading Brexit *(SEE: BREXIT)*, said that people had had enough of experts, he seemed to be articulating a new populist contempt for a metropolitan elite who had got so many things wrong in the past they shouldn't be trusted now. The same attitude was seen when the *Daily Mail* regularly sneered at the people who know what's best for you.

But it's an old argument in new clothes. The famous 1920s debate between John Dewey and Walter Lippmann hinged on whether the press's function was to enable a more informed democracy (Dewey) or whether, in the end, in the words of the media academic Michael Schudson, 'experts were the best hope to save democracy from itself'. As Schudson has written, the debunking of the professional authority of experts had its roots in Marx, Nietzsche and Freud, 'but reached a high point in the egalitarian fever' of the 1960s.

So Gove was wading into long-muddied waters regarding the value of experts.

But no sooner had the first stage of his Brexit project been accomplished at the end of 2019 than the world was hammered by a pandemic so strange and devastating that suddenly experts were back in fashion. At a time of such mass mortal danger politicians and media alike turned to (or hid behind) epidemiologists, respiratory physicians, microbiologists, public health officers, virologists, economists, immunologists, behavioural scientists, vaccine testers and more. Suddenly everyone else was out of their depth . . . only this time it really mattered. So most news organisations suddenly remembered the value of listening to figures of real authority. Most, but not all. There were still news outlets which found it difficult to understand what genuine expertise amounted to. An example: on 11 April – about three weeks into the lockdown of the British population – the Murdoch-owned *Sun* pitched two 'experts' against each other on the issue of when the lockdown should be lifted. One was Jimmy Whitworth, Professor of International Public Health at the London School of Hygiene & Tropical Medicine (in favour of maintaining the lockdown). The other was Toby Young, a gadfly columnist and friend of Boris Johnson who is not any kind of scientist. They were presented head to head as if Young was every bit as expert as Professor Whitworth.

Of course, Covid-19 reminded us that 'experts' are not infallible – nor do they always agree with each other. If politicians or reporters had been hoping for 'science' to lead them, they soon had a rude awakening to the complexity of interpreting evidence at urgent speed. Some advocated 'herd immunity': the idea that once enough people had been infected the disease would stop spreading. Others argued a total lockdown was the only reasonable response. Others still that testing and surveillance was the correct approach. Swedish epidemiologists were at the relaxed end of the spectrum. Some pathologists thought coronavirus wasn't much worse than seasonal flu. Scientists, it turns out, are not themselves immune from having their own hidden cognitive frames.

So scientists do need to be challenged and ought to be as transparent as any other public figures (including journalists). Gove's critique was specifically targeted at the ones from 'organisations with acronyms' who, he said, get things 'so wrong' – and it's not hard to think of examples. Economic experts failed to predict the 2008 financial crisis, which left many livelihoods in ruin. British health ministers repeatedly denied the possible risk of transmission of the cattle-borne illness BSE (bovine spongiform encephalopathy) to humans, but ate their words when it caused a public health crisis and collapse of beef sales in the 1990s – as well as a major crisis of public trust. In the worst cases, of course, experts can hide the truth and intentionally harm the public for personal gain, as Exxon's scientists did when they understood human-made climate change in the 1980s.

Experts may even defend the idea of experts getting things wrong. Isn't that what the scientific method is all about: hypothesise, be wrong, try again? It does take a leap of faith to trust experts to tell the truth. But the question of honest wrongness is more complex. The public tends to be highly averse to risks related to unknown unknowns: the gulf between public and scientific support for GMOs, for example, is a result of public concern for future disasters that scientists can't predict, while scientists and policymakers are often content with evaluating *known* unknowns. Perhaps for the public, the real definition of an expert is someone who has dived so deep into a topic they know how much they don't know, and are prepared to take that ignorance seriously *(SEE: FOOTNOTES)*.

F

FACTS

One of the most quoted aphorisms about journalism is the seven-word pronouncement of the *Manchester Guardian*'s longest-serving editor, C.P. Scott, in 1921: 'Comment is free, but facts are sacred' – nicely subverted by Tom Stoppard some fifty-odd years later in his play, *Night and Day*: 'Comment is free, but facts are on expenses.'

Scott was making a plea for accuracy, honesty and fairness. Facts are powerful. A single fact can make a story. A single fact can change society. Facts form the core of any story, deployed by reporters as evidence to back up conclusions.

There are basic facts – a name, an age, an address – that are for the most part indisputable. There are photographs that, if verified, are factual – such as overviews establishing the relatively small size of the crowd at Trump's inauguration, disputed by the president himself and his adviser Kellyanne Conway, who claimed, in an interview, that there were 'alternative facts'.

There are no alternative facts. Only facts. While basic facts are either right or wrong – such as the size of the crowd at an inauguration – judging the accuracy of the body of an article can be more difficult. Has the reporter correctly interpreted the information? Has he or she understood the context? The longer journalists research an issue, and the more informed people they speak to, the better will be their understanding and the higher the chances the piece will be accurate.

This much they will teach you in journalism school. Nevertheless, some facts – like 'truth' – are sometimes not quite so easy to feel entirely certain about. For one thing, they are often merely the starting point for a story. 'There is,' wrote the great American essayist Walter Lippmann, 'a very small body of exact knowledge, which it requires no outstanding ability or training to deal with.

'The rest is at the journalist's own discretion. Once he departs from the region where it is definitely recorded at the county Clerk's office that John Smith has gone into bankruptcy, all fixed standards disappear. The story of why John Smith failed, his human frailties, the analysis of the economic conditions on which he was shipwrecked, all of this can be told in a hundred different ways.'

Back on the ground, where it all goes wrong is when a reporter is not sure of his/her facts and lazily tries to fudge it. One of the pluses of the internet is that readers can quickly tell the world if they have found a mistake. Within seconds of a 'fact' entering the digital ecosystem (a mis-statement by the president, say) someone, somewhere, will point out (for instance) that Kansas City is not in Kansas but Missouri. Wrong facts are often exposed instantly.

C.P. Scott would have approved.

FACT-CHECKERS

In a perfect world journalism would not need fact-checkers. Reporters would report infallibly. Every fact would be as perfect as the placing of each comma and every single correct spelling.

But – surprise! – not all reporting is perfect. If money and time were no object, it would nearly always be a good idea to have a second pair of eyes double-check the work of the original writer. Almost anyone who has ever been fact-checked will know that the painstaking process does, indeed, usually pick up slips, a lack of clarity, maybe a slight distortion through compression.

The most thorough fact-checking processes were legendary. For big magazine pieces the fact-checker would practically move in with the writer, sometimes for days on end. The checker would pore over tran-scripts, notebooks, recordings and original documents. They would demand the names of sources and, on occasions, re-interview those sources about whatever it was they had told the reporter.

The very knowledge that everything in a piece of copy had to stand up to independent scrutiny provided an extra layer of discipline for writers. The second eye on a piece of copy can spot things the first eye missed. The *Sunday Times* investigations unit, Insight (in the days of editor-in-chief Harold Evans), used to try reading copy aloud to the whole team before publication. Sometimes the ear catches things the eye skates over. Sometimes a third party can bring distance and rigour to a story where a reporter may be close and invested. At the end of the process both the editor (and, more to the point, the reader) could have a high degree of faith that the article held water and could, at least in its own terms, be trusted. Plus, it saved on legal bills.

In some publishing houses – notably the *New Yorker*, with its team of seventeen – the tradition of rigorous fact-checking persists to this day. There was even a recent Broadway play, *The Lifespan of a Fact*, about the skirmish between an intern fact-checking at the *Believer* magazine and a veteran writer who – as the *New Yorker* phrased it in its review of the play – had 'more of a watercolorist's approach to the truth'.

But, of course, the second eye or ear is a hefty additional publishing cost – and the speed of modern digital journalism doesn't really allow for practices that were once routine in the best American magazine journalism. All of which explains why fact-checking (along with copy editing in general) is now in decline.

The 2003 case of Jayson Blair caused a paroxysm of shock to both public and in-house confidence about the thoroughness of editing systems. Blair resigned from the *New York Times* after being exposed for lying, faking and fabricating his way through scores of stories over many years. One result of an internal inquest was to create the role of the public editor *(SEE: OMBUDSPERSON)* so that readers could appeal directly to someone if they had doubts about journalistic integrity. The paper also created a full-time standards editor and established a programme to thoroughly and regularly evaluate journalists' work.

In theory repeated fabrication by a reporter would these days be found out by bloggers and social media. In 2017 the *NYT* closed down the role of public editor, with the then publisher Arthur Sulzberger arguing that the job was superfluous because 'our followers on social media and our readers across the Internet have come together to collectively serve as a modern watchdog, more vigilant and forceful than one person could ever be. Our responsibility is to empower all of those watchdogs, and to listen to them, rather than to channel their voice through a single office.'

With Stephen Glass, who was found to have fabricated numerous articles at the *New Republic*, part of the problem was that he had been the head of the fact-checking department at the magazine, and, according to a 2014 article by Hanna Rosin, his former colleague, 'he went to extreme lengths to hide his fabrications, filling notebooks with fake interview notes and creating fake business cards and fake voicemails'.

Over the past few years numerous publications have let go fact-checkers as outlets have haemorrhaged employees. When, in April 2017, American Media Inc. (owners of the *National Enquirer*) purchased *Us Weekly* from the media company of Jann Wenner (founder of *Rolling Stone*), the fact-checkers were among the first out the door. The team had comprised two staffers and a large team of freelancers, but within a year the operation largely relied on writers and editors to check their own stories.

One of those dispensed with, Stephanie Fairyington, subsequently wrote about the cull in the *Columbia Journalism Review*, quoting *Us Weekly*'s former editor-in-chief Michael Steele justifying his robust fact-checking operation: '"Even small mistakes, like copy errors and misspellings, undermine the reader's confidence," he said. "Getting as many facts right as possible helps bolster the authority of the journalism."'

Fairyington continued: 'To sustain rapidfire publishing, it was more effective to entrust designated checkers, as opposed to editors and writers, with sussing out mistakes. Steele said: "If I wanted the writer and editor to move quickly onto the next story, it was a much more efficient system to rely on checkers."' It was, wrote Fairyington, 'perhaps, the irony of all ironies: in the age of post-truth and alternative facts, America's second-best-selling gossip magazine [had] made accuracy a top priority'.

Fairyington queries whether dumping the fact-police at the moment of the greatest crisis in trust about journalism makes sense: 'It's a bad time in history to skimp on fact-checking – and not just because we have a president who will milk every opportunity to disparage the press as "fake news". The public, including the subjects of high-profile stories, can easily call out magazines' mistakes to their followers on social media, potentially sullying a brand's reputation. Slimmer editorial staffs and the higher pace at which content is published both raise publications' vulnerability to error.'

FAIRNESS

All the words that seem to describe desirable qualities in journalism are laced with difficulties. Objectivity is lauded by some, ridiculed as impossible by others. Impartiality *(SEE: IMPARTIALITY)* can live in the eye of the beholder. Balance can lead to distortion if, for instance, you give as much weight to soundly-based evidence as to crackpot theories.

How about fairness? In general, it is a good thing to be fair in your reporting. But what does that mean? It could mean looking for evidence that doesn't fit with any presuppositions you might have had. It could mean looking for nuance and shades of grey. It could mean you give your subject the opportunity to respond to the things you, or others, are saying about them. It could mean that you include their response in full, or at length. It could mean that you try to balance one view with another . . . but already the term is becoming a little slippery.

Suppose you are exposing the activities of a drug baron, or a tax cheat, or a habitual sexual harasser or a corrupt politician. How fair should you try to be? How much of the 'other side' do you have to include in your report?

In the eyes of Bill Kovach and Tom Rosenstiel, it is better to think of fairness and balance as techniques rather than high principles. 'They should never be pursued for their own sake or invoked as journalism's goal,' they write in *The Elements of Journalism*. 'Their value is in helping to get us close to more thorough verification and a reliable version of events.'

FAKE NEWS

Fake news is a particularly problematic term. Depending on the speaker, it can have at least two entirely different meanings:

1) News that is false or invented
2) News that someone wants you to believe is false or invented

Both are bad, but in different ways. It's obviously a deeply undesirable thing for people to be fabricating and circulating 'news' that is wrong or untrue. It's just as undesirable to use a generalised term to discredit real news by simply labelling it fake.

There is precedent for the latter use of the term in Nazi Germany and elsewhere *(SEE: LÜGENPRESSE)*. Donald Trump's tweet on 17 February 2017 was firmly in this tradition: 'The FAKE NEWS media is not my enemy, it is the enemy of the American People!' He named the 'failing' *New York Times*, as well as NBC, ABC, CBS and CNN – all broadly reputable news organisations – as fake news.

This was, itself, fake news.

FALSE AMPLIFIERS

Facebook's definition: 'Coordinated activity by inauthentic accounts that has the intent of manipulating political discussion (e.g., by discouraging specific parties from participating in discussion or amplifying sensationalistic voices over others).'

FALSE INFORMATION

'News articles that purport to be factual, but which contain intentional misstatements of fact with the intention to arouse passions, attract viewership, or deceive.' This is how Facebook defines the problem. The House of Commons Digital, Culture, Media and Sport Select Committee found itself abandoning 'fake news' *(SEE: FAKE NEWS)* as a term that had any real meaning. In its interim report in 2018 it suggested a variety of more specific types of false information:

- Fabricated content: completely false content
- Manipulated content: distortion of genuine information or imagery, for example a headline that is made more sensationalist, often popularised by 'clickbait'

- Imposter content: impersonation of genuine sources, for example by using the branding of an established news agency
- Misleading content: misleading use of information, for example by presenting comment as fact
- False context of connection: factually accurate content that is shared with false contextual information, for example when a headline of an article does not reflect the content
- Satire and parody: presenting humorous but false stories as if they are true. Although not usually categorised as fake news, this may unintentionally fool readers.

FINANCIAL REPORTING

In financial markets, news – positive or negative – equals money.

Picture the scene: Franco's on Jermyn Street, London, an upscale Italian restaurant favoured by minor-league oligarchs and the various ancillary personnel who hide their money and protect their reputations. Lunch is between a respected financial journalist and a businessman who made his money in plastic coat hangers, only to lose most of it in the 2008 financial crisis. He's holding out the promise of an intro-duction to a source who claims to have documentary evidence of fraud and industrial-scale money laundering at a large German institution. But there's a catch.

'Dave,' says the source with the information, 'needs a payday. All he needs is four or five days' notice of when you are going to print the story.'

It doesn't work like that, explains the journalist, mumbling something about editors and sub-editors and lawyers, and all the other variables that get in the way of a story about German fraud actually seeing the light of day. There seems little point at the time in highlighting the obvious: that offering up the planned publication date would be sharing price-sensitive information. 'Dave' would have inside knowledge, since revelation of the fraud in the press would surely send shares in the German institution sharply lower.

But then Dave doesn't actually exist. He is a character dreamt up by the German institution doing the defrauding, or by one of the three corporate security firms it employs in the UK to investigate, harass and silence its journalist critics. The Franco's lunch is, in short, a set-up, a sting operation aimed at harvesting evidence that the journalist involved is corrupt and working in league with those in financial markets manipulating the German firm's share price for financial gain.

It has become almost routine for financial journalists to be accused of having ulterior motives when writing critically about the companies or institutions under their watch. The sneering dismissal of hard-reported facts as 'fake news' is widely seen as a Trumpian phenomenon. But in financial markets the charge of journalistic corruption goes back decades.

Broad public knowledge of the financial world is poor and there is a widely held assumption that anyone and everyone working in or around finance has some sort of sneaky access to the money. And that includes financial journalists. In the experience of most of the best practitioners, however, corruption amongst financial journalists is extremely rare – and also very obvious when it has happened.

What has changed is that, say, thirty years ago financial journalism was widely trusted, even though corrupt journalists were readily identifiable; now, conversely, there's no evidence of corruption and yet their work is widely mistrusted.

One leading financial journalist remembers how, at the start of his career, the editor of a closely followed investment column asked him to act as a witness, signing documentation for a Swiss company he was secretly using for stock trading. Nowadays new, young colleagues are regularly warned that even the slightest misuse of price-sensitive information will instantly end their careers. What's also worth noting is that while trust has dissolved – despite ethics improving progressively over the years – the technical skill of financial reporters has had to keep pace with an increasingly complex business and financial environment.

Prior to the financial crisis in 2008, the repertoire of the average financial hack was pretty limited. Company results were covered, usually with a parochial focus on the UK side of any story. Corporate takeover battles were about personality clashes and little else. 'Market reporters' knew about stocks and shares, and where to get a stiff gin and tonic in the City. The crisis changed all that. Suddenly financial journalists had to understand how the actual system worked. What was money?

How did it move around? What was structured finance? How were liabilities settled across the Eurozone? It was an uncomfortable adjustment, but one that forced a step change in technical competence on business desks across the media industry.

But if financial journalism is much cleaner and technically adept than it was, other challenges have limited improvements in the end product.

The first of these is regulation. Cleaning up markets in the UK and other advanced economies has meant the authorities imposing stringent controls on the flow of information. This has had a chilling effect on the ordinary working relationship between journalists, corporate executives, bankers and other finance types. Access is reduced, and when communication does happen interactions are carefully managed, lessening understanding and insight.

This, in turn, has fuelled a second broad challenge: the rise of an often combative relationship between journalist and subject matter, along with the inevitable involvement of lawyers. A generation ago newspapers didn't feel the routine need for an internal specialist libel lawyer. If a sticky issue between the paper and a company or individual looked to be turning legally toxic, an outside law firm could help. But it wasn't a common occurrence.

Fifteen years on, the case of the German institution involved in running the Franco's sting operation caused the *Financial Times* to hire the services of three external law firms to work alongside the paper's stretched (but skilled) internal team. That's not healthy, if only because the costs involved reduce the ability of financial media to hold corporate and financial power to account.

If that sounds a grand claim for the role of financial journalism, consider who else there is policing these esoteric worlds. And it's a pressing matter, especially after a decade when money funnelled into business and finance has essentially been free, when a colossal investment bubble in tech has inflated, and when flows of management and capital have become genuinely international.

Some financial journalists reckon it all adds up to fraud on a gigantic scale. And post-coronavirus, we are likely to find out that that is the case.

FISK, ROBERT

Robert Fisk (b. 1946) is a legendary British writer and journalist, renowned for a career of exceptional work in Northern Ireland and the Middle East. He has been garlanded with awards for his work, mainly in the *Times* and *Independent*. He was voted International Journalist of the Year no fewer than seven times and has at least half a dozen books to his credit, as well as documentary films. To some he is virtually a cult figure – the only person brave enough to 'tell the truth' about the Middle East. His writing is often fluent, dramatic and compelling. To many *Independent* readers he was, for a generation, one of the main reasons for buying the paper.

And yet, whenever Fisk's colleagues gathered to compare his reporting with theirs, doubts were often voiced. It boiled down to one American correspondent's careful phrase: 'He sees things we don't.'

This could be the description of an extra-vigilant reporter who goes off the beaten track and is more enterprising than his fellow journalists. It could be jealousy. Or it could be something a bit more disturbing: an unusually 'inventive' reporter – but not in a good way. Journalists shake their heads in wonder: they were with him on the same trip, in close proximity all day long. And yet he managed to find some crucial piece of evidence or eyewitness that eluded everyone else. And then wrote rings around them.

This low-level grumbling broke out into the open in 2011 with the publication of a book by his one-time *Independent* colleague Hugh Pope. A review by the *Guardian*'s veteran Middle East hand Ian Black praised Pope's bravery in giving voice to other journalists' 'envy and irritation' at how Fisk 'managed to get an amazing-sounding story from a dull day we all spent staking out Israeli anti-insurgency troop movements in south Lebanon'.

Other reviewers jumped on the passage. A leading Cairo-based blogger, Issandr El Amrani, wrote about Fisk's 'overactive imagination'. Catherine Philp of the *Times* was reported to have said on a Facebook group of foreign correspondents that Fisk 'makes it up'.

Another experienced correspondent, Claude Salhani – author of three books on the Middle East and someone who had frequently worked alongside Fisk – weighed in on the side of Pope, saying that 'more often than not Robert Fisk's description of these events were very different from what either myself or my colleagues had witnessed. Eventually I stopped reading Robert Fisk.'

Yet another American foreign correspondent, Jamie Dettmer, reviewed Pope's book with the question: 'Why does Fisk get away with it? It has been common knowledge for years among British and American reporters that Bob can just make things up or lift others' work without attribution and embellish it. I recall him doing it to me on a story in Kuwait about the killings of Palestinians at the hands of Kuwaitis following the liberation of the emirate. I remember also the time Fisk filed a datelined Cairo story about a riot there when he was in fact at the time in Cyprus.' *(SEE: DATELINE)*

Fisk's response to these attacks was blunt: 'I do not make stories up, full stop. This is being put together in order to harass me and possibly *The Independent*.'

Disquiet broke out again in 2018, when Fisk reported from the Syrian city of Douma in the wake of a reported chemical warfare attack on 7 April, which had resulted in the deaths of between forty and fifty people. Most western governments and correspondents attributed the attack to the Syrian army: the Syrian and Russian governments responded by claiming that the 'gas' videotape which had horrified the world was fake news. The incident was used as justification for a series of retaliatory military strikes by the US, France and UK on a number of government sites in Syria on 14 April.

Fisk was one of a small group of journalists (described in the *Guardian* as comprising 'many favoured by Moscow') taken to the scene, where he interviewed a doctor who lived nearby. On 17 April 2018, Fisk – who said he walked around the town with no minders – announced the findings of his own 'search for truth'. His own unique witness, a Dr Assim Rahaibani, reportedly denied there had been gas poisoning and said the 'gas' video in fact showed people suffering from hypoxia (dust and dirt inhalation from air bombs) rather than gas poisoning.

Fisk found other citizens happy to supply him with 'a few words of truth'. He found that his 'earnest questions about gas were met with what seemed genuine perplexity. How could it be that Douma refugees who had reached camps in Turkey were already describing a gas attack which no one in Douma today seemed to recall?'

The conclusion many readers would have taken away from this piece was that the so-called gas attack on Douma never happened.

The *Guardian*'s Martin Chulov reported from Beirut on the same day that a number of doctors he had spoken to had been subjected to 'extreme intimidation' by Syrian officials who seized biological samples, forced them to abandon their patients and demanded their silence. One doctor who had treated victims told Chulov: 'The testimony of people under pressure cannot be relied on. Imagine if you spoke out while under the control of those that you were speaking out against, what will your fate be?'

Fisk's report enraged other correspondents. The *Times* – Fisk's old paper – published a scathing piece about Fisk's Douma report the following day, listing other incidents where Fisk's reporting was at variance with other journalists'. The paper said: 'In 1999 he reported finding fragments of an American missile among the blood and guts of a refugee convoy in the Kosovo war zone. NATO denied bombing a refugee column, and no other journalist found any missile fragment.

'In 2006 in a front-page story, Fisk reported that Israel used depleted uranium shells in Lebanon. UN and Lebanese scientists found that there was no evidence to support the claim.

'Five years later, in 2011, *The Independent* issued a correction to a Fisk story that referenced an order allegedly issued by Prince Nayef bin Abdul-Aziz al-Saud, the Saudi minister of the interior, instructing security forces to show no mercy and to use live rounds on unarmed demonstrators. *The Independent* admitted the "order" was a forgery.'

Other journalists weighed in to attack Fisk. The Intercept carried a column by Mehdi Hasan ridiculing what he called 'atrocity denial' by people who dismissed numerous reports of murderous activity by Syria's President Assad. 'Dear Bashar al-Assad Apologists,' he wrote in an open letter. 'Sorry to interrupt: I know you're very busy right now trying to convince yourselves, and the rest of us, that your hero couldn't possibly have used chemical weapons to kill up to 70 people in rebel-held Douma on April 7. Maybe Robert Fisk's mysterious doctor has it right – and maybe the hundreds of survivors and eyewitnesses to the attack are all "crisis actors."'

To add to the confusion, others rushed to defend Fisk, including the anti-corporatist 'media criticism' website Media Lens, whose exoneration began: 'UK corporate media are under a curious kind of military occupation.' The reader was invited to believe that Fisk's critics were largely stooges who were influenced, if not controlled, by British intelligence. Meanwhile, Russian officials claimed the entire event was a hoax staged by British spies.

Who to believe, and why does it matter? How can an ordinary reader pick sides when even those who have spent a lifetime reporting from the Middle East are in such violent disagreement?

It couldn't matter more. After the misuse of ropey intelligence to soften up the public to support the attack on Iraq post-9/11, we should all be super-alert to any attempts to mislead people about evidence which could be used to justify a particular political line or the threat of military intervention.

But in the case of the Douma incident it is extremely difficult, if not impossible, for any general reader to know whom to believe. A year after his original report, Fisk returned to the theme in the wake of a report by the Organisation for the Prohibition of Chemical Weapons (OPCW), which represents 193 member states throughout the world. The main report of more than a hundred pages, published on 1 March 2019, concluded that two cylinders were dropped by an aircraft – probably Syrian. 'All the . . . evidence provides reasonable grounds of the use of a toxic chemical as a weapon . . . likely molecular chlorine.'

Fisk alleged in his article on 23 May 2019, however, that the OPCW had deliberately concealed a dissenting fifteen-page assessment which claimed that the damning evidence was more probably placed manually.

To Fisk, this was a dangerous act of censorship and a piece of outrageous deceit. 'It can lead to only one conclusion: that we must resort once more to the Assanges and the Chelsea Mannings – "traitors" who harm Western security in the eyes of their enemies – and the revelations of groups like Wikileaks, if we want to know the truth of what happens in our world and the real story behind the official reports.'

This is a remarkable statement by a man who had been working for a national newspaper for the best part of fifty years.

Was Fisk onto something with his report in April 2018? Or was he highly selective in his presentation of what he found? Why is he so mistrusted by so many of his colleagues and yet revered by so many readers? What does it say about trust in mainstream media when even a veteran correspondent like Fisk states that in future we will have to rely on the Assanges of this world to give us the real truth?

The British journalist James Harkin spent six months trying to work out fact from propaganda over this story for the Intercept. Harkin's own conclusion couldn't be more urgent: 'Investigative reporting now needs to be about breaking through the noise of electronic information in a climate thick with propaganda, conspiracy-thinking, and reassuring half-truths. Otherwise, the next world war might begin with a grainy, contested image launched online from some distant and inaccessible outpost right onto the pages of a newspaper that has recently sacked all its journalists.'

'FLOOD THE ZONE WITH SHIT'

The phrase is attributed to the former head of Breitbart News, Steve Bannon, who briefly had a role in the inner circle of the Trump White House.

'The Democrats don't matter,' Bannon reportedly said in 2018. 'The real opposition is the media. And the way to deal with them is to flood the zone with shit.' As explained by Vox's Sean Illing: 'The press ideally should sift fact from fiction and give the public the information it needs to make enlightened political choices. If you short-circuit that process by saturating the ecosystem with misinformation and overwhelm the media's ability to mediate, then you can disrupt the democratic process. What we're facing is a new form of propaganda that wasn't really possible until the digital age. And it works not by creating a consensus around any particular narrative but by muddying the waters so that consensus isn't achievable.'

This leads to what Illing has termed 'an age of manufactured nihilism. The issue for many people isn't exactly a denial of truth as such. It's more a growing weariness over the process of finding the truth at all. And that weariness leads more and more people to abandon the idea that the truth is knowable.'

FOOTNOTES

Are footnotes one answer to regaining trust in journalism?

For academics writing up their research, footnotes are a routine part of the craft. Initiation into the sacred rite starts early: students in their first year of university classes are introduced to the alphabet soup of citation and footnoting styles – MLA, APA, Chicago – and sternly warned of the punishments for plagiarism should facts, quotes and paraphrases not come accompanied by an entry detailing their source. Those who stay in academia will carry the habit to their dissertations and journal articles, where peer reviewers will look for the required robust set of footnotes.

Beyond forcing authors to show their work, footnotes are meant to help the reader. They often include commentary to contextualise a claim, clarify methodology or explain a complex term or idea in more depth. They also provide a menu of further reading: many researchers will share the experience of following footnotes down fascinating – or painfully useless – rabbit holes.

But journalism, though equally dependent on facts and their sources, has no such practice. Each publication sets its own standards for citation and attribution, and additional commentary to supplement an article is extremely rare. (Even when contributors write notes for their editors, these normally go unpublished.) One major reason is the space constraints in print publications: an annotated issue of the *New York Times* would resemble a novella instead of a newspaper. But digital platforms don't have that problem, and the practice of including links to sources in online articles is (slowly) becoming commonplace *(SEE: LINKS)*.

Links, however, won't always suffice: they only go to one, already-online place. A journalist's commentary on how they accessed their source or corroborated a claim can't be linked. If, for instance, they mention 'environmental justice' in an article and want to explain that big idea, must they choose just one URL or else squeeze a definition inside the text?

Which brings up deeper questions: is it a journalist's job to ensure readers understand all the issues in an article? Must they constantly prove to readers they have reported accurately? Where would the footnotes end? These are the same questions academics ask themselves when they footnote: journalists would not have to reinvent the wheel.

They might need a quicker wheel than academics', though, to match the breakneck speed of the news. Chris Cillizza, a former *Washington Post* politics reporter, suggests that footnoting or annotating could democratise the news in an era of increasing distrust of journalists. Footnotes could help bust the myth that reporters are the sole 'gate-keepers' *(SEE: GATEKEEPERS)* of information, and offer windows into their process and the nuance in their ideas.

FREDDIE STARR

Freddie Starr (1943–2019) was a moderately successful singer and comedian, remembered today mainly for a *Sun* headline 'FREDDIE STARR ATE MY HAMSTER'. The story was untrue: Starr had never eaten a hamster. The *Sun*'s editor, Kelvin MacKenzie, knew the story was false. But he published it anyway, and the splash headline on 13 March 1986 went down in history.

Starr's publicist at the time was Max Clifford (1943–2017), who was later to die while serving a prison sentence for eight counts of indecent assault on four girls and women aged between fifteen and nineteen. Clifford had told MacKenzie before publication that Starr denied the story, but that he (Clifford) was relaxed about the *Sun* running it because it would help drum up publicity for Starr's forthcoming tour. He was right: the story led to a £1 million increase in ticket sales. The story also made readers laugh. Everyone was happy.

Today we would call such inventions 'fake news'. *(SEE : FAKE NEWS)* Then, it was all considered a bit of a joke. That's what the red tops did. MacKenzie later reflected on the headline: 'Remember this is the first draft of entertainment history, and entertainment history is mainly bollocks anyway created by rather ho-hum PRs who don't really care whether it's kosher or not.'

A classical view of the role of editor would be to expose 'bollocks' rather than promote it. But MacKenzie didn't appear then to care, any more than he did three years later when he crafted a two-word headline 'THE TRUTH' to run over a pack of lies about the behaviour of

Liverpool fans on one of the darkest days in football history, the Hillsborough Stadium catastrophe of 1989.

Does it matter? Well, the *Sun* at the time sold 4.1 million copies a day and was read by about 11.6 million people – roughly one in three of those over the age of eighteen. The supreme 'success' of the tabloid was its mix of news and fun. It was not in the tradition of the American supermarket tabloids, which generally spurned hard news for outrage or fantasy. The *Sun* – from Thatcher onwards – was regarded as the main newspaper to whom would-be prime ministers paid court.

That didn't mean that *Sun* readers necessarily believed the Starr story. But they didn't necessarily disbelieve it either. An era had been born when editors and publicists worked in collusion to promote (and often subsequently destroy) 'talent'. Truth took a back seat to sales. 'The fabricated story which resulted in Freddie Starr Ate My Hamster . . . filtered into the national consciousness,' wrote the BBC broadcaster Andrew Marr nearly twenty years later. 'For a long time it simply didn't seem to matter. *The Sun* was a good read, and a bit of fun, and sales kept rising . . . All this was bought at the price of a general disbelief in anything that tabloid newspapers now say.'

Twenty-three years after Hillsborough the *Sun* finally repudiated its 'TRUTH' headline, saying it was 'deeply and profoundly sorry'. That was in September 2012. The *Sun* had hired MacKenzie as a columnist from 2006 to 2011, apparently not minding much about his indifference to the truth. Notwithstanding the paper's belated 'profound regrets' at the lies MacKenzie had presided over, the *Sun* hired him yet again to write a column twice a week in 2014. That came to an end in May 2017 after MacKenzie compared a mixed-race football player, Ross Barkley, to a gorilla. Once more, the *Sun* apologised.

MacKenzie's journalistic brand was cheeky, populist – often bigoted – outrage. Chastised by the Press Council for homophobia in 1987 (he had 'revealed' in a front-page splash that 'SIXTY-FIVE MPS ARE POOFTERS'), MacKenzie was contemptuous. 'Readers of the *Sun* KNOW and SPEAK and WRITE words like poof and poofter. What is good enough for them is good enough for us.'

MacKenzie's job wasn't to elevate or educate. If he could make you smile, he had you. Truth? MacKenzie himself told the Leveson inquiry into press standards and ethics that he didn't have much time for the concept: 'Basically my view was that if it sounded right it was probably right and therefore we should lob it in.' *(SEE: MURDOCH, RUPERT)*

Freddie Starr never ate the hamster. It wasn't true: it was too good to check. Just lob it in, it was just a bit of fun. The *Sun* made stuff up, but it sold millions of copies, earned Rupert Murdoch eye-watering sums of money and made people laugh. And it was called journalism.

G

GATEKEEPERS

In the past, if you owned a printing press or a TV station, you were a gatekeeper. You – along with the people you hired – got to decide what people were allowed to know. You were able to determine what they could know, what they should know – and also what they needn't know or even shouldn't know.

There are arguments for and against this form of gatekeeping. The pro-gatekeeper arguments go something like this:

1) People are (increasingly) busy. There is too much information out there. It is useful to have someone sift the wheat from the chaff and serve up the wheat *(SEE: CHAFF)*.
2) We need people to tell us what matters and what to focus on, even if we don't think something is of direct relevance to us (climate change, ebola, financial derivatives, new viruses in China, etc.).
3) In a world of fake news, we need someone to tell us if something is true or not. And to publish it legally, responsibly and safely.

The anti-gatekeeper argument runs something like this:

1) Who gave you the right to be a gatekeeper? Is the role of gate-keepers broadly limited to multi-millionaires who can afford the enormous financial outlay in equipment and (for many, these days) funds to stay afloat?

2) If rich proprietors and publishers control the conversation, what kind of conversation will result?

3) We no longer live in an age of so-called enlightened paternalism. Why not give us the information and let us decide?

One of the most notable examples of the gatekeepers conspiring to decide people should not know something was the abdication crisis of 1936. King Edward VIII had fallen in love with an American divorcée, Wallis Simpson. Though the American press was full of excitable coverage of the relationship, the British public was kept in the dark.

Who decided? The two most powerful gatekeepers of the day were the press barons Lords Rothermere and Beaverbrook, who stitched up a deal with their fellow proprietors that nothing would be printed (SEE: PROPRIETORS). It was left to an obscure bishop – the Bishop of Bradford – to spill the beans in an address to his clergy. The dam then broke.

Our own age has thrown up characters who challenge, subvert and undermine the idea of gatekeepers. In starting Wikileaks, Julian Assange wanted to scatter information around the digital ecosphere – at times in a quite anarchic way (SEE: JOURNALIST). He would occasionally (and generally unhappily) partner with mainstream media organisations in redacting, editing and releasing a small selection of the material he possessed. But he seemed at his happiest simply publishing all the material in its rawest form – and letting the public decide for themselves what they considered interesting or important. He didn't really believe the public needed, or wanted, gatekeepers.

Then came the so-called Steele dossier on Trump and the Russians – a private intelligence dossier produced by a former MI6 officer, Christopher Steele. Several traditional gatekeepers got hold of the dossier during the late stages of the 2016 US election but decided not to publish it while they worked on attempting to verify its allegations. Traditional view: journalists act as the arbiters of what's true and what isn't, and don't publish anything until they've done the sifting. But along came a new media player, BuzzFeed, which decided to publish it in January 2017, too late to influence the presidential vote. In publishing, BuzzFeed noted that the claims in the report were unverified and that the report contained errors.

Alternative view: who are you to sit on such important material? Publish it and let the public decide. The *New York Times* (and several others) didn't publish: BuzzFeed did. Who was right?

The future of journalism depends on whether the wider public decide gatekeepers are necessary and/or desirable; on who gets to call themselves a gatekeeper; and on what the rules of gatekeeping are. But there is now also a world out there without any gates.

'GOTCHA'

This was the headline used by the *Sun* on 4 May 1982 to celebrate the torpedoing of an Argentine warship, the *General Belgrano*, carrying 1,138 men. Within a short period the *Sun*'s editor, Kelvin MacKenzie, had second thoughts about the taste of gloating at so much loss of life and changed it for later editions to 'Did 1,200 Argies Drown?' (His boss, Rupert Murdoch, was reported to have been less concerned – 'Seemed like a bloody good headline to me.' In the end 323 lives were lost.)

It was no more or less tasteful than much of the *Sun*'s approach to the Falklands War. It was the paper that paid £5 (plus a can of non-Argentine corned beef) for every 'anti-Argie' joke sent in by readers. It was the paper that marketed 'Stick it Up Your Junta' tee-shirts, and sponsored a missile with the same message inscribed on its side. (A *Sun*-sponsored missile downed an Argentine bomber: the paper boasted of this as an 'exclusive'.) The paper caused vital signals to be delayed in their transmission from the HMS *Invincible* while the *Sun* reporter on the spot sent back stories about naked Page 3 girls being sent to the troops. Its editorials accused other papers of treason and treachery when they expressed doubts about the course of the war. So the headline 'GOTCHA' was of a piece with the newspaper's overall approach to war reporting.

More generally, the headline inspired a new editorial category – 'gotcha journalism' – a vague term encompassing everything from tough questions to journalism which rejoices in trapping or humiliating its victims.

One issue of the *Sun* from seventeen years later (25 May 1999) was a classic example of gotcha journalism, as it developed. Pages one, two and three were given over to the alleged 'love romps' of a man who had once (some nineteen years previously) captained England at cricket.

Pages four and five were devoted to the night a popular comedian was reported to have spent in the company of a 'blonde' who was not his wife. Pages six and seven examined the allegations of drug use levelled against a man who once captained England at rugby. Three gotchas in seven pages.

But politicians, faced with difficult questions, have also harnessed the term to imply there is something 'unfair' in asking tough questions. Bill Clinton said questions about marital infidelity were 'a game of gotcha'. George W. Bush complained of 'gotcha' questions about his use of cocaine. Vice-presidential candidate Sarah Palin complained of gotcha journalism when questioned on a range of domestic and foreign policy issues by CBS News anchor Katie Couric in 2008. To this day journalists find themselves having to assure subjects that they are not out to do a gotcha job on them. Even if they should be.

GRENFELL

In the middle of the night on 14 June 2017, fire engulfed a tower block in the heart of the Borough of Kensington and Chelsea. The twenty-four-storey building was a pocket of poverty within an extremely affluent area of London. When a throng of reporters arrived to see the smoking remains the following morning they were greeted by furious local residents, not welcoming them, but in bitter denunciation.

Jon Snow, the veteran news anchor for C4 News, devoted much of a keynote lecture at the Edinburgh TV Festival a few months later to reflecting on the gulf between the lives of the reporters and those they were reporting on that morning, and in the subsequent weeks and months. He reflected on the indisputable fact that 'the echelons from which our media is drawn do not for the most part fully reflect the population, amongst whom we live and to whom we seek to transmit information and ideas. Grenfell speaks to us all about our own lack of diversity, and capacity to reach into the swathes of Western society with whom we have no connection . . . We the media report the lack of diversity in other walks of life, but our own record is nothing like good enough.'

The UK figures are reasonably familiar: the national media is disproportionately white, privately schooled and educated at elite universities

(SEE: ELITE). Nearly half the opinion-formers – columnists – went to Oxbridge: only 19 per cent went to a comprehensive school. A 2016 piece of research from City University found that the British journalism industry was 94 per cent white. Just 0.4 per cent of British journalists were Muslim and only 0.2 per cent black, compared with the UK population of respectively 5 per cent and 3 per cent.

The US figures are marginally better. According to a Pew Research Center analysis from 2018, newsroom employees are 77 per cent non-Hispanic white and 61 per cent male – both figures considerably higher than the percentage of US workers as a whole (65 and 53, respectively). Only 7 per cent of newsroom employees are non-Hispanic black, and 10 per cent are Hispanic, both lower than the national averages in the US workforce.

All this has long been known but usually remains the stuff of academic papers or pressure group research. Jon Snow – liberal to his roots and married to a Zimbabwean-born scientist – knew it. But there was something that clearly shook him in the simmering rage of that bitter crowd outside Grenfell Tower on 15 June. A video posted on Twitter shows one man furiously jabbing a finger at him: 'You didn't come here when people were telling you the building was unsafe. That isn't newsworthy. You come here when people died.' Snow was not the only journalist to be berated that morning. A number of similar videos of reporters being verbally abused went viral.

How could British journalists have known that there was a problem with the cladding on Grenfell Tower? Well, on 15 June reporters turned to Google and found a Grenfell Action Group blog published eight months previously which highlighted the dangers of the building. The story had been there to write. It was, as Snow said, 'a chronicle of death foretold . . . it was hidden in plain sight, but we had stopped looking. The disconnect complete.'

One of Snow's points was that a thriving, healthy local press was no longer there to pick up on the signals from street level. Even an affluent London borough had become a news desert or (in the contentious US phrase) 'flyover zone' where little in the way of community news found its way into even the local press, never mind national media coverage. The feedback loop had broken.

Thirty years ago there had been four reporters covering the borough for the local newspaper, now closed. These days there are no news reporters dedicated to reporting the area: one reporter covers three of the main London boroughs – K&C, Westminster and Fulham – while based in Surrey, an hour's drive away. Another reporter, working for the local freesheet, told the BBC's Gemma Newby he did all his reporting from his home in Dorset, 150 miles away. He had been to the borough only twice in two and a half years.

At a November 2017 debate organised by *Press Gazette*, a former reporter in the area, Grant Feller, said: 'I'm convinced that if the paper I worked on existed today there is no way that Grenfell could have happened. We would have been part of that community at the time. We felt part of the community. You were the glue that kept things going.' Local residents welcomed reporters, instead of regarding them as hostile intruders.

The lack of British media diversity was painfully highlighted by the sight of so many white reporters suddenly visible in one of the most ethnically and culturally mixed areas of the capital (and reinforced all over again by the Black Lives Matter summer of 2020). The discovery by reporters that the residents of Grenfell were, and had been, pillars of the community – artistic, altruistic, working in key parts of London's economy, skilled, thoughtful and organised – was treated as a revelation. To people from BAME and working-class backgrounds this was a given. The gulf was obvious.

The two great hazards resulting from the paucity of BAME journalists at all levels of the British media are that stories are missed or badly reported – arguably including reporting of domestic terrorism and its roots – and that the few BAME reporters there are, are predominantly used in stories perceived to be about ethnic minorities or subjects like Islam and racism. 'Muslims can do Islam but not architecture' runs the complaint. This then stops knowledge and familiarity about other communities from flourishing in white-dominated newsrooms. And, as always, the majority failure to integrate journalistically with minorities means the usual waste of talent, unique perspective and brilliance which the closed shop always brings.

H

HEADLINES

Anyone who tried to write a tweet in the distant days of the 140-character limit on Twitter would have had some idea of what's involved in writing a good headline. You're aiming for something that will crisply and accurately encapsulate an idea, story or thought while also seeking to intrigue/shock/amuse/tease. A headline must faithfully represent the article beneath it while simplifying and capturing its salient points. Get it right and it flies; get it wrong and it sinks.

A front-page tabloid headline is aiming to sell copies. It has to be arresting and dramatic: it is shrieking 'Buy me!' A sub-editor on a more upmarket paper will have more words to play with and is seeking not to sell copies, but to help a reader understand at a glance what the text is about: either lure them into reading it or save them time by not having to read further.

For that great craftsman of journalism Harold Evans, good headline-writing was crucial to a good newspaper: 'Where headlines are wordy, vague or confused, the newspaper seems to be in its dotage. Where every headline goes unerringly to the point with precision or wit, the whole newspaper comes alive. The art of the headline lies in imagination and vocabulary, the craft lies in accuracy of content, attractiveness or appearance and practicality.'

These days *(SEE: SUB-EDITORS)*, a headline is also there to snag the attention of search engines and internet crawlers *(SEE: METRICS)*. In law, some leeway is given to expecting readers to take both the headline and text into consideration rather than just the headline. But the headline itself must strive to be completely accurate.

The best satire on headline-writing was penned by the columnist-turned-writer/dramatist Michael Frayn, whose 1965 novel *The Tin Men* imagined a newspaper research department inventing UHL, or Unit Headline Language, a comprehensive lexicon of all the multi-purpose monosyllables used by sub-editors. The inventors realised that the grammar of words such as 'ban', 'dash', 'fear' etc. was so ambiguous as to be useful in almost any sentence. (Linguistics students regularly get headlines to parse in their syntax classes, half as a joke, half as tough homework.) Forty years before anyone seriously imagined the use of AI to put a paper together, Frayn's researchers imagined a random headline generator:

Say, for example, that the randomiser turned up:

STRIKE THREAT

By adding one unit at random to the formula each day the story could go:

STRIKE THREAT BID
STRIKE THREAT PROBE
STRIKE THREAT PLEA

And so on. Or the units could be added cumulatively:

STRIKE THREAT PLEA
STRIKE THREAT PLEA PROBE
STRIKE THREAT PLEA PROBE MOVE
STRIKE THREAT PLEA PROBE MOVE SHOCK
STRIKE THREAT PLEA PROBE MOVE SHOCK HOPE
STRIKE THREAT PLEA PROBE MOVE SHOCK HOPE STORM

Or the units could be used entirely at random:

LEAK ROW LOOMS
TEST ROW LEAK
LEAK HOPE DASH BID

~~RACE HATE PLEA MOVE DEAL~~

With UHL, in other words, a computer could turn out a paper whose language was both soothingly familiar and yet calmingly incomprehensible.

Half a century later there are a number of random *Daily Mail* headline generators on the internet which rather brilliantly mimic the *Mail's* signature use of the 144pt interrogative:

ARE THE UNEMPLOYED GIVING
MIDDLE BRITAIN DIABETES?

COULD DUMBING-DOWN GIVE
YOUR PENSION SWINE FLU?

WILL FOXES RIP OFF BRITAIN'S FARMERS?

ARE PAEDOPHILES GIVING
TAXPAYERS' MONEY CANCER?

HAS FACEBOOK GIVEN
THE CHURCH CANCER?

ARE CYCLISTS DESTROYING
BRITISH SOVEREIGNTY?

And so on. In an age of AI, sillier things could happen.

HEALTH

Anyone who doubted how fundamental people's interest is in health has only to look at the coverage of the novel coronavirus that emerged from China and spread around the world in early 2020. The story was huge, the virus apparently a threat to the entire planet and certainly the global economy as countries locked down cities and recession loomed. It was hard to know who was more obsessive about it – the news media or their readers.

Crucially, SARS-CoV-2 (the virus) and Covid-19 (the disease it caused) appeared to be threats to all of us. There was no treatment, no vaccine and the virus spread invisibly and unstoppably across borders. Some initially claimed that 80 per cent of the disease was mild and that those who would suffer most would be the elderly and those with damaged immune systems, who would be at almost as much risk from flu. But this was fiercely contested by medical experts. It was hard to strike the right balance between alarm and reassurance.

That tells us something about health stories. The interest is personal. It is a lot harder to get readers excited about a disease laying waste to part of the Democratic Republic of the Congo, as ebola was just before Covid-19 emerged, than it is to attract attention to HRT shortages, obsessive-compulsive disorder or the evils of a diet filled with sugar – in other words, the everyday health issues facing people in the affluent comfort of the UK. Global health threats emerge all the time – think zika, which deformed babies in Brazil, and multi-drug resistant tuberculosis. Even though the issues underlying these diseases should be of concern to all humanity (mosquitoes spreading viruses and resistance potentially rendering all our antibiotics useless), they don't get much play in our newspapers until a Brit gets very sick.

So much of newspaper health coverage is aimed at the worried well. The *Daily Mail*, which knows its audience, produces pages and pages of health features, all aimed at its largely female readership's anxieties and concerns. It's broadly what you could call consumer health, appealing to parents worried about their children but also to those interested in 'wellness' and those of a hypochondriac tendency. Articles will range from how to adopt a gluten-free diet (which only people with coeliac disease or gluten sensitivity actually need), to symptom checks for heart disease, to cosmetic surgery.

When it comes to front-page hard news, there are just two themes: miracle cures and killer diseases. Those labels are usually untrue, but most newspapers rarely do caveats or nuance so they skip over the scientific detail, doing their readers a major disservice. Immunotherapy, for instance, really is a miracle cure – for a very small proportion of patients with specific advanced cancers. It will fail more people than it cures and some will suffer very unpleasant side-effects. Covid-19 is a killer, but for a very small percentage of people, most of whom are vulnerable and could easily be killed by other bugs they encounter.

But scientists *(SEE: SCIENCE)* don't run newsdesks, and detail gets in the way. Newspapers thrive on human interest. What could be more emotive than the attractive young woman or innocent child who is suffering because they are not getting the treatment they need? Miracle cure denied to photogenic patient with killer disease.

Most often these are cancer stories, which are well-read because people are scared of the disease. Breast cancer gets far more coverage than any other cancer, just because it's mostly about women. The great majority of breast cancers are in older people, but the photographs and interviews of case studies are invariably of those who are young and attractive, significantly distorting public perception of the disease.

These case studies are supplied by patient groups. They are charities, but they are single-issue groups whose agenda is not always helpful to the NHS or the population as a whole. NICE, the National Institute for Health and Care Excellence, is charged with making cost-effectiveness decisions on drugs to try to contain NHS spending. A charity such as Breast Cancer Care or Bowel Cancer UK is only interested in obtaining the latest, very expensive, new drugs for its clientele. It isn't interested in the plight of people with hepatitis C, who may not get the cure they need because the NHS is spending all its money on cancer drugs. Charities lobbying for new drugs have a keen ally in the manufacturing pharma companies, which often give them funding. In the past, the companies have also tried to court health journalists with lunches, dinners, overseas trips and paid 'workshops'.

Newspapers have bashed NICE mercilessly over the years for blocking drugs that may offer just a few weeks or months of extra life at huge cost, running emotive stories about mothers who will not live to see their children grow up. They rarely look beyond the individual tragedy to examine why the cost of the new miracle medicine is extortionately high. In the long-running scandal over drugs for cystic fibrosis, a horrible disease which affects children and young people's lungs and shortens lives, most newspapers attacked NICE and the government for their refusal to pay £100,000 a year per patient. Few investigated the US company Vertex, which had received charitable money to develop the drugs, was making vast profits and was refusing to do a deal.

Human stories trump scientific facts time and again. It happened over vaccines, where the plight of children with autism and their desperate families who were looking for explanations drove the cause of anti-vaxxers inspired by the theories of the discredited doctor Andrew Wakefield in 1998. Newspapers have achieved great things by taking up the cause of the common person. But populism is now challenging scientific orthodoxy. Health journalists, however diligent, can put together a story full of facts, evidence and the opinions of distinguished scientists only for it to be rubbished on social media by people who hold alternative views. Some of those people – such as anti-vaxxers – have scientific qualifications themselves, albeit not primarily in the contested field. Wakefield was not an immunologist, but a gut specialist. Others might be psychologists. They have the language and they know how to frame the argument. It makes the health journalist's job ever more difficult – and even more important.

HERSH, SEYMOUR

Seymour 'Sy' Hersh (b. 1937) would, for much of the past fifty years, be included in any conversation about the best American investigative journalists. He was a lone wolf, preferring to go it alone, scorning the safety and consensus of the crowd. There has been no Bernstein to his Woodward; no investigative team into which he could easily blend. He broke some of the biggest stories of his times. He fell out with editors. He threw typewriters through windows. He could be petulant, unreasonably stubborn and prudish. But, boy, could he report.

As a thirty-two-year-old freelance reporter in Vietnam, he broke the story of the My Lai massacre, winning a Pulitzer and becoming a household name during a golden age for investigative reporting. When the Watergate story unravelled a few years later, he covered it for the *New York Times*. He didn't receive the level of acclaim of Bob Woodward and Carl Bernstein, but would certainly be included in the same tier. He broke a number of other nationally and internationally significant stories over the next several decades and became one of the leading journalistic voices covering the Iraq War and Bush administration. In 2004, he revealed the Abu Ghraib scandal.

Societies need reporters like Hersh – sceptics who take nothing on trust and who will go to exhaustive lengths to dig beneath the ever-thicker veneer of gloss, dross, fakery and spin. 'If your mother says she loves you,' an early news editor advised him, 'check it out.' He did, time and time again.

And yet. Throughout his career Hersch has been the subject of crit-icism on fact-finding and sources, especially from within the journalism community. The first major public scandal came in 1997, when Hersh claimed to have found documents proving that Marilyn Monroe had blackmailed President John F. Kennedy. According to *Newsweek*, Hersh received a $2 million TV deal before later admitting that the documents had turned out to be forged. When confronted he replied 'Big deal', even though reporting from *Vanity Fair* revealed that he had ignored numerous red flags in the course of his reporting.

After receiving many awards for exposing the Abu Ghraib scandal, including the National Magazine Award for Public Interest and his fifth George Polk Award, Hersh became embroiled in more scandals, to the point where he's now regarded as a conspiracy theorist by many main-stream journalists.

In 2005, less than a year after the Abu Ghraib story broke, *New York Magazine* reported that Hersh – then the national security correspondent for the *New Yorker* – had a history of embellishing the truth in speeches he delivered at college campuses, often for as much as $15,000. According to the article, Hersh would often say, 'I'm just talking now, I'm not writing,' before making unsubstantiated allegations regarding TV censor-ship, money disappearing in Iraq, and possible war-crimes bombshell stories that the *New Yorker* wouldn't print. In an interview, Hersh told the reporter: 'I can't fudge what I write. But I can certainly fudge what I say.'

That changed in 2015, when the *New Yorker* refused to print a 10,000-word piece penned by Hersh claiming that the Obama administration's narrative of the killing of Osama bin Laden was largely a lie. His editor, David Remnick, had been a supporter of Hersh but his reporter's habit of asking readers (and his editors) to take on trust his heavy reliance on anonymous sources got him into scrapes. Many of his sources were

– as the passage of time has shown – impeccably informed. But his more recent sources have also included, for instance, Syrian president Bashar Assad. Some of his writing on who should bear responsibility for chemical weapon attacks in Syria has been vehemently contested *(SEE: FISK, ROBERT)*. In his autobiography, *Reporter*, published in 2018, Hersh admits to being enraged – 'editors get tired of difficult stories and difficult reporters' – and took the bin Laden story and subsequent investigations off to the *London Review of Books* or to the German paper *Die Welt*.

His piece on Osama bin Laden attracted immediate scepticism. One of the most outspoken critics was Max Fisher for Vox, who wrote, 'The story is riven with internal contradictions and inconsistencies' and 'simply does not hold up to scrutiny'. Among the criticisms was Hersh's use of only two sources, one of whom was anonymous. The damage was done. The *Washington Post* published a piece headed: 'Sy Hersh, journalism giant: Why some who worshiped him no longer do'. He received criticism again after writing another piece in the *London Review of Books* about Syria which Max Fisher described as a 'bizarre new conspiracy theory'.

Hersh's 2018 memoir led to many outlets revisiting his legacy. Profiles in the *New York Times* and the *Nation* laud his contributions to American journalism and status as a top investigative reporter, but agree that his work has suffered in what the *Nation* referred to as the 'disappointing denouement' of his career.

As with Robert Fisk, pity the innocent reader not knowing who to believe.

HORIZONTAL

The old world – in which a few billionaire individuals or corporations owned printing presses – was, if you like, arranged vertically. Those lucky enough to have a printing press almost literally handed down the truth – or a version of it – from above. It was sometimes referred to as the 'tablet of stone' model. But then the world began to rearrange itself, with four billion people online and able to publish, distribute, talk and respond to each other. Suddenly the world began to look more horizontal: how we talked to each other, how we informed ourselves, how power became remoulded.

The historian Niall Ferguson examined the transformative effect of this shift in his 2017 book *The Square and the Tower*: one (a tower) vertical, the other (a public space) horizontal. The vertical was about hierarchies (a downward cascade of power and knowledge) *(SEE: GATEKEEPERS)*; the second was about networks of networks – a more equal connectivity of power and knowledge.

Any journalist born into the age of the printing press and broadcasting studio will have assumed that what they did fitted into some sort of vertical structure. Anyone under the age of thirty will experience the world in a different way. They may not use the words, but having the visual metaphor in their minds might help.

HOT TAKE

A one-line opinion designed to be controversial, usually related to a news story and usually found on Twitter. However, when specifically labelled as a hot take: usually sarcasm.

HYPOCRISY

Are journalists required to live by the rules they set for everyone else? The genius of some of the best tabloids was to sell smut dressed up as moral rectitude. Their imperative was to shame. And, of course, to make money out of it.

The most classic exposition of this almost biblical purpose was artic-ulated by Paul Dacre, editor of the *Daily Mail*, in a fire-and-brimstone speech he delivered in 2008. Parts of it would not have been out of place from a Wee Free pulpit on a Sunday morning.

'Since time immemorial,' he thundered, 'public shaming has been a vital element in defending the parameters of what are considered acceptable standards of social behaviour, helping ensure that citizens – rich and poor – adhere to them for the good of the greater community. For hundreds of years, the press has played a role in that process. It has the freedom to identify those who have offended public standards of decency – the very standards its readers believe in – and hold the transgressors up to public condemnation.'

Dacre simply could not comprehend why judges did not believe it was in the public interest to expose the sex life of the former Formula One boss Max Mosley, which he considered 'perverted, depraved, the very abrogation of civilised behaviour . . . squalid purgatory'.

Mosley – we know this thanks to the *News of the World* – was into S&M. But once upon a time the *Mail* and other titles would have similarly railed at homosexuals or anyone else who transgressed a moral code determined by the editor. Dacre singled out the *News of the World* for exposing 'sexual wrong-doing' – and, indeed, they were very good at it, as numerous gay people, transgender people, adulterers and sexual transgressors found out to their cost every single Sunday morning.

Did the *News of the World* employ no gay people? Did no one on the editorial staff ever break their marriage vows? As it turned out, the editors did. During the criminal trial for phone hacking, it emerged that for eight years the two leading figures in red-top naming and shaming, Rebekah Brooks and Andy Coulson, both in their time editors of the *News of the World*, had been having an affair with each other. Both were married to other people.

A loving email from Brooks to Coulson in 2004 (when Brooks had moved on to edit the *Sun* and Coulson was exposing adulterers at the *NoTW*) was read out in court during Brooks's trial. At the time she was quite happily exposing people such as the leader of the firemen's union, Andy Gilchrist, for being a 'lying, cheating, low-life fornicator . . . We need men we can trust. Not a hypocrite who lies about his family so he can drop his trousers.'

When News International came under intense parliamentary scrutiny over phone hacking, one of the company's leading critics, the MP Tom Watson, was put under surveillance for a week in 2009, hoping to catch him having an extra-marital liaison. The three unnamed News International bosses who ordered up the hit job knew the value of naming and shaming.

'Do what we say, not what we do.' It was 'hypocrisy' when exposed in others, but it was 'only human' in a newsroom.

Hypocrisy is not limited to sex, of course. At a time when Fox News viewers (average age sixty-five) were being reassured that coronavirus didn't amount to much, Rupert Murdoch himself *(SEE: MURDOCH, RUPERT)* called off his eighty-ninth birthday party in Bel Air, California, out of concern for his health. This cancellation was reported by Ben Smith in the *New York Times*, who added that his source had supplied the information in order to highlight the disconnect between the family's prudent private conduct and the reckless words spoken on air at their media company.

Unlike sex, this was a matter of life and death. As Murdoch himself recognised only too well.

I

IMPARTIALITY

The BBC is – as a condition of its licence fee – required to achieve 'due impartiality'. What does that mean? The BBC defines 'due' as impartiality that is 'adequate and appropriate to the output, taking account of the subject and nature of the content, the likely audience expectation and any signposting that may influence that expectation'.

It is, says the BBC, not simply about 'balance' between opposing viewpoints. It doesn't require absolute neutrality on every issue (such as the right to vote, freedom of expression and the rule of law). It does mean including a wide range of viewpoints: it takes account of different cultural views.

The question has become more complicated over time, as Peter Pomerantsev argues in his book *This Is Not Propaganda*: 'During the Cold War the BBC defined "impartial" as a balance between left-wing and right-wing opinions. In the 1990s and 2000s things got more complicated. There was no clear left or right any more. In the late 2010s audiences have fractured even more, seeing the world through the distinct values and causes that define them.'

How did the BBC measure the centre-ground? According to Pomerantsev: 'The BBC used to determine what to be impartial about by following the agendas set by the political parties and, to a much lesser extent, newspapers. These were meant to be representatives of greater interests. But what happens when newspapers are no longer read and parties are so fractured that they no longer represent anything coherent?'

Pomerantsev might have added the conundrum of how to maintain impartiality in a situation like Brexit, where the polling (and the eventual result in the referendum) was very roughly fifty-fifty (52–48 on the night) but the pro–Brexit coverage in newspapers outgunned pro-Remain coverage roughly 2:1. How do you weave an impartial thread through differing metrics, especially when, during the referendum campaign, the mainstream political parties (the official line of the Tories, Labour, Lib-Dems, SNP) were all in favour of Remain. Pity the poor head of news trying to navigate that.

Impartiality is not the same as balance (the allocation of equal space to opposing views) or objectivity. You can be 'balanced' about the danger of health from smoking – giving equal airtime to a lobbyist from the tobacco industry and a leading cancer specialist. But that would not feel like impartiality. And it would amount to false balance.

What was simple a generation or more ago is more complex today. As the former ITV producer David Cox has written: 'As society has fragmented, it has become harder to set the parameters within which impartiality is to be exercised. Individualism and multiculturalism have made people less willing to accept any kind of consensus or dominant culture. The political landscape has altered too, as lobbyists and single-issue groups have transformed the once easily mediated world of Westminster party conflict. All of this threatens the legitimacy of the supposedly neutral broadcaster.'

Climate change is an example of an issue where 'impartiality' can collide with editorial judgement *(SEE: CLIMATE CHANGE)*. For some time, BBC producers and executives struggled with how to interpret the doctrine, feeling obliged to 'balance' scientists with deniers. In September 2018 the broadcaster admitted it had 'got it wrong too often' and stated unequivocally in a briefing note: 'Manmade climate change exists: If the science proves it we should report it.' This followed on from a series of challenges over the BBC allowing the former Chancellor of the Exchequer, Lord Lawson, to spout false statements about climate change without adequately contradicting him – or at least signalling to the listener that he was wrong.

The corporation decided that it was legitimate to allow contrarians or sceptics to debate the speed and intensity of global warming, but demanded that presenters had to be prepared with reliable information in order to challenge speakers, as well as to expose any potential sources of funding.

INCREMENTAL

Many of the most famous newspaper investigations did not begin and end in a day. In films, big stories tend to arrive oven-ready and explode immediately, with satisfying results. Mayor resigns, goes to prison, job done.

In real life, a story more usually builds painstakingly, piece by piece. Harold Evans, as editor of the *Northern Echo*, helped secure a posthumous pardon for Timothy Evans (no relation), hanged in 1950 for a murder committed by the serial killer John Christie – but only after several years of repeatedly returning to the issue, long after most readers had tuned out. Evans was hugely admired for his subsequent, years-long campaign to secure justice for the children born with appalling deformities after their mothers had been prescribed an anti-nausea pill, thalidomide, during pregnancy. The story of Watergate, which would eventually bring down a president, was told in many single-column or down-page bites. Nick Davies's long *Guardian* investigation into phone hacking ran over several years, as did David Leigh's work on the bribes involved in selling arms to Saudi Arabia.

Here is an area where metrics *(SEE: METRICS)* are of no help. It is likely that 99 per cent of readers will be uninterested in each incremental build of a story. But a skilled investigative reporter will know that each article may flush out another piece of vital information, or provoke a whistleblower to emerge from the woodwork.

All investigative reporters console themselves with the advice of the founder and editor of the *New-York Tribune*, Horace Greeley, who observed that the point when a newspaper began to tire of a campaign was the point where readers were just beginning to notice it.

There is, to date, no algorithm for that.

INFLUENCERS

In the vertical world, influence came from the scarcity of information. In the new horizontal, or peer-to-peer, world *(SEE: HORIZONTAL)* there sprang up a new category of people whose individual following could only be gawped at in disbelief by many mainstream journalists.

Gawpworthy and galling, to put it mildly. Journalists had done the hard
graft, learned the trade, practised their craft — and then along came a
seventeen-year-old filming in her bedroom who called herself an 'influencer', with a vast audience and revenues to match.

Who did they think they were? Most reporters would never have
heard of Arshdeep Soni, a twenty-four-year old TikTok (and Instagram
and YouTube) star with a cool seven million followers, who was 'working
with' Burger King and a select number of record labels. Or the Harfin
family from Edinburgh, with their two million followers, who discreetly
drop clients' names into their videos. Or Jeffree Star (née Jeffrey Lynn
Steininger Jr), who has built a beauty empire through YouTube, attracting
more than 16 million subscribers and earning an estimated $18 million
in 2018. That placed him fifth on one list of influencers, topped by a
motley crew of kids in their twenties talking about fashion, video games,
toys or food, or performing tricks or pranks.

Is influencing a real job? How does the industry work and how is
the money made?

Even a fledgling influencer may find themselves approached by talent
management agencies who help them with everything from content
strategy to sourcing and negotiating brand deals. The agencies also deal
directly with the contracts, invoicing and payments. They will offer to
handle all emails and all correspondence with brands and external help,
with a standard revenue split of 80/20 influencer/agent.

Cue disdain from hard-nosed reporter. But is the world of influencing
that different from the realm of native advertising (SEE: NATIVE
ADVERTISING), which increasingly pays our reporter's salary in the
realm of mainstream media? PR agencies and brands have large budgets
to put the way of young would-be digital stars, whose role is to promote
a product in a way that seems authentic, and not at all like advertising.
Just like native 'content', in fact.

A new breed of search engines for influencers has sprung up, such
as Traackr, via which a would-be advertiser can specify age, audience
demographic, content and 'passion points' in order to find a 'relevant'
influencer to work with.

As with native advertising, influencers are supposed to adhere to
guidelines requiring them to declare sponsored content. They are
supposed to have a legal obligation to declare whether they have received

free gifts for promotion. Influencers are also supposed to be honest about the products they are promoting, e.g. they should not promote products they have not personally used without making that explicit to their audience. They're advised to use hashtags such as #AD #sponsored #gifted #collab and #paidpost.

In the UK this new landscape is regulated by the Advertising Standards Authority, along with the Competition and Markets Authority, which have released their own guidelines on the conduct of influencers (comparative guidelines are currently looser in the US).

Covid-19 hit the world of influencers just as it did more mainstream forms of media. Their revenues dried up as the global economy went to sleep. Some were praised for broadcasting responsible messages about social distancing to vast audiences whom mainstream media was missing. Others were panned for spreading rubbish.

Economic fragility. Dilemmas about trust while seeking authenticity. New media, old problems.

INFORMATION OPERATIONS

Information (or Influence) Operations: actions taken by governments or organised non-state actors to distort domestic or foreign political sentiment, most frequently to achieve a strategic and/or geopolitical outcome. These operations can use a combination of methods, such as false news, disinformation or networks of fake accounts aimed at manipulating public opinion *(SEE: FALSE AMPLIFIERS)*.

INVERTED PYRAMID

The inverted pyramid is a metaphor instilled in rookie journalists in their first week: it is a visual image to train them to include all the most important information at the top of a story (need to know), moving on to the supporting details and background information lower down (nice to know). It is, in many ways, the opposite of academic writing, which may begin with an abstract and then quite often progress to a review of the existing literature before moving on to a conclusion at the end. Journalists may well include the conclusion at the beginning. A piece written in an inverted pyramid is also easier for an editor to cut for length: it should be safe to trim from the bottom.

INVESTIGATIVE JOURNALISM

The charm of life for many conventional reporters and commentators lies in the way they are allowed to mingle with celebrities, chief executives and Top People, who pretend to like them and treat them as near-equals. But investigative journalists don't really benefit from this glamorous atmosphere. They specialise in the exposure of concealed wrongdoing. This doesn't make them particularly popular with their contacts.

Indeed, investigative reporters occasionally get killed. Maltese anti-corruption writer Daphne Caruana Galizia was blown up by a car bomb in 2017; Veronica Guerin was assassinated by an Irish drugs gang in 1996; and in 2006 a Chechen gunman shot Anna Politkovskaya of *Novaya Gazeta* four times as she stepped out of a lift in Putin's Moscow.

That happens only rarely. However, many investigative reporters have to weather barrages of personal abuse, establishment pressure, official complaints and ugly, not to say potentially career-ending, legal fights. To take just one dispiriting example: during a period of uproar in Britain about sexual predators, BBC journalists at first struggled vainly to expose a guilty celebrity, Jimmy Savile, and then managed wrongly to accuse an entirely innocent man, Tory treasurer Lord McAlpine, of the same crimes. A journalistic website called Exaro simultaneously pursued misguided sex-abuse allegations against a retired field-marshal and the former UK prime minister Edward Heath.

These follies cost a number of investigative journalists their livelihoods (as well as that of the then director-general of the BBC itself, George Entwhistle). And one of the most dismaying aspects of the saga was that the reporters who got it right seemed to end up being punished alongside the ones who got it wrong.

So why do people sign up so keenly for this dangerous and blundering game described by Australian Bruce Page, one-time editor of the famous old *Sunday Times* Insight team, as 'Blind Man's Buff played with open razors'?

The answer for a whole generation of Anglo–American reporters can be summarised in one word: Watergate. This David-and-Goliath struggle in the 1970s, in which two young *Washington Post* journalists brought down US president Richard Nixon for assorted political burglaries and cover-ups, became iconic on both sides of the Atlantic. Watergate came to symbolise the capacity of the media to provide accountability to societies that were badly in need of it, to give a voice to the powerless, and to fearlessly replace lies with truths.

These were intoxicating ideas. And their practitioners have been rewarded by another kind of glamour – they get to be played by movie stars. The Watergate pair, Woodward and Bernstein, started the trend, transformed by the silver screen into Robert Redford and Dustin Hoffman. Al Pacino followed in *The Insider*, playing the US TV journalist Lowell Bergman, who challenged the falsehoods of Big Tobacco. More recently, in 2015, Liev Schreiber played former *Boston Globe* editor Marty Baron in the film *Spotlight*, which lionised journalists' dogged exposure of sex abuse by powerful priests.

People thus admire the work of investigative journalists – in principle, at least. And in some ways, the task of investigative reporting has become much more rewarding in the internet age. Vast databases are now publicly available at the click of a mouse: global news archives, company filings, electoral and property registers. Even more significantly, whistleblowers have discovered how easy it is to leak vast troves of electronic information; media organisations have likewise learned how to mine such enormous sets of data for journalistic gold *(SEE: DATA)*.

Investigative worlds have opened up dramatically as reporters in different countries realise they can now co-operate, not only sharing research instantaneously, but also by organising multinational operations that can inflict hammer-blows of worldwide publicity on their often equally multinational targets. Those exposed to unexpected daylight by these means have included politicians looting their own people, global corporations dodging national taxes, state-backed murderers and torturers, and intelligence agencies secretly surveilling the internet.

Unfortunately, the obvious social importance of this kind of investigative work does not protect it from coming under attack from three directions.

The first is well-known: the collapse of conventional media business models as online advertising hoovers up the money. Journalistic investigations are expensive.

The second is the ever-swelling armoury of laws designed to tie newspapers up in preparing pieces for publication, and then defending them against attack. As news organisations become financially enfeebled, they can afford to take fewer risks against well-resourced subjects who can launch injunctions, libel suits and privacy cases with the click of their fingers.

The third assault is even more dangerous: the Wild West of the online age is destroying the hierarchy of credibility that gave Watergate-era investigative journalism its special potency. On the screen of an iPhone, fake news and real news look the same. Yet one may come from the *Washington Post* while the other may be a Russian bot. The real struggle for the future of investigative reporting may therefore not be about how to unearth truths. The two great questions for investigative journalists instead will probably be these: how can we be believed? And how is anyone going to afford it?

An unimaginative finance director will probably not see the point of running an investigative team. They tend not to be very productive, because digging takes time and there will be many false leads. They may well incur huge costs in legal fees. Their articles may not attract huge traffic *(SEE: INCREMENTAL) (SEE: METRICS)*. In many news organisations they are the first to go.

The counter-argument is this: that many readers and viewers see investigative reporting as the highest form of journalism and will, if pressed, support it. In a period of five years the *Guardian* produced a string of extremely high-profile stories covering tax avoidance, rendition and torture, toxic dumping, undercover policing, modern slavery, surveillance, phone hacking, food safety and more. A conventional accountant would not see the point. But when the *Guardian* turned to its readers and invited them to give money to keep the paper's content available to all, the readers – now 'members' – responded. The paper, in turn, did more remarkable reporting on the Panama Papers, the treatment of the Windrush generation and Cambridge Analytica.

The readers were saying: 'If you do more reporting like that, we'll back you.' Investigative reporting – far from being a drain on resources

– became the paper's defining characteristic. It became the business model.

INVISIBLE MENDING

The former readers' editor of the *Guardian*, Ian Mayes, coined the term 'invisible mending' to describe the practice of amending a website without actually acknowledging the act. So, an error might be corrected without the reader ever fully understanding there had been another version – or what had been corrected.

In the hurly-burly of web-first journalism it's often understandable for journalists to tweak things as they go. Nevertheless there is, by the end of a 24-hour news cycle, a 'final' version of a story which may be published, printed or stored in an online archive. Some news organisations are meticulous about logging different versions of a published story. In correcting an article, they will note the fact of the amendment either at the end or the beginning of the piece. The best newspapers will give some indication of what has been changed, along with when, and why, the change was made.

But the practice of many news organisations is the opposite. If they can get away with changing a piece without too many people noticing, they will. Why wash your own dirty linen in public?

Here's a tiny but illustrative example of the mess created when a news organisation can't quite bring itself to acknowledge that a mistake was made and that you have – rightly – corrected it.

In March 2018 the *Daily Mail* ran an article about a small Gloucestershire village. The story originally reported on the graves of local Polish war heroes in Blockley being vandalised, apparently as a racist act. The headline read: 'Sick thugs smash graves of Poles and Polish soldiers'. The story was mostly not true. Some gravestones had been damaged, but by a falling tree in a storm, not by racists.

The *Mail* became aware of its mistake and then set about a re-writing of the story to include the true reason for the damage while indicating that 'it had originally been thought' that there had been vandalism. The local MP was still quoted saying how sickened he was by the destruction and hoping that the perpetrators would quickly be brought to justice. A new quote was added saying that he was relieved to hear the true story.

But whoever made the invisible corrections didn't bother to look at the forty or so comments beneath the article, which continued to refer to the original version. They included remarks such as:

- I hope the perpetrators are found and given harsh prison sentences.
- Give them 10 years with no remission, when they are caught.
- What a sorry country we have become.
- This is absolutely disgusting, I can't imagine the uneducated vile creatures who would do this.
- Youth of today . . . disgusting self-absorbed idiotic scum with parents that entitle them.

At some later stage, once the piece had been referred to Ipso, the independent press regulator, the comments disappeared. But the invisible mending of the story left a patchwork of story and responses which would, for a long time, have confused anyone stumbling across the story. It was neither fish nor fowl.

A more straightforward approach would have been to acknowledge frankly that the original story was plain wrong. An editor's note could have been appended listing the original allegations, acknowledging they were unfounded, and being explicit about the changes in the current version.

The editor of MailOnline, Martin Clarke, told the Leveson inquiry that he thought it was not really possible to record changes in this way. 'I think it would be impractical to record every single change you make as you go along,' he said in evidence. 'We're editing constantly, we're improving, we're polishing, we're changing headlines, we're changing intros. We're constantly – it's an evolving organic animal of a product. So you couldn't record every single change you made as you went along, it would be impractical.'

One journalist who later wrote about his time on MailOnline, James King, disclosed another approach to 'correction' at the website. He had mistakenly sourced a picture of a deceased woman, only to be contacted by the woman herself, very much alive. She begged for a correction, but the editors decided 'a disappearing act would be much better for business, so the Mail just removed the photos from the story as if the whole thing had never happened'. The ultimate in invisible mending.

Others differ. They believe that *visible* mending is a good thing in its own right and (like all forms of correction) should lead to greater trust that a news organisation is willing to be honest and upfront about its mistakes. But there are other archival reasons for being explicit about corrections.

Any story today may live in various forms. One version may have ended in print, which is – obviously – impossible to mend invisibly. Another might exist in a version for iPad or Kindle. It may turn up in a LexisNexis commercial archive. All of these are difficult to mend individually without leaving an incoherent trail behind.

Journalism is no longer simply the first draft of history. It is better to think of it as a draft of a number of drafts, with numerous Track Changes. If journalism prides itself as being some sort of record, it should probably think harder about what sort of record that is – and will be.

J

JOURNALIST

Who or what is a journalist? The question becomes harder, not easier, to answer the more other people do stuff that looks and feels like journalism, and the more that journalism itself dilutes the clear purposes and methods which would make definitions simpler.

First, consider the range of acts that feature in the big top we call journalism. The *Sun* or *Daily Star* have something, but perhaps not very much, in common with the editorial standards and preoccupations of the *Financial Times* or *Economist*. The *Daily Mail* has its virtues – including professional and technical skill – but under its former editor Paul Dacre its editorials, ethics and outlook on balance (let alone its digital edition *(SEE: SIDEBAR OF SHAME)* did not overlap much with the BBC or the *New York Times*. The *Daily Express* and the *Frankfurter Allgemeine Zeitung* both call themselves newspapers, but their idea of what a newspaper is could hardly be more different.

So that's the first problem with codifying what a journalist is. You have people flying under the same flag who, when they go into work in the morning, do something almost completely different. That is not, by and large, true of lawyers or dentists or teachers or scientists or plumbers or soldiers.

There is training for journalists *(SEE: TRAINING)* but you don't have to be formally trained to be one, and some of the best practitioners weren't. There is – thankfully – no licensing. Almost anyone can call themselves a journalist, and there's no register from which anyone can be struck off. Indeed, the UK's biggest private news corporation, News

UK, is led by someone who was reinstated after terrible ethical failings under her watch were very publicly exposed.

Journalism is, at its highest, a very skilful occupation. But since the age of digital it has been in competition with amateurs who, at their best, are equally informative, entertaining, expert and forensic – if not more so. News organisations now jostle with millions of other institutions, corporations and bodies which effectively behave like media companies.

If something is so hard to define, perhaps it's best not to try. But that comes with severe downsides, two in particular: access and protection.

The access question relates to who gets the ringside seat – on culture, politics, sport, war. Who gets to become a member of the Westminster lobby, or attend White House or State Department briefings? Who's allowed into a war zone? Who gets embedded? Who gets the theatre tickets and the holidays and the fashion giveaways?

Some of these questions are more profound than others. If a jewellery company wants to prioritise YouTube stars over newspaper style desks, little turns on it. But privileged access to the corridors of power or combat zones is a consequential decision, and one that authorities the world over are grappling to determine. So long as Westminster politics depends on private off-the-record briefings, it really matters who is allowed into the inner sanctum.

Elsewhere, simple market forces are gradually moving the boundaries. If a theatre finds that an enthusiastic and knowledgeable blogger has a larger and more devoted following than a lacklustre critic on a newspaper that has all but bailed on cultural coverage, then the blogger is soon going to get those plum seats in the stalls.

And then comes protection. There are, in theory, few special favours dished out to journalists above other citizens, in law or on the ground. The state – in theory – used to respect the obligations of confidentiality a reporter owed to his or her source *(SEE: SOURCES)*. That's less true today, even in countries regarding themselves as mature democracies. The law makes few distinctions between the rights of journalists and others. There was a time when warring nations did their best not to kill journalists. That's much less true now.

Nevertheless, the courts have over time often taken quite bold steps to give protection to journalists who behave responsibly in the pursuit of some form of higher public interest. The big landmark press freedom cases – *New York Times Co.* v *Sullivan*, Pentagon Papers, Distillers, Reynolds, Jameel, Spycatcher and more – have gradually built some form of shield around good reporters doing good things.

But what happens when someone like Julian Assange comes along – calling himself a journalist – and demands similar protections?

Assange was something of a chameleon: a publisher, but also a (kind of) source. He could be a disciplined editor, but was also, at heart, an information anarchist. He was a secretive hacker, but also a camera-loving performer. He hugged the documents in his possession close, but also acted as a leaks impresario, sharing them, or even apparently selling them, when it suited him. He wanted to be thought of as a journalist, but was also a political activist.

In uneasy partnership with mainstream media organisations, he helped bring into the open information that any news organisation would have been proud to publish. But he also behaved recklessly at times, needlessly dumping unredacted documents onto the internet. And he lost the sympathy of many when he appeared to act as a conduit for the Russian military intelligence (GRU) in distributing emails stolen from Democratic Party organisations and the Clinton campaign chair, John Podesta, in the run-up to the 2016 election. That's not particularly journalistic – but neither did it stop a great many journalists poring over every leaked email, and publishing many. His behaviour in this matter led many journalists to wash their hands of him. He wasn't one of them. So when the US authorities eventually came to indict him in 2019, they turned their backs.

The problem was that, by indicting Assange, the US government was attempting to criminalise things 'proper' journalists regularly do when they receive and publish true information given to them by sources or whistleblowers. Assange was accused of trying to persuade a source to disclose yet more secret information. Most reporters would do the same. Then he was charged with behaviour that, on the face of it, looked like a reporter seeking to help a source protect her identity. If that was indeed what Assange was doing, you might think 'good for him'.

He was finally accused of repeatedly publishing material that 'could harm the national security of the US'. Whenever you read about jour-nalists harming national security *(SEE: NATIONAL SECURITY)*, massive alarm bells should start ringing. Think no further than Richard Nixon trying to prosecute the Pentagon Papers whistleblower, Daniel Ellsberg, for harming national security in 1971. Ellsberg, an intelligence analyst, found that the Vietnam War had been prosecuted on the basis of a web of lies and thought the public deserved to know. To Nixon, Ellsberg's commitment to the truth was treason. He reached for the Espionage Act.

Today Ellsberg is celebrated as a principled whistleblower – but he came close to being jailed for his courage. That the *New York Times* was free to publish the leaked papers was down to judges. Murray Gurfein, a federal judge, refused an injunction, saying: 'The security of the nation is not at the ramparts alone. Security also lies in the value of our free institutions. A cantankerous press, an obstinate press, an ubiquitous press must be suffered by those in authority in order to preserve the even greater values of freedom of expression and the right of the people to know.' Gurfein's ringing judgment was subsequently endorsed by the Supreme Court.

But where does that leave a more complicated figure such as Assange? The point is that yesterday's definitions of what a journalist is can barely stretch to cover the new breed of people performing journalistic acts today. That may be bad for such figures – but the new precedents that may be set by turning our backs on these new players may well end up damaging more conventional forms of journalism.

'If Assange is found guilty of conspiring with Manning under this indictment, which incorporates the Espionage Act, this will be a blow to the First Amendment,' commented James Goodale, who was the *NYT*'s counsel at the time it fought the Pentagon Papers case. 'It will criminalise the news-gathering process and will be a precedent for future cases concerning leaks. This will be particularly so since substantially all leaks in the future will be computer-generated . . . All we are seeing now is the tip of the legal iceberg.'

Journalists will have to work harder to persuade a sceptical public that there is a common craft at the heart of what they do, regardless of whether they work for a red-top tabloid or a public service broadcaster. In time, as revenues shrink, there will be a premium on journalism that performs some kind of public service, rather than being entertainment or forceful expressions of political ideology.

J

And then professional journalists have to decide how they work with the oceans of non-professional content all around. Rather than sneering at the outpourings of amateurs, they should work harder at harnessing the expertise and goodwill which lives outside newsrooms. Should journalistic privileges, access and protections extend, say, to some players on social media, or to bloggers – that much-derided breed who include some of the most articulate and expert writers (as well as idiots and fakes and trolls and hatemongers)?

Finally, there are some basic fundamentals that should be true of anything a journalist does: honesty; independence; verification; responsiveness – including a readiness to clarify and correct; transparency; and acting in accord with personal conscience. Most decent journalists have all those qualities. Some journalists don't. For the sake of anyone trying to cultivate a broader understanding of what 'journalism' is, the ones that don't behave professionally and decently need to be called out.

K

KREMLIN

It is now beyond reasonable doubt that, in place of the cold war, the Kremlin has for some time been waging a different kind of war – covertly infiltrating the digital sphere to influence and corrupt democratic processes in Europe, the US and beyond. The hacking and leaking of internal Democratic Party communications during the 2016 US election were simply one high-profile symptom of the new warfare, which saw widespread covert political disinformation as well as the use of troll farms and bots to infiltrate and sway public debate.

In some ways Putin's agenda was not dissimilar from the tactics used by Donald Trump, Steve Bannon and other populists in seeking to undermine faith in any kind of evidence-based reality. If you can, for instance, convince enough people that the *New York Times* is completely fake, then (they imply) you might as well believe Bannon's reality, and Trump's alternative facts.

The targets of disinformation are not always the obvious ones. The writer Peter Pomerantsev explored the odd-seeming behaviour of the Kremlin in choosing to crawl inside American protest movements online. The rationale? 'One starts doing a double take at everything one encounters online. Was that American civil-rights poster actually produced in St. Petersburg? Is anything what it says it is? Getting caught is part of the point, making it easier for the Kremlin to argue that all protests everywhere are just covert foreign-influence operations.'

Pomerantsev even found online a 2011 Russian manual called *Information-Psychological War Operations: A Short Encyclopedia and Reference*

K

Guide. He wrote, 'The book is designed for "students, political tech-nologists, state security services and civil servants" – a kind of user's manual for junior information warriors. The deployment of information weapons, it suggests, "acts like an invisible radiation" upon its targets: "The population doesn't even feel it is being acted upon. So the state doesn't switch on its self-defence mechanisms."'

How to combat this kind of operation? 'If all information is seen as part of a war, out go any dreams of a global information space where ideas flow freely, bolstering deliberative democracy,' writes Pomerantsev. 'Instead, the best future one can hope for is an "information peace", in which each side respects the other's "information sovereignty": a favoured concept of both Beijing and Moscow, and essentially a cover for enforcing censorship.'

But 'information peace' feels illusory in a world in which, increasingly, the suspicion of Kremlin-inspired disinformation pollutes virtually everything, most recently Brexit and conspiracy claims about coronavirus. The pandemic which swept the world in 2020 was bad enough without being complicated by what the World Health Organization termed an 'infodemic'. Both were, in their own ways, viral and deadly.

L

LAMESTREAM MEDIA

To some, MSM (mainstream media) is insult enough, with its whiff of surrender to corporate capitalism and the cloying consensus of elites. But LSM (lamestream media) makes the point more emphatically. It was originally coined around the end of the twentieth century to describe a media that – in the face of digital disruption – was dying on its feet. Alternatives were to refer to 'dead tree media', 'dinosaur media' or 'legacy media'.

MSM began as a critique from the left: a loathing for what it perceived as a vice-like grip on information by the rich ('Corporations sell audiences to other corporations. In the case of the elite media, it's big businesses,' said Chomsky).

'Lamestream' was used increasingly as a term of sneering contempt by the alt-right: it implied a failed attempt by fundamentally dishonest big media outlets to be blandly mainstream in an attempt to appeal to, and probably mislead, everyone. It became a favourite insult of Sarah Palin, former governor of Alaska, in her abortive run for vice president in the 2008 election.

LSM was, of course, an irresistible word for Donald Trump as he repeatedly promoted the idea of a giant media conspiracy against him. Near the start of the Covid-19 lockdown in the US, on 25 March 2020 he contemptuously tweeted: 'The LameStream Media is the dominant force in trying to get me to keep our Country closed as long as possible in the hope that it will be detrimental to my election success. The real people want to get back to work ASAP. We will be stronger than ever before!'

In further taunts at LSM he accused them of knowingly inventing information and of being 'dangerous and corrupt people'. They were, inevitably, the Enemy of the People. Only by people taking power into their own hands would America be great again: 'Never has the press been more inaccurate, unfair or corrupt! We are not fighting the Democrats, they are easy, we are fighting the seriously dishonest and unhinged Lamestream Media. They have gone totally CRAZY.'

LINKS

Links are – or should be – commonplace in digital journalism today, peppering articles with underlined portals to elsewhere. They have been lauded as the solution to journalism's greatest woes, and blamed for destroying readers' already-stunted attention spans. Which is it? The debate shows a press grappling with the opportunities and challenges of an interconnected web.

First, the dissent: in 2006, TechCrunch contributor Steve Gillmor swore off hyperlinks and technology writer Nicholas Carr likened them to 'little textual gnats buzzing around your head' and 'violent footnotes'. Carr worried that distracted, superficial reading has become the norm as our brains remain suspended in the constant decision to click or not to click. His suggestion to 'delinkify' – to move links to the bottom of an article *(SEE: FOOTNOTES)* – sparked, well, lots of angry links to his post. But some readers and bloggers embraced a switch to text without the clutter. (Carr went on to write the best-selling book *The Shallows: What the Internet Is Doing to Our Brains*.)

In the fallout, many rallied around links. Harvard's Nieman Lab responded by compiling four ways they might make the news better and more useful. Jonathan Stray argued:

1) Links are good for storytelling: they allow journalists to stay concise online by linking to background and sub-stories. This solves the problem of re-telling long, complex sagas in print.
2) Links keep the audience informed: they allow journalists to efficiently share the source of their knowledge, pointing readers to other good reporting.

3) Links are a currency of collaboration: they offer a story's external sources a vote of confidence, or at least some web traffic, like a payment for contributing. Stray reckons this could facilitate the production of good journalism amongst different players.

4) Links enable transparency: they give journalists an easy route to attribution and citation. Gone are the days of 'a study shows' or 'it has been reported': readers can follow journalists to their sources, when those sources have URLs.

But many news organisations – especially ones where the primary output is print or broadcast – are still bad at linking. That document or report of a legal judgment you're writing about? Could you just let us click through to it so we can read it for ourselves? You'd be amazed how often reporters can't be bothered.

This may be a hangover from Age of Paper habits wherein (as the internet philosopher David Weinberger has written) we got used to the idea 'that authority comes in the form of a stop sign: You've reached a source whose reliability requires no further inquiry.' But, as Weinberger continued: 'In the Age of Links . . . transparency – the embedded ability to see through the published draft – often gives us more reason to believe a report than the claim of objectivity did . . .

'In fact, transparency subsumes objectivity. Anyone who claims objectivity should be willing to back that assertion up by letting us look at sources, disagreements, and the personal assumptions and values supposedly bracketed out of the report.

'Objectivity without transparency increasingly will look like arrogance. And then foolishness. Why should we trust what one person – with the best of intentions – insists is true when we instead could have a web of evidence, ideas, and argument.

'In short: Objectivity is a trust mechanism you rely on when your medium can't do links. Now our medium can.'

No standardised system of citation for journalism has emerged yet, even in a press awash with links. But many major news outlets have guidelines for their reporters on how to link well.

Does it make us better consumers of news, or do we now put the 'hyper' in hyperlink? Filtering lots of information is part of what makes

us human. Perhaps we just need a little help prioritising, and finishing
~~what we start: for that, there's 'open in new tab'.~~

LISTICLES

Seven Facts About Listicles That Will Make You Want To Write One

1) People love lists
2) The optimum length of a listicle is 29 according to a Betaworks analysis
3) Listicles break down their subject into bite-size factoids
4) Reading a listicle requires less concentration than a traditional article, so they are more widely clicked on and shared
5) Martin Luther's '95 Theses' could be considered an early listicle
6) So could the Ten Commandments
7) Martin Luther's '95 Theses' would be a better listicle if it included gifs

LÜGENPRESSE

The term Lügenpresse – 'lying press' – was used by the German National Socialist Party before and during the Third Reich to discredit new media and undermine public trust. It was thus similar in intent to the phrase 'fake news' *(SEE: FAKE NEWS)* which became current in the USA and elsewhere in the early twenty-first century. A 2019 study by academics Michael Koliska and Karin Assmann found that reports of verbal and physical attacks on journalists and news organisations by individuals calling them Lügenpresse had again become a frequent feature of the public discourse in Germany. Editors responded by thinking deeply about how to counter these accusations of lack of trust. They focused on improving established processes and on making professional standards and practices more visible to the audience.

LYING BASTARDS

'Why is this lying bastard lying to me?' was the *Times*'s Washington correspondent Louis Heren's approach when talking to politicians, and is often (mis)credited to the British TV presenter Jeremy Paxman. In fact, Heren's maxim was qualified, and read in full: 'When a politician tells you something in confidence, always ask yourself, "Why is this lying bastard lying to me?"' The qualification implies – rightly – that there may be reasons to distrust a politician who does not want to be on the record as the source of information. But many journalists would agree with the advice, regardless of qualification. They lie; we tell the truth.

Paxman was asked about the credo in 2005. 'Do I think that every-body you talk to is lying? No, I do not. Only a moron would think that,' he responded. 'But do I think you should approach any spokesman for a vested interest with a degree of scepticism, asking "why are they saying this?" and "is it likely to be true?". Yes, of course I do.'

Paxman's erstwhile boss, former director general of the BBC Michael Grade, had a different view of the relationship between journalist and politician, advising BBC reporters to avoid 'slipping into the knee-jerk cynicism that dismisses every statement from every politician as, by definition, a lie. Scepticism is a necessary and vital part of the journal-ist's toolkit. But when scepticism becomes cynicism, it can close off thought and block the search for truth.' *(SEE: SCEPTICISM)*

But some reporters undoubtedly prefer the simplicity of cynicism. Paxman was also (again, wrongly) credited with saying that the rela-tionship of a journalist to a politician should be that of a dog to a lamppost. The former BBC presenter did use the quote approvingly, attributing it to the American columnist H.L. Mencken. The evidence that Mencken coined the saying is thin. It seems more likely that it originated from (or described) one of Paxman's colleagues on *Newsnight*, the late Vincent Hanna.

Politicians do sometimes lie – perhaps increasingly so. The *Washington Post*'s dedicated Trump team claimed to have found him making 13,500 false or misleading claims in his first three years in office. As the press became more economically enfeebled, so politicians may have felt a sense of freedom to lie with impunity. In 2019 Britain re-elected as prime minister a man who was widely considered to be serially untruthful.

Regarding all politicians as liars and seeing it as the journalist's role to (albeit metaphorically) piss on them elevates the press into a position of moral superiority. There are two problems with this. One is that a great many readers look at a great deal of journalism and can't see why newspapers feel entitled to occupy the higher ground. The other is that, however much the public may distrust politicians (and they do), they also feel legislators are publicly accountable in a way that most jour-nalists seem not to be.

A few politicians are certainly lying bastards. But cocking a leg at every passing lamppost is no more attractive in reporters than it is in dogs.

M

METRICS

On 1 December 2009, Mark Contreras, senior vice president for newspapers for E.W. Scripps and incoming chairman of the then Newspaper Association of America, gave a statement to the Federal Trade Commission under the title 'How Will News Media Survive the Internet Age?'.

'More than 15 years after the widespread adoption of the Internet there are no universally accepted definitions that both publishers and advertisers agree upon,' he said. 'Creating one gold-standard definition should help assist publishers in deriving a more fair value for the online inventory all publishers create.'

More than a decade later there is still no universally accepted definition and there remains huge debate about the dangers and benefits of even the act of measuring what people are reading online. New business models and metrics have come and gone. Metrics have been consistently attacked as toxic, and corrosive to the act of journalism itself. But the use of audience metrics in newsrooms, for better and for worse, has become business as usual.

A decade ago, if metrics entered newsrooms they did so in quite a standard way. Tools such as Adobe Omniture were set up to automate the delivery of email reports to small groups of senior editors. These reports would typically outline the number of daily unique visitors that came to the site the previous day, along with a list of the articles most clicked-on by those visitors. The topline numbers might be read out in a daily meeting, with peaks and troughs usually linked only to the liveliness of the news agenda. The list of top articles would be considered worth mentioning if it included pieces editors particularly liked. Nothing really happened in response to the numbers.

This status quo began to shift as publishers became aware of the implications of the web in terms of unbundling the news package *(SEE: ATOMISATION)* and the potential for search engine and social optimisation to help individual articles find vast audiences. More and more, newsrooms began to employ people to focus on writing headlines *(SEE: HEADLINES)* that maximised reach. Inevitably, these individuals needed to know what worked. They also brought a muddying of church and state *(SEE: CHINESE WALLS)*: the driver was often a commercial one linked to advertising revenue and with little thought for editorial implications.

In 2010, the former *New York Times* media reporter David Carr (1956–2015) wrote the ur-text for the SEO resistance: 'Headlines in newspapers and magazines were once written with readers in mind, to be clever or catchy or evocative. Now headlines are just there to get the search engines to notice. In that context, "Jon Stewart Slams Glenn Beck" is the beau ideal of great headline writing. And both Twitter and Facebook have become republishers, with readers on the hunt for links with nice, tidy headlines crammed full of hot names to share with their respective audiences.'

It's an enjoyable irony that the *New York Times* chose to publish Carr's virtuosic and acidic piece with a headline – 'Taylor Momsen Did Not Write This Headline' – that attempts to illustrate his argument but condemns it to be found only by those who already know of its existence.

It's an extremely useful piece, full of contradictions. It captures the suspicions of the time (some well-founded) as well as the reluctance to recognise that giving a worthy news article a headline that allows it to be discovered and read by more people might be a laudable aim *(SEE: SUB-EDITORS)*. There's the winsome lament for print headlines despite their total inappropriateness for a radically different medium which strips articles of their context. And it articulates a fundamental and undying trope: that optimisation is somehow for robots rather than humans, despite the fact that Google and other search engines are the tools most humans use to navigate the open web.

As the focus on optimisation began to emerge, so too did the measurement tools to support it. Platforms such as Omniture typically had long lag times, rendering them useless to those trying to spot poorly performing articles and act before it was too late. Chartbeat, still one of the biggest real-time analytics tools, emerged from Betaworks in 2009 and launched their news platform in 2011. The *Guardian's* bespoke real-time tool Ophan began at a hack day in the same year.

Almost overnight, these products radically increased the number of staff who had access to this kind of data. In newsrooms which had thought carefully about how the data was discussed, communicated and responded to this led to a huge growth in understanding amongst journalists, editors and production staff of how readers arrived at any given piece of journalism and how to help journalism find an audience. But where the data was injected mindlessly and without guidance, a whole range of insidious side effects sprang up.

In 2014, Tony Haile, the then CEO of Chartbeat, wrote a piece for *Time* that captured these side effects and articulated a case for an alternative. 'Here's where we started to go wrong,' he wrote. 'In 1994, a former direct mail marketer called Ken McCarthy came up with the clickthrough as *the* measure of ad performance on the web. From that moment on, the click became the defining action of advertising on the web . . . However, the click had some unfortunate side effects. It flooded the web with spam, linkbait, painful design and tricks that treated users like lab rats. Where TV asked for your undivided attention, the web didn't care as long as you went click, click, click' *(SEE: CLICKBAIT).*

The fundamental danger of pure reach metrics in the newsroom was an advertising model disconnected from the wider aims of journalism. When page views, clicks or unique visitors were being set as targets, editorial values ceased to lead commissioning.

Instead, articles were commissioned on the most popular topics and optimised in ways that misrepresented subjects or sensationalised them. Some publishers employed whole new teams of journalists to produce a separate stream of content created as a response to Google Trends or social media monitoring data.

But the impact could be more insidious: the presence of visible analytics in a newsroom could make journalists feel under pressure to respond even in the absence of explicit instructions from executives. If a weatherman was blown over on live television in Kansas and subsequently went viral, you could be sure that hundreds of news organisations worldwide would publish their own version of the story within hours in a desperate grab for clicks.

Some newspapers put very odd incentives in place. In June 2019 it came to light that reporters on the Murdoch-owned *Herald Sun* in Australia were being offered financial bonuses of between $10 and $50 for driving digital subscriptions and traffic through their own stories. If readers landed on a paywalled story and then decided to buy a subscription, the reporter would be financially rewarded after a certain target had been reached. This might have been welcome news to the crime reporter, less encouraging to someone writing gritty pieces about penal policy or social care.

Haile's proposed solution was to place more value on what readers did when they got to a page rather than focusing on the click itself. This in itself wasn't necessarily groundbreaking – publishers and platforms including the *Guardian* and Medium were looking at the time people were spending on pages already – but Haile's ability to inject metrics into multiple newsrooms through Chartbeat and his attempt to promote attention time as a metric that brought benefits to advertisers and publishers made it an ambitious and meaningful intervention.

'Articles that were clicked on and engaged with tended to be actual news,' his 2014 *Time* article continued. 'The most clicked on but least deeply engaged-with articles had topics that were more generic . . . The best performers captured approximately five times the attention of the worst performers. Editors might say that as long as those topics are generating clicks, they are doing their job, but that's if the only value we see in content is the traffic, any traffic, that lands on that page. Editors who think like that are missing the long game. Research across the Chartbeat network has shown that if you can hold a visitor's attention for just three minutes they are twice as likely to return than if you only hold them for one minute.'

The advertising side of the argument was never won, sadly. But even though clickbait has remained a surprisingly stubborn stain on the publishing industry (despite digital advertising revenue providing less and less incentive), Haile's work undoubtedly pushed attention metrics to the fore and more and more publishers began to at least pay lip service to their value as a better proxy for journalistic quality and an important means of establishing loyalty.

As the debate around reach and attention raged, another interesting front was opening up. By 2015, CEO Jonah Peretti had grown BuzzFeed to 200 million unique monthly visitors. But at that year's SXSW gathering in Austin, Texas, he explained that those metrics were irrelevant. They were dwarfed by the people who saw BuzzFeed's content in social streams: 847 million views on Twitter, 6 billion on Pinterest, and 11.3 billion on Facebook.

The rise of BuzzFeed had already led to publishers paying more and more attention to very different engagement metrics: likes and shares. A broad case was made that they represented a sense of endorsement from users that elevated them above the flat click or page view.

Peretti's message at SXSW was clear: trying to develop direct and loyal audiences through social platforms was an outdated irrelevance. The game was now about capturing huge audiences on the platforms themselves. That meant paying more attention to the platform's metrics than your own. TechCrunch observed, 'That won't necessarily make business sense unless a media property has a similar revenue model to BuzzFeed. But maybe everyone should be moving in that direction.' By 2016 Emily Bell, professor at the Tow Center at Columbia University, was capturing the general sense of the time in saying, 'The prognostication game has hitherto been about the speed at which newspapers will go out of print. Now it shifts up a gear to the more pressing question of which companies will start to jettison websites and other digital infrastructure accumulated in the past two decades.'

At the start of 2015, Mark Zuckerberg and senior Facebook executives were making some bold claims. 'We're entering this new golden age of video,' Zuckerberg told BuzzFeed News. 'I wouldn't be surprised if you fast-forward five years and most of the content that people see on Facebook and are sharing on a day-to-day basis is video.' This was the starting gun for the infamous pivot to video.

In September 2016, the *Wall Street Journal* reported that 'big ad buyers and marketers are upset with Facebook after learning the tech giant vastly overestimated average viewing time for video ads on its platform for two years'. Four days later Facebook themselves detailed the specifics:

'About a month ago, we found an error in the way we calculate one of the video metrics on our dashboard – average duration of video viewed. The metric should have reflected the total time spent watching a video divided by the total number of people who played the video. But it didn't – it reflected the total time spent watching a video divided by only the number of "views" of a video (that is, when the video was watched for three or more seconds). And so the miscalculation overstated this metric.'

If this sounds arcane, the outcome for the industry was clear: a mass delusion had led to significant resources being re-routed into video, with the loss of numerous jobs. A delusion sustained by a broken and misleading metric. The implications for Facebook were still rumbling late into 2019 when it agreed to pay $40 million to settle a class action lawsuit brought by advertisers.

While the pivot to video remains the most eye-catching example of bad metrics leading to bad decisions and serious damage, BuzzFeed and others' shift to publishing direct to platforms and reliance on those platforms' metrics above their own has also aged poorly. The idea that a like on Facebook somehow represented engagement when it was entirely possible that the user hadn't actually read the related article was increasingly undermined.

In June 2017, Peretti could be found telling traditional news businesses 'opportunistically' attacking Facebook and Google that they only had themselves to blame. Less than a year after criticising traditional media, Peretti was making the case that Facebook should be willing to share the revenue it made since, along with Google, it had hoovered up advertising revenue and put 'high-quality creators at a financial disadvantage'. By the start of 2019, BuzzFeed was laying off hundreds of staff. Increasingly, publishers are paying less attention to platform-specific metrics, or at least treating them with appropriate scepticism.

The most recent shift in newsroom metrics coincided again with a shift in business models: the second era of paywalls and reader revenue. While it's broadly recognised that multiple revenue streams, including advertising, will be crucial for most publishers, there are signs of significant success across a range of models, from the *NYT* to the *Guardian*. The industry has seen an increasing focus on reader payments, a premium on signals of on-site engagement and a view of the role of platforms as being explicitly to bring readers into the top of the funnel through referral.

The shift is exciting for publishers because it promises an explicit link between the journalism and payment that simply doesn't exist in the advertising model, and therefore a set of metrics relating to loyalty, trust and engagement that feel linked to quality and affinity with a news organisation's values. Most of the publishers who are successfully adapting to this model have built metrics and systems that connect frequency of visit and time spent to propensity to pay. And most are seeing a positive link between what they would consider quality journalism and revenue.

But seductive metrics need to be treated with care. The reader-revenue model brings with it many of the issues related to page views but accentuated by the explicit connection to money. Many organisations have begun to use internal screens to show league tables of the articles that generate the most money. But readers are often inclined to pay more for a piece they strongly agree with than a piece they consider 'quality'. A reader may make a payment or subscribe after reading a particular article, but this approach, known as last-touch attribution, obscures the value of the individual's wider reading and connection with the broad sweep of the journalism.

Finally, much of the data around this kind of model shifts the focus from pieces of journalism to the individual readers and subscribers. This reader-focused view has often been championed as a necessary change for publishers. But it brings real challenges in terms of editorial response. Article-level metrics can be acted on in real time and can inform longer-term editorial behaviour. But it's much harder for an editor to know what to do about data showing that a particular reader is visiting less often.

Despite the caveats and the dangers, the reader-revenue era has been welcome if only because it requires publishers to reappraise the metrics that are disseminated in their newsrooms and underpin their businesses. A range of models requires a range of metrics. But it's also notable how many of the questions around metrics in newsrooms remain unchanged from a decade ago and the similarities between the organisations that have navigated this space most successfully and responsibly over the years.

These can be boiled down to six broad principles:

1) **Focus on editorial aims**

Editorial values must be at the heart of any metric that's driving a news organisation. The reason the *Guardian* continues to use page views as one of two key article metrics (along with engaged time) is directly linked to its commitment to open journalism and the active desire to find the widest, most relevant audience. A wider point is also crucial: data should inform, not lead, a newsroom.

2) **Clear metrics with clear actions**

Any decent metric needs to be understood. One of the reasons unique visitors can be challenging is simply because, for most people, there is a significant gap between what it sounds like and what it actually means. Things get even worse when you start to look at the difference between daily and monthly uniques. One of the downsides of straight engaged time as a metric is that it's hard for even experienced audience editors to know if 1m 13s is good or bad. But even if the metric is fairly straightforward, like a page view, the newsroom needs to understand what it should do in response to it. If you don't have a clear idea of what a good reaction is, you end up with potentially very bad ones or utter bafflement and confusion, as in the case of Franklin Foer at the *New Republic*: 'My master was Chartbeat . . . Sometimes, I would just stare at its gyrations, neglecting the article I was editing or ignoring the person seated across from me.'

3) **A positive culture around metrics in the newsroom**

Journalists don't always use audience data in the best way possible. That's not surprising, because it takes skill and rigour. All too often it's easy for people to ignore the disappointing results (where most of the learning is) and accentuate only the good. Any organisation that makes data meaningful has a way of modelling good practice around its use. This might be an individual, a team or a regular email. Most important is the propagation of a culture that can talk transparently and constructively about things that didn't go to plan.

4) **Editors who see data as a fundamental part of their job**
Many publishers have been tempted to make data the sole responsibility of siloed teams. Having data analysts as partners is crucial
in ensuring good handling of data but organisations that succeed
here are explicit in their expectation that audience data is central
in informing editorial decisions. The best in class have cultivated
a very positive engagement. This is also important because only an
editor can really understand the context of a given piece. That's
crucial in making the data meaningful and identifying how to
respond to it.

5) **Metrics that tell journalists what they don't know**
One response to metrics that have been perceived as lacking
editorial value has been to propose other metrics that explicitly
attempt to measure quality or impact *(SEE: QUALITY)*. While
on the surface a worthy aim, this idea founders on two key points:
quality is subjective and impact is hard to define. Some publishers
have tried to aggregate other metrics as a poor proxy. Some hold
up machine learning as a way of solving the problem, but this
approach still requires an objective truth and a clear definition to
achieve it. Ultimately, it seems a more sensible approach is to use
metrics that inform editors of things they couldn't possibly know
and rely on the editorial engine and process itself to deliver and
monitor quality.

6) **Long-term thinking**
An organisation that continually shifts core metrics is likely to be
one confused about its aims and identity. Setting up metrics that
relate to really fundamental principles and aims helps, as does a
healthy scepticism around metrics from other platforms.
If there's one certainty about the news industry's future, it is that
it will be continually disrupted. Mistakes will continue to be made.
But the organisations that succeed will be those that think deeply
about the measurements and targets they ascribe to and the fundamental editorial and business principles behind them.

MILLER, JUDITH

Judith Miller (b. 1948) is a Pulitzer Prize-winning and best-selling journalist who covered alleged Iraqi weapons of mass destruction for the *New York Times* before being forced to resign in 2005 for flawed reporting methods.

Miller won a Pulitzer Prize in 2002 with the *New York Times* as part of a team covering global terrorism around the 9/11 attacks and released a best-selling book, *Germs: Biological Weapons and America's Secret War*, after being the recipient of a hoax anthrax letter.

Over the next two years, Miller wrote a series of articles on Saddam Hussein's journey to produce weapons of mass destruction. She faced criticism for her reporting, both for accepting official administration claims too easily and for publishing unsubstantiated information from dubious sources. *Washington Post* reporter Howard Kurtz later revealed that the information provided to Miller for the articles came from Ahmad Chalabi, an Iraqi politician who supplied top US officials with false intelligence *(SEE: SOURCES)*. According to an article in *New York Magazine* in 2004, while the *New York Times* published a number of pieces questioning Chalabi's credibility, it did not acknowledge the role of Chalabi in its own reporting – and that of Miller's. The article called Miller 'a star, a diva' and 'a newsroom legend', but used the terms disparagingly, calling her ambition and reliance on faulty sources reasons for her fame. In May 2004, the *Times* published a note from the editors saying, 'Some critics of our coverage during that time have focused blame on individual reporters. Our examination, however, indicates that the problem was more complicated.'

In 2005, a federal judge held Miller in civil contempt for refusing to reveal her source – who turned out to be Vice President Cheney's chief of staff, Scooter Libby – in the ongoing case surrounding the leak of Valerie Plame as a CIA officer. Miller spent three months in jail. Maureen Dowd wrote a column in the *Times* alleging that Miller had misled her editors about her involvement in the Plame leak, and questioning whether the *Times* should 'turn Judy's case into a First Amendment battle'. Miller was forced to resign in 2005, supposedly because of her politics, the embarrassment she brought the paper, and her personality.

After leaving the *New York Times* Miller wrote independently, mostly for right-wing organisations such as the Manhattan Institute, before joining Fox News as a writer and on-air analyst in 2008. A flurry of articles came out in 2015 after Miller released a memoir entitled *The Story: A Reporter's Journey*. Most coverage focused on her role in misreporting the build-up to the Iraq War and her unwillingness to admit to any mistakes. A review in the *Columbia Journalism Review* admitted Miller was correct when she alleged her 'mistakes were magnified by Web-spread attacks that were "relentless, sexist, and ugly."'

Miller and the *New York Times* played a fascinating role in the mainstream media's support for the Bush administration's decision to start the Iraq War. Although the *Times* offered apologies for its coverage – as early as 2004 – Miller continues to stand by her reporting, writing a column for the *Wall Street Journal* in 2015 subtitled: 'officials didn't lie, and I wasn't fed a line'. While she seemed to skirt partisanship for the majority of her career, she certainly found a more appropriate home at Fox News. And left behind many bewildered and disappointed readers at the *NYT*.

MISINFORMATION

False information which is imparted without malice or an intention to deceive. The sender may or may not know the information is false.

MISTAKES

Journalism is riddled with errors. The work is generally done at speed, and often in the dark. Some people will try to help a reporter get at the truth, but many others will do their best to confound them. They will conceal things, lock them away, mislead, dissemble and lie. There is, for those with the resources, an armoury of law to block an inquiring news hound.

So it's hardly surprising that journalists make mistakes. The question is, should they be more open about the flawed nature of what they do? And, having acknowledged that errors are inherent in the process of journalism, what will they do about it?

The most honest description of the intrinsic messiness of much journalism was written by the *Washington Post* columnist David Broder in a speech honouring the 1979 winners of the Pulitzer Prize. Some editors liked the text well enough to reprint it; others criticised Broder for telling tales out of school and giving ammunition to journalism's critics *(SEE: DOG EAT DOG)*:

'If we treated our audience with the respect its members deserve, and gave them an accurate understanding of the pressures of time and space under which we work, we could acknowledge the inherent limitations and imperfections in our work – instead of reacting defensively when they are pointed out. We could say plainly what we all know to be the case, that the process of selecting what the reader reads involves not just objective facts but subjective judgments, personal values and, yes, prejudices. Instead of promising All the News That's Fit to Print, I would like to see us say – over and over, until the point has been made – that the newspaper that drops on your doorstep is a partial, hasty, incomplete, inevitably somewhat flawed and inaccurate rendering of some of the things we have heard about in the past 24 hours – distorted, despite our best efforts to eliminate gross bias, by the very process of compression that makes it possible for you to lift it from the doorstep and read it in about an hour. If we labeled the product accurately, then we could immediately add: *but it's the best we could do under the circumstances, and we will be back tomorrow with a corrected and updated version.*

'If we did that, I suspect, not only would we feel less inhibited about correcting and updating our own stories, we might even encourage the readers to contribute their own information and understanding to the process. We might even find ourselves acknowledging something most of us find hard to accept: that they have something to tell us, as well as to hear from us. And if those readers felt that they were part of a communications process in which they were participants and not just passive consumers, then they might more easily understand that their freedoms – and not just ours – are endangered when the search warrants and subpoenas are visited on the press.'

In other words, our readers are not stupid. They know that journalism aspires to be a perfect representation of the truth, but is almost always bound to fall short. If we levelled with them (and corrected our mistakes), they would – so the theory goes – trust us more.

MURDOCH, RUPERT

First, consider the positives – and there are several. Murdoch loves newspapers and respects journalists. A lot of immensely rich men have bought their way into publishing houses without such affection or instinct. He turned the *Sun* into an immensely successful and profitable title in the UK. He virtually single-handedly created Sky News, which is an impressively professional and (albeit by law, rather than Murdoch's choice) impartial broadcaster. He has ploughed untold millions – probably billions – into propping up struggling titles, and broadcasters thereby giving employment to thousands of journalists over the years.

And then there is the Wapping dispute, which any fair observer would now place in the plus column, whatever the past negatives. It was inconceivable that any publisher could carry on for ever producing newspapers with printing techniques that had changed little in a hundred years. The Fleet Street unions – like their counterparts elsewhere – were implacably opposed to change and indulged in notorious and corrupt practices which defied the inevitable cost-effective introduction of computer typesetting. Any management which tried to take them on faced ruin. Murdoch did exactly that, with the incredibly daring gambit of building a parallel production capability and facing down the unions. One can criticise the ruthlessness with which he did it. One can frown on the relationship with Margaret Thatcher that allowed him to do it – along with any implicit political paybacks – but Wapping was ultimately to the benefit of the media business, even if it was painful and brutal at the time.

So much for the positives. The negatives comprise a longer list. Yes, the *Sun* was successful but, boy, did it diminish, coarsen and brutalise public discourse. The Murdoch tabloids led the way in exploiting private lives for profit and were intrusive in a way that redefined the profession of journalism. That it should have resulted in the hiring of criminals to dig up dirt on targets was only the logical conclusion for newsrooms run in pursuit of profit, without ethical guidance and ruled by fear.

Just as the newsroom staff felt cowed, so did anyone in public life who had any indiscretions in their past or present lives – i.e. a great many people. When the phone hacking scandal broke, a lot of otherwise admirable figures in public life – MPs, police, regulators, other journalists – ran for cover. This was a bad organisation to make an enemy of. Better to keep your head down.

And that, in a way, was the point. Murdoch had built up a dominant position in ownership of UK press titles and was keen to increase his dominance of privately-owned broadcast media (it was even worse in Australia, where Murdoch built up a 60 per cent share of the newspaper print market). Once someone acquires that concentration of muscle you would have to be very brave or foolhardy to take him on.

In each of the three main territories in which he operated (swapping nationalities where it suited his business) there was a pattern. He wanted an upmarket paper for respectability and to open doors (*Times/Sunday Times*, *Wall Street Journal*, *Australian*). He wanted a TV business to make money (Sky, Fox, Foxtel and Network Ten). And he wanted tabloids (*Sun/News of the World*, *New York Post*, *Herald Sun* and (Australian) *Daily Telegraph*) to make money, for political influence – and maybe to frighten people.

Because it was his company he could behave how he liked. In a normal situation, the chief executive of a company which had experienced a near-fatal ethical, legal, criminal, regulatory and financial meltdown would be banished for ever – even if they escaped conviction. But no, in the wake of the hacking trial Murdoch promptly reinstalled Rebekah Brooks, fresh from embarrassment (if not a guilty verdict) at the Old Bailey, to run his British newspapers – even though her best defence was that she had no idea what had been going on inside the company she was supposed to be running, along with James Murdoch.

What does Murdoch hope to get out of any of this? And how far can a Murdoch reader or viewer trust what they read or watch?

If only there were simple answers to these questions. There are those who argue that Murdoch – though instinctively of the neo-liberal right – is driven primarily by business pragmatism. He likes creating, or backing, winners. A politician who believes he or she partly (or considerably) owes their success to the support of Murdoch papers is likely to smile on changes to the regulatory framework that would allow his companies to flourish.

Does that translate into direct editorial control? Again, it's complicated. It is a fair assumption that any significant political argument in the *Sun* or the now-defunct *News of the World* or the *Australian* would closely reflect the views of the owner. Their editors are not, in other words, entitled to think for themselves. There may be more leeway granted to other titles – though it would be a brave editor of the *Wall Street Journal* or *Times* who did not listen to a small voice in the back of their minds regarding how far they felt able to stray from the current orthodoxy of the more directly 'influenced' titles.

And then there's Fox News, which, under Donald Trump, has felt like the nearest thing that America has ever had to a state broadcaster. In the words of the *NYT*'s James Poniewozik, it was a 'noise machine that amplified conservatism and then devoured it . . . [Fox CEO] Roger Ailes, a onetime campaign operative, programmed our current political environment. Rupert Murdoch, the Fox mogul, bankrolled Ailes's furious vision in America while imposing his own in Britain. Together, they created a smash-mouth version of conservatism that married plutocracy with populism, reactionary politics with showbiz values. They exploited fear, prejudice and, in Ailes's case, women.'

The pattern persisted over years. Most recently, look at the news channel's coverage of coronavirus in late February/early March 2020 to see how the almost perfect correlation in numerous Fox hosts mirrored the White House line – a journey from outright scepticism to belated acknowledgement of the gravity of the pandemic.

By April 2020 the channel's coverage of Covid-19 was sufficiently misleading that a group of seventy-four professors of journalism and journalists wrote an open letter condemning the coverage as 'a danger to public health . . . Indeed, it is not an overstatement to say that your misreporting endangers your own viewers – and not only them, for in a pandemic, individual behaviour affects significant numbers of other people as well.' *(SEE: HYPOCRISY)* The disquiet was evidently shared by James Murdoch, who resigned from the board of News Corp in July 2020 citing 'disagreements over certain editorial content'.

Ben Smith in the *New York Times* pointed out that the channel was notionally run by Murdoch's other son Lachlan, and questioned why Rupert Murdoch himself hadn't got a grip. Maybe, at eighty-nine, he was simply no longer up to it. Maybe he no longer cared. Maybe it was more important to Murdoch to stick with the president than insist on rigorous editorial standards. Or was he now, nearing his tenth decade

M

on earth, so ideologically aligned with elements of the populist right
that he no longer knew science from slant?

How would we know? Apart from Murdoch's humiliating 2011
appearance before the House of Commons select committee investigating phone hacking ('the most humble day of my life'), the most
powerful proprietor *(SEE: PROPRIETORS)* on the planet is rarely seen
in public – far less interviewed or in any way held accountable in the
way the journalists he employs would consider desirable of anyone else.
They hold power to account, remember? *(SEE: DOG EAT DOG)*

Books about him range from the flattering (Shawcross) to the patchy
(Wolff). But it is worth reading two little-noticed pieces of testimony
about the way he operates, given to the Leveson inquiry by two of his
most successful former editors, Andrew Neil (*Sunday Times* (1983–94)
and Kelvin MacKenzie (*Sun*, 1981–94). Both were instructive on the
way Murdoch exercises the immense power he knows he wields.

For Neil, the Murdoch newspapers' brutal treatment of the Labour
leader Neil Kinnock in the 1992 election was 'the seminal development
in relations between British politicians and the media . . . seared into
the minds of a future generation . . . [it showed] what could happen if
they ended up on the wrong side of the Murdoch press. They vowed
to themselves not to let it happen again.'

Kinnock, a centre-left politician who had helped purge the Labour
Party of the Militant faction of left-wing infiltrators, was subjected – in
Andrew Neil's words – to brutal, personal, uncouth and vicious coverage
by his 'most virulent tormentors' (the News International tabloids). 'Neil
Kinnock learned the hard way what it was like to be on the wrong
end of a press out to get you, day in, day out.'

In Andrew Neil's mind (though he concedes it is unprovable), the
Murdoch press played a significant part in Kinnock's defeat. More
important was what a subsequent generation of British politicians
believed: that in order to get elected in the UK, you had to make nice
with a multi-billionaire who wasn't even British and who spent most
of his time in New York, California or Australia.

Neil goes on to describe the unwritten deal between Tony Blair's
New Labour and Murdoch. He even quotes Blair as telling him in
1996: 'How we treat Rupert Murdoch's media interests when in power
will depend on how his newspapers treat the Labour Party in the run-up

to the election.' Which was more or less how it panned out. Blair allowed Murdoch a near 40 per cent share of the newspaper market, avoided introducing a privacy law, allowed Murdoch's TV interests to grow unhindered and repelled tougher cross-ownership rules preventing powerful newspaper groups from also becoming powerful broadcast groups.

It went further. A Labour minister told Neil that, when it came to two major issues of public policy – Iraq and Europe – 'Rupert Murdoch was the 24th member of the Blair cabinet.' According to Neil, Murdoch let it be known in Downing Street that his papers could not support New Labour's re-election for a third time if the government was going ahead with the Lisbon Treaty.

The same with Iraq. 'In the prolonged run up to the Second Gulf War,' writes Neil, 'Mr Murdoch was a regular and consistently hawkish voice in Mr Blair's ear, as were his newspapers. He would share inside information with the Prime Minister from his extensive Washington contacts. Mr Blair was almost certainly inclined to war anyway; but Mr Murdoch was a powerful voice propelling him in that direction and overcoming any doubts. I understand that in the last days before the Iraq invasion began Mr Blair spoke to Mr Murdoch more often than he spoke to his defence or foreign secretaries. All Mr Murdoch's British papers supported the PM's pro-war stance. Indeed Murdoch papers across the globe spoke with one voice on this contentious matter: on war with Iraq the Murdoch organisation was more united and more disciplined than either the Bush or Blair administrations.'

The full extent of the relationships between the Blair government and the senior executives running the Murdoch operation have, said Neil, 'never been fully revealed or exposed and, I believe, is unprecedented in the history of press proprietor/government relationships'.

A similar picture is painted by MacKenzie, for so long himself a loyal part of the Murdoch machine. In his account to Leveson, the post-Blair era was marked by exactly the same kind of incestuous behaviour between the Murdoch top team and whoever was aspiring to, or in, power. 'There was never a party, a breakfast, a lunch, a cuppa or a drink that [David] Cameron & Co would not turn up to in force if the Great Man or his handmaiden Rebekah Brooks was there,' MacKenzie told Leveson. 'There was always a queue to kiss their rings. It was gut wrenching.

'An American with a disdain for Britain, running a declining industry in terms of sales, profitability and influence, was considered more important than a meeting with any captain of industry no matter how big their workforce or balance sheet.'

Murdoch's unique power, according to Neil, derives from his willingness to be politically promiscuous. Whereas most British titles stay loyal to their tribes, Murdoch is a swing voter – 'up for grabs, depending on the circumstances'. He was pro-Labour in the seventies, pro-Thatcher in the eighties, just about loyal to the Tories in the early nineties, then switched to New Labour before the 1997 election – a pact that lasted until the autumn of 2009. At that point, as Gordon Brown struggled to find his feet as prime minister, Murdoch flipped back to the Tories.

As MacKenzie recorded, under Cameron a familiar nexus of chummy relationships developed between the Murdoch team and the new Cameroonians, a bond that was only shattered by the revelations of widespread criminality within the Murdoch organisation which Murdoch's son James had tried to cover up.

The pattern was the same in Australia, where Murdoch papers have been, in recent years, instrumental in dethroning at least three prime ministers – Kevin Rudd, Malcolm Turnbull and Julia Gillard – and in providing election coverage so shrilly one-sided that it led in 2019 to protests from News Corp insiders. 'I wasn't going to run my government in partnership with Rupert or Lachlan Murdoch or their editors, and I knew they'd resent that,' wrote Turnbull in his 2020 memoirs, acknowledging that this meant that he would sooner or later be dispensed with.

Nearly seventy years of living with Murdoch media oligarchy has doubtless blunted us to the sheer oddness of allowing one old man such extraordinary sway over civil and democratic life and processes on three continents. His heirs and successors may or may not be very different: it's a lottery. According to an extensive 2019 *New York Times* series on the Murdoch family, James began in recent years to express near-open rebellion against what he felt Fox News had become: 'a political weapon with no editorial standards or concern for the value of truth and a knee-jerk defender of the president's rhetoric and policies'. His eventual resignation was no surprise.

No rational system of informing the public about political choices would tolerate such a polluter of public discourse and honest evidence, let alone on the mass scale at which Murdoch operates. Equally, any leading politician who moved to regulate, diminish or break Murdoch's hold on our democratic processes would make themselves a target for vilification, intrusion, condemnation and destruction.

We have allowed it to happen.

Murdoch employs a great many decent journalists: even the ones who have sold their professional souls to him know how to produce popular and crowd-pleasing newspapers and programmes. At their best, Murdoch's editorial employees are as good as any on the planet. Journalism does owe him some sort of debt. It also has the absolute duty of holding him and his family to account. If the general public were ever to confuse Murdoch's general idea of news values and ethical standards with what journalism should be, then the news business really would be in trouble.

N

NATIONAL SECURITY

National security reporting is difficult in virtually every way – morally, ethically, editorially, legally, technically, politically . . . and more. Get it wrong and, at best, you may be accused of being unpatriotic ('Do you love this country?' the chairman of the Home Affairs Select Committee asked the editor of the *Guardian* during the Snowden revelations). At worst, an editor may end up with blood on their hands, or in jail – or both.

In few other areas of reporting is so little material openly available. You are writing about people who, by the nature of their job, guard their secrets closely. The main intelligence agencies may choose to spoon-feed information to trusted journalists. An editor has few ways of independently verifying the work of a reporter. There are increasingly fearsome laws to deter any form of determined inquiry. Under some proposed laws the mere receipt of unauthorised information could place journalists in jeopardy.

And yet it is surely obvious that the world of intelligence and national security cannot be off-limits to scrutiny in any democratic society. These are agencies that, today, have untold powers to place millions of people under some form of surveillance. We don't need to re-read George Orwell to see what can happen when things go wrong: there are numerous examples of societies which take pride in their ability to keep a close watch on citizens.

Journalists covering the spy agencies in the UK, the US and other democracies do so in hugely different ways. At one end of the spectrum are reporters extremely close to the spy agencies. These are favourites, the trusted ones who can be relied on by the agencies to relay information to their readers and viewers largely unfiltered and unquestioned.

At the other end of the spectrum are reporters who see their job as holding the intelligence agencies to account. They work through victims, lawyers, human rights organisations, whistleblowers, disenchanted spies and a host of other alternative sources to document agency abuses, blunders, misinformation and outright lies. Such reporters tend to be contemptuous of their counterparts at the other end of the spectrum.

The rest fall somewhere in between, balancing access to the agencies while retaining a sense of scepticism. They see much to admire – from Bletchley Park in the past to foiling terrorist attacks at present – but do not hold back from documenting the dark side. Some of the biggest scandals in both the UK and US have involved the intelligence agencies.

UK reporters have three intelligence agencies to cover: the Secret Intelligence Service, better known as MI6; the Security Service, MI5; and GCHQ. Covering the agencies is not usually a full-time job so they often combine it with covering defence. There is overlap with the work of crime correspondents, particularly in covering counter-terrorism.

Spies operate in a world where lies and black propaganda are commonplace. The agencies, by their nature, are secretive and want to stay that way. National security reporters, at least the less pliable ones, want to disclose – without putting lives or operations at risk – their secrets.

The tension is evident in competing definitions of 'national security'. The agencies, both in the UK and US, have since their inception cited 'national security' as a reason for preventing disclosure of information. Reporters counter that 'national security' is a convenient excuse for hiding things the agencies would be embarrassed to see made public.

Trying to find out what the agencies are doing is much harder in the UK than in the US, where there is more of a culture of openness throughout government, or even elsewhere in Europe. Spies in Europe seem more relaxed about talking to journalists. They are also subjected to greater government scrutiny.

Neither MI5 nor MI6, unlike their US counterparts, have press offices (though GCHQ does). Almost all the major UK news organisations have one or two journalists who are designated to speak off-the-record to the agencies. The agencies might confirm the name of a terrorist or volunteer who they think is behind a cybersecurity attack. MI5 and MI6 usually refuse to be quoted or even identified by such vague constructs as 'a security source' or 'a Whitehall source'. This is problematic for journalists working for news organisations that will not use information without some sort of attribution. By contrast, the CIA, the FBI and other US agencies do have press offices. A call to the CIA press office will probably produce no comment but sometimes they can be surprisingly open off-the-record.

US reporters have an advantage over their UK counterparts in that there is a much bigger pool to work in, with sixteen agencies. They also have a large community of talkative former intelligence officers to tap into, many of them just recently retired and potentially willing to talk about what they have been doing. Another rich source is members and staff from the Senate and House intelligence committees, which tend to be well-briefed in comparison with the UK's limp parliamentary Intelligence and Security Committee.

In spite of all the sources available to its press, however, the US has witnessed catastrophic failures in national security reporting over the last two decades, most notably publication by the *New York Times* and others of bogus reports of Iraq holding weapons of mass destruction in the run-up to the 2003 invasion. The *NYT*, although it has a fine record of breaking national security stories, was also culpable in 2004, suppressing for more than a year at the request of the White House a story about a secret Bush administration programme to snoop on Americans without warrants.

In the years after 9/11, when the kidnap and mistreatment of terrorism suspects became commonplace, journalists in the US and UK who sought to report on the secret state needed to realise that they were reporting, to an extent, on criminal enterprises. This realisation came more quickly in the US than it did in the UK. No doubt this was, at least in part, because the US is a less secretive society than the UK: Washington DC is a remarkably leaky city compared to London. While American journalists enjoy the backing of the First Amendment – and the culture of free expression that this has promoted for centuries – British journalists encounter the Official Secrets Acts, and the culture of concealment that these laws has engendered for generations. That is not to say that American journalists do not face state secrecy measures:

just that they appear to be regarded in the US as exceptional, rather than the norm, as they are in the UK.

There are almost no unauthorised leaks by those working within the British secret state. The experiences of David Shayler (a former MI5 officer), Richard Tomlinson (a former MI6 officer) and Katharine Gun (a former GCHQ translator), show what happens to those who attempt it: they are arrested, prosecuted and usually imprisoned.

The US authorities wanted their robust approach to be seen during the weeks and months after 9/11: the first photographs showing men in orange jumpsuits being dragged across the ground at Guantanamo, their hands, ears and eyes covered, were taken by a US Navy photographer and distributed via Associated Press.

The British government was soon complicit in similar abuses, but subject as it is to European as well as British courts – and rooted in a different domestic political climate – it could never be seen to be involved in mistreatment in any way. After the 7/7 bomb attacks on the London transport network, however, Tony Blair said publicly that 'the rules of the game are changing'. But the British public – and the journalists who inform the public – were not supposed to see all that that actually entailed.

While MI5 and MI6 do not run traditional press offices, they do have regular contact with journalists, usually one or two people at each media organisation, who receive briefings on the understanding that the public will never learn the source of the information. These journalists are known in agency parlance as 'accredited media contacts'. MI5 officers who brief them will often have had experience of handling informers in Northern Ireland. These encounters are backed up by agency chiefs' lunches and dinners for senior editors.

Accredited media contacts fall into one of three categories. Some do a very good job of attempting to determine whether they are being misled, and always run the risk of being cut adrift for doing so. Others, while not gullible, appear at times to suspend their disbelief in the hope of picking up a good story. The people in this group are guilty in my opinion of a rather British journalistic vice: deference.

While American national security reporters are drawn from a society that has a tendency at times to look down on its governments, their British counterparts emerge from one which frequently respects authority and, as a consequence, does not always closely question it. A security reporter was recently heard telling a group of journalism students in London that, in dealing with MI5, 'you play the game, and every now and again they'll give you something'. The students would have been well-advised to discount such advice. MI5 and MI6 are agencies of the executive branch of government, and need to be reported on like any other government body. Furthermore, the secrecy surrounding their activities is such that journalism is often the only way in which they are held accountable.

The journalists in the third category are those who are so impressed by the supposed mystique of the agencies that they appear to go weak at the knees at the thought of an off-the-record briefing. These people do not realise that their agency contacts – people whom they unaccountably believe to be friends – are actually engaged in information operations, and that frequently they are being used to launder half-truths or downright lies.

And so, for more than a decade after 9/11, many British journalists assured their readers, listeners and viewers that there was simply no truth in the allegations that the UK was engaged in the rendition and mistreatment of terrorism suspects. The invasion of Iraq was justified by Saddam's WMD programme, or by his links with al-Qaida. British troops in Afghanistan and Iraq had not been encouraged to abuse their prisoners; the real problem lay with ambulance-chasing human rights lawyers. These journalists had allowed themselves to become what the historian E. P. Thompson once termed, in relation to the late Chapman Pincher of the *Express*, 'a kind of official urinal' before which MI5, MI6 and the Ministry of Defence stood side by side, leaking.

A surprisingly small number of journalists did attempt to discover the truth about the UK's activities in the so-called war on terror, however, and found that it was not impossible.

Details of abuse in counter-terrorism operations emerged during litigation brought by the victims and sometimes during legal argument that preceded terrorism trials. Some confirmation could also be found in open sources, such as the reports of Parliament's Intelligence and Security Committee (ISC), although for many years these were written for those who were already 'in the know' – the cognoscenti of the secret state – and needed to be read against the grain. Some public officials who worked closely with the agencies would offer hints, insights and encouragement. Then there were the terrorists themselves. Some were behind bars, some were at large, and with patience they could be persuaded to give their accounts of how they had been interrogated by British intelligence officers at prisons across the Middle East and Asia, detention centres where torture was commonplace. These accounts could then be studied to see whether any pattern emerged to suggest that the terrorists were telling the truth. Finally, in a serendipitous moment during the Libyan revolution, human rights workers discovered documents detailing MI6's involvement in the kidnap and rendition of two families. It was only in June 2018, however, that the ISC finally published a report that set out the full extent to which the UK's intelligence agencies had been involved in human rights abuses of that nature.

The terrorists had been telling the truth. MI5 and MI6 officers had not. And many British national security reporters had either been fooled or simply looked the other way.

Although journalists in the US enjoy more protection under the First Amendment, both they and whistleblowers have found those freedoms under strain since 9/11. That the Bush administration would be intolerant of unauthorised security leaks after 9/11 is not surprising. The surprise was that his successor, Barack Obama, a professor of constitutional law and a liberal, would be even more active in harassing national security journalists and leakers.

Among those on the receiving end was John Kiriakou, a former CIA officer who in 2007 revealed the US had waterboarded an al-Qaida captive, treatment which he described as torture. This is what whistleblowers are supposed to do: reveal abuses. The security agencies were unhappy. Kiriakou was not prosecuted for the torture revelation but the administration took its revenge in another way, sentencing him to thirty months in jail for passing classified information to a reporter.

Others who felt the anger of the Obama administration included national security reporter James Risen, a *New York Times* veteran, who was hounded for seven years and threatened with jail for refusing to disclose a confidential source *(SEE: SOURCES)*. The case against Risen was dropped in 2015. The alleged source, former CIA officer Jeffrey Alexander Sterling, was jailed under the 1917 Espionage Act. It is one of the few times in US history that anyone has been punished under the Espionage Act for allegedly being in contact with a journalist.

Both Bush and Obama took a heavy-handed approach to National Security Agency whistleblowers such as William Binney and Thomas Drake before going on to charge the most famous of them, Edward Snowden, who leaked tens of thousands of documents disclosing the capabilities of government for mass surveillance in the US and UK.

Snowden is a case study of the competing definitions of 'national security'. The agencies claimed the leaks damaged 'national security'. Snowden and the journalists involved in the story countered that the leaks showed the governments in the US and UK were acting illegally and the public had a right to know about the scale of mass surveillance.

Without Snowden's whistleblowing, the public would never have known about mass surveillance. The agencies not only hid what they were doing: they lied about it. The US Director of National Intelligence, James Clapper, in response to direct questions at a Senate hearing, twice denied there was any mass surveillance of US citizens.

While the US charged Snowden under the Espionage Act, it took no action against journalists – unlike the UK government, which threatened to close down the *Guardian*'s reporting and oversaw the destruction in the *Guardian* basement of computers used for the Snowden stories. The London Metropolitan Police's counter-terrorism section also launched a six-year investigation into the journalists involved before shelving it.

The British security agencies would not admit it publicly, but since Snowden and the resulting damaging image that emerged of them as snoopers they have embarked on a series of public relations exercises, including the heads of agencies giving media interviews. The UK agencies are still remote but not quite as remote as they had been. They remain, however, much more secretive than they need to be, and much more secretive than their US equivalents or those elsewhere in Europe.

NATIVE ADVERTISING

Once upon a time there were Chinese walls *(SEE: CHINESE WALLS)* in newspapers. On one side of the wall lived journalists, and on the other the people who sold advertising. It was considered essential to keep the two halves of the company insulated from each other. The integrity of a newspaper is – supposedly – all it has to sell. So the wall was there to protect the journalists from suspicion that the purity of their words or pictures could have in any way been influenced by the people who, in effect, paid for much of it.

That was mainstream media. That was then.

There is now, however, a new generation for whom Chinese walls mean nothing. One of the earliest new media start-ups was Vice Media *(SEE: VICE)*, which – like all bright young disrupters in the early part of the century – was wondering how to make ends meet with the paltry sums companies were then willing to pay for digital advertising.

In 2009 the company was approached by the tech company Intel, who thought Vice could help them reconnect with millennials. The deal, according to Vice co-founder Shane Smith, was worth a staggering $40 million. The outcome was a series across print, TV and Vice's own website devoted to the work of contemporary artists. The Creators Project featured Intel's logo, though not so prominently as to put off millennials suspicious of covert messaging or product placement. It was 'editorial'. But Intel – of course – had an ulterior marketing motive.

'That program built the company,' Smith later told Quartz. 'You learn, holy shit, we could do a $40 million deal with Intel where we actually create content that we like, and they don't give notes! Why were we doing banner ads? Those $40 million deals have turned into $100 million deals.'

These kinds of deals eventually acquired a name: native advertising.

Old-style advertising was identifiable as such. The whole point of native advertising is that it is less easy to spot whether or not it is advertising. The term 'native advertising' has come to mean paid 'content' designed to mimic, or blend into, the editorial material on platforms on which it is placed. Its defenders claim that consumers are able to appreciate it for what it is (and that it brings in life-saving amounts of revenue for otherwise struggling journalism); its detractors claim that it is undermining trust in media still further by pretending to be some-thing it's not.

The very term 'native advertising' (the phrase was probably coined in 2011 by the technology investor Fred Wilson) is a sleight of hand.

Advertisers are drawn to the concept for the very reason that journalists are suspicious of it: the more the promotional 'content' looks like editorial, the more authority it will have. Like it or loathe it, it relies on a degree of confusion.

And in that respect it works – at least for the advertisers. A consumer survey in 2019 by Michelle Amazeen and Bartosz Wojdynski found that fewer than one in ten people could recognise native ads (or 'branded content') for what they were. It also works in revenue terms, at least as long as consumers either don't notice or don't mind. But Amazeen and Wojdynski did find that readers' trust in a publication declined when they discovered that some of the content was actually 'branded' and therefore not quite what it seemed. This mirrors disillusion found in Reuters Institute research, which identified misleading forms of advertising and sponsored content – along with fake news – as part of a wider discontent about the information landscape.

But doubts fade in the face of money. As late as 2013 the then editor of the *Wall Street Journal* Gerard Baker was describing native advertising as a 'Faustian pact' and urged resistance to the blurring of clear delineation between news and advertising. Within six months, however, the Murdoch-owned *WSJ* had published its first native ad (a story titled 'Cocainenomics', sponsored by Netflix) and then soon launched WSJ. Custom Studios to produce 'sponsored content'. In 2019 the division daringly rebranded itself 'the Trust' ('experiences powered by intelligence'). It sold itself on the fact that the team was composed of not mere advertising copy-writers or marketeers, but journalists. 'We have led newsrooms, headed major consumer titles, and produced award-winning films.' Trust, you see.

An early output from the Trust was a series on 100 Modern Britons, coyly describing itself as a 'paid programme' ('this content was paid for by advertisers and created by the WSJ . . .'). The only clue to the advertisers was the British Airways logo at the top of the page nuzzling alongside the Murdoch titles, *Times* and *WSJ*, a flash of the BA logo and an end-credit for BA ('Made by Britain. What a time to be a Brit.').

Native advertising has become almost ubiquitous over recent years: a 2018 study found that 92 per cent of the most visited online news sites engaged in native advertising in 2015–16. By 2019 it accounted for some 60 per cent of the US advertising market, or around $41 billion. Little wonder, in a world of highly intrusive pop-ups or 'banner blindness' in which readers either become irritated by conventional forms of advertising or filter it out altogether.

'On the one hand,' says Amazeen, 'journalists are trying to fight fake news, but on the other hand, the publishers at their organizations are participating in this practice that some find misleading or ethically challenging.' She found that there was a lack of disclosure standardisation. Other studies found publishers playing down the labelling of sponsored material in response to advertisers protesting that it was too prominent. But as conventional advertising revenues drained away and new players such as BuzzFeed, Quartz, Mashable, Facebook, Twitter and *Forbes* embraced this new commercial/editorial hybrid, native advertising became irresistible.

In 2011 Facebook started featuring 'sponsored stories' in news feeds. Twitter calls them 'promoted tweets'. On Instagram brands started mimicking the kinds of images users were used to seeing in their feeds – first-person PoV, naturalistic shots, casual hashtags, filters, a conversational tone and so on. Many mainstream companies launched their own creative operations made up of editors, designers, producers and creative strategists: the *Guardian* (Guardian Labs), *New York Times* (T Brand Studio, with a hundred staff by 2016), the *Atlantic* (Re:think), Condé Nast (23 Stories).

Even the publicly funded BBC was at it with StoryWorks – a 'creative studio with newsroom values'. A what? It says it is an 'agile content production agency from BBC Global News, embodying the BBC's creative spark and rigorous editorial quality to help brands connect through beautifully crafted storytelling.' In other words, a client pays to be associated with the journalistic and ethical standards of one of the most trusted news organisations in the world.

At least the BBC attempts a degree of openness about the various types of arrangements it enters into – up to a point. Its website describes different grades of native advertising or branded content:

- 'Custom production' is, it says, 'paid commercial content that is created to promote an advertiser' and produced by a BBC division which is separate from the BBC editorial teams.

- 'Branded content', which seems to allow commercial clients to create, or contribute to, 'published content with an editorial style which runs "natively" on BBC.com'. That apparently means that it is designed to feel like BBC content, though it will be labelled as 'paid and presented by [brand logo]' or 'advertisement feature presented by [brand logo]'.
- 'Sponsored content', which is BBC editorial content that an advertiser pays to associate with. The content is 'commissioned by the BBC's editorial teams' and is 'independent of the sponsor'. It is usually labelled 'sponsored by' or 'in association with'.

The question is whether the average viewer or user of the BBC's websites can easily differentiate between these categories of content, particularly on a small mobile screen. Academics have spent some time analysing 'disclosure characteristics' (proximity, visual prominence, wording clarity and logo presence). Studies suggest that more than a third of readers of a sponsored news story have never even glanced at the disclosure label.

Some of the native advertising projects have bigger 'editorial' budgets and smarter, younger teams than their counterparts in the newsroom. The main *Telegraph* news website, for instance, has a bog-standard traditional presentation of the sort found on thousands of news sites around the world. But its 2017 Nikon-sponsored native advertising content offering 'tips for serious photographers' was of an entirely different order of design, ambition and creativity.

Similarly, a UBS-sponsored campaign for the *New York Times* ('what it takes to be human') was a deeply immersive and stylish experience involving many interviews with leading experts in AI and a generous foreign travel budget. The toilers in the news department may sometimes grit their teeth at the disparity of available resources.

Ava Sirrah is someone who worked for two years in the T Brand Studio (and then went on to work on a PhD on native advertising). She has voiced concerns about what she saw as the increasingly blurred lines and lack of transparency as clients sought to leverage the *NYT*'s skills and – especially – credibility.

In her view it is up to journalists to police the divisions. 'When the newsroom wants to work on a special series of stories, they may reach out to T Brand to see if it will be easy to underwrite the editorial initiative with advertising dollars,' she wrote in October 2017. 'When T Brand gives editors feedback on what clients want . . . the editors may decide to pay more attention to such topics than they would have initially. Now, this isn't something that will ever be explicitly stated. Rather, it will be baked into the larger partnership between advertiser and publisher . . . Editors and reporters in the newsroom know the revenue generated by T Brand helps secure their job. We should stop painting advertisers as the problem and start realising that journalists are also responsible and need to stand up to editorial interference.'

Is there a difference in expectation between so-called legacy players and the new kids on the block? The spectacular initial growth of new sites such as Vice or BuzzFeed – which were, initially at least, virtually creative advertising teams with a newsroom attached – caused many commercial directors in legacy media to suck their teeth. How come they had to live with Chinese walls when it seemed that younger readers in particular weren't too choosy?

The future of native advertising is being closely scrutinised by regulators, who, in the past, frowned on what was then known as 'deceptive advertising'. In 2015 the US Federal Trade Commission (FTC) issued guidelines aiming to prevent consumers from being misled by the commercial nature of apparently editorial content. 'The more a native ad is similar in format and topic to content on the publisher's site,' it warned, 'the more likely that a disclosure will be necessary to prevent deception.'

Disclosures, said the FTC, had to be presented clearly and prominently – i.e. in front of or above the headline of the native ad. It frowned on ambiguous terms such as 'promoted', 'presented by (x)'; 'brought to you by (x)', or 'sponsored by (x)' if the implication was that a sponsoring advertiser 'underwrote' but did not influence the content.

So the regulators are actively on the case of native advertising. The same newspapers which publish regular articles on how to spot 'fake news' must be alert to the suspicion of some readers that fakeness comes in many forms.

NEWS AMNESIA

The syndrome – familiar to us all – that when journalists write about something we actually know about, we may find it superficial or actively misleading. And yet we continue to read journalism about other people and subjects with our scepticism suspended.

The novelist and director Michael Crichton described the habit in 2002, even naming it after the particle physicist, Murray Gell-Mann:

'Briefly stated, the Gell-Mann Amnesia effect is as follows. You open the newspaper to an article on some subject you know well . . . You read the article and see the journalist has absolutely no understanding of either the facts or the issues. Often, the article is so wrong it actually presents the story backward – reversing cause and effect. I call these the "wet streets cause rain" stories. Paper's full of them.

'In any case, you read with exasperation or amusement the multiple errors in a story, and then turn the page to national or international affairs, and read as if the rest of the newspaper was somehow more accurate about Palestine than the baloney you just read. You turn the page, and forget what you know. That is the Gell-Mann Amnesia effect. I'd point out it does not operate in other arenas of life. In ordinary life, if somebody consistently exaggerates or lies to you, you soon discount everything they say. In court, there is the legal doctrine of falsus in uno, falsus in omnibus, which means untruthful in one part, untruthful in all.

'But when it comes to the media, we believe against evidence that it is probably worth our time to read other parts of the paper. When, in fact, it almost certainly isn't. The only possible explanation for our behaviour is amnesia.'

NUMBERS

Until recently, reporters were typically hired for their literacy rather than their numeracy. The ability to write quickly, clearly and entertainingly was considered among the main skills the job required. But it is rather belatedly dawning on editors that numbers are quite an important thing in life. This is partly because, with the rise of social media, so many people enjoy pointing to the elementary howlers journalists keep making.

Numbers are everywhere in the news. No matter what their area of specialty, journalists will inevitably be faced with data such as population statistics, employment and crime figures, house prices, health performance measures, exam grades, survey results, earnings, wages, taxes, interest rates, opinion polls . . . and more *(SEE: DATA).* The penny is therefore dropping that journalists are going to have to get a better grasp of the basic statistical patterns and behaviours that they are likely to see, as well as acquiring the tools they need to help make sense of these numbers.

Scepticism helps *(SEE: SCEPTICISM).* Numbers can be invented or falsified just as malignly or carelessly as words can. They can mislead, and they may be misreported deliberately or through ignorance. Too often statistics are trusted because they imply a level of precision, without an investigation of their validity.

An important part of a journalist's craft is to establish the incentives to report particular results. Governments can dislike uncomfortable news, particularly close to elections. Academics can be rewarded for new or exciting results, leading to publication bias – particularly if negative results do not see the light of day.

A striking feature of public services across many countries has been the rise of performance monitoring, which records, analyses and publishes data in order to give the public a better idea of how systems or policies are implemented and can be improved.

Done well, performance monitoring can be a critical part of a democratic process of shedding light on the performance of public bodies. But it is vital to appreciate the incentives involved when statistics are used to reward, or punish, individuals or organisations. Deliberate misreporting can have unintended consequences if attention is paid to the things that are measured at the expense of those that matter. A hospital trust hitting its waiting targets? A good thing – unless it means that less important cases are prioritised over more complex cases because they have waited longer and a target could be missed. A well-performing school? Yes, but is it filtering out less well-performing pupils and not permitting them to take exams in order to improve its league-table position? These are cases of hitting the target but missing the point.

So understanding why data has been collected and what happens as a result of particular findings will help a reporter judge its likely quality.

Similarly, understanding the source or provenance of the data is an important step towards deciding whether it is fit for purpose. How, why and when was the data collected? By whom? What quality assurance processes took place? How big was the sample? How representative? Did a poll use non-probability or quasi-probability sampling? Did the reporter think to ask?

We should also take care whether too much attention is paid to the sample size, in these days of hype around 'big data'. Big isn't always better – a smaller balanced sample may provide better insights than a large skewed one. Is there someone in the newsroom who can properly interrogate the polling company and its methods? Who understands correlation does not mean causation? How many reporters might mix up their millions with their billions? How do you make billions meaningful to anyone? (One answer: try dividing a huge sum by the number of items they relate to. The NHS annual budget of £134 billion sounds vast, but this relates to £2,000 per person or £37 per person per week.)

Is the newsroom good at not confusing absolute risks and relative risks? Example: a report of 2007 concluded that eating 50g of processed meat per day increases the risk of colorectal cancer by 20 per cent. This sounds worrying: cue news headlines warning 'Careless Pork Costs Lives' – but in practice it means that a cancer rate of 5 people in every 100 getting colorectal cancer (the absolute risk) would rise to 6 in 100 if every one of those 100 people ate three rashers of extra bacon every day.

Numbers have grown more complex. One reporter on the *Guardian* admitted: 'I live in constant fear of making a whopping error because I don't truly understand credit default swaps, the mechanics of a bond auction, etc.'

The speed of modern journalism doesn't help. But public trust is easily lost. And you can, alas, measure that.

O

OMBUDSPERSON

Most modern organisations believe in some form of customer service. If their product or service is deficient, a good company or institution usually wants to hear about it because:

1) It's the right thing to do
2) You can only learn from your mistakes if you know about them
3) It's better – especially in an age of social media – to have a satisfied customer than one who will use all available means to slag you off.

The world of customer service has to some extent moved on from directly-employed human beings on the end of a telephone to impersonal globalised call centres; from email to text messages; from live chat to social media; from remote desktop support to AI and predictive intelligence tools.

Companies which are honest about mistakes, as well as finding a way of talking authentically to their customers, are likely to be valued and trusted more.

Many media companies invest heavily in keeping at least some of their customers happy – especially if they are subscribers or can easily switch elsewhere. If a Sky Broadband router is on the blink, or the Wi-Fi keeps dropping or the app doesn't download, there will soon be someone on the case. But if it's the journalism that is faulty, many media companies don't want to know. Well, that's not quite fair. If there's genuine unavoidable trouble – the sort that could end up in court, or on Twitter, or with a regulator – they will, with a sigh, set about doing the minimum possible to make amends. While often making the process of correcting a mistake as difficult as possible.

Sky Broadband and the *Sun* newspaper are both owned by Rupert Murdoch. You can be sure that a complaint about a problem with a Sky TV subscription will be treated with greater alacrity and courtesy than a complaint about an article in the *Sun*.

Why is this?

A character in *Pravda*, the 1985 Hare/Brenton play about a Commonwealth-born press baron, has a fictional journalist who comes out with the following speech: 'If every time we got something wrong we published a correction, then a newspaper would just be a footnote to yesterday's newspaper.' The character adds: 'A newspaper isn't just a scrap of paper, it's something people feel they have to trust. And if they can't trust it, why should they read it?' In other words, owning up to errors could encourage readers to stop trusting the journalism – as opposed to not owning up to errors *(SEE: MISTAKES)*.

The truth is that journalists find it hard to admit to their mistakes. It is not only about the size of a journalist's ego: there is often a legitimate need for steely self-belief in the face of overwhelming forces trying to stop them revealing what needs to be revealed. Therefore, the life of an ombudsperson, the man or woman tasked with confronting the journalists with complaints and queries from readers and others about their work, is not an easy one.

At the heart of the ideal of the ombudsperson system is that a willingness to admit error is a strength, not a weakness.

The concept of the ombudsperson was established in 1922 in Japan. Today the membership of the Organization of News Ombudsmen and Standards Editors (founded in 1980 and known as ONO) comprises news ombudspeople, readers' representatives and standards editors from around the world, working online, in print, and in television and radio. It has more than fifty members in North and South America, Europe, and parts of the Middle East and Asia.

The idea of the ombudsperson really took off in America, where the principles of objectivity *(SEE: IMPARTIALITY)* and news you can trust were established in the battles over yellow journalism in the 1920s.

In the decades that followed, the American Society of News Editors inculcated American journalists with the principles of 'sincerity, truthfulness, accuracy and impartiality' and so it was a natural cultural progression to the idea of ombudspeople. In the UK, meanwhile, media self-regulation was wrenched, kicking and screaming, from a press desperate to fight off government press legislation.

Watergate brought a burst of enthusiasm for the role in North American news organisations. That, combined with Americans' great respect for the First Amendment, saw a slew of appointments of ombudspeople in the 1980s.

In Canada, the first appointment was at the *Toronto Star* in 1972, and in the 1980s the Pierre Trudeau government passed a Canadian Charter of Rights and Freedoms which validated in law the rights and obligations of a free press.

The number of ombudspeople grew until there were twenty-nine in North America, but began to fall when the press felt the squeeze on revenues brought about by the rise of the internet. Things really took a turn for the worse in 2008 at the time of the financial crash. Now, there are no major newspaper titles with ombudspeople in the US.

In the UK the idea was much slower to take off. Ian Mayes became the *Guardian*'s first readers' editor in 1997. The inclusion of the role of 'standards editor' in the full title of ONO sheds light on the varied ways in which the role of ombudsperson is interpreted. All herrings are fish but not all fish are herrings. All ombudspeople care about ethics but some focus on accuracy and a code of practice, some on standards, and some take on the role of writing an opinion column based not just on alleged breaches of a news organisation's code but the wider issues of editorial decisions.

For instance, the *New York Times* introduced the role of public editor in 2003 after the reporter Jayson Blair was discovered to have been fabricating large chunks of major stories. At that time the *NYT* had a team focusing on corrections and one on standards. The role of the public editor sat alongside those other two functions as a readers' representative charged with investigating complaints about the *NYT*'s journalism 'with an eye to protecting journalistic integrity and good practice'. However, it wasn't the role of the *NYT*'s public editor to deal with day-to-day corrections or issues of standards.

P

PHILANTHROPY

Is news a public service or a means to large profits? For a long time the question seemed largely redundant: it was possible to make extremely healthy margins while still keeping communities informed. As profits declined or disappeared, however, thoughts turned to what other sort of economic model might support the supply of the sort of truthful and reliable information any society needs in order to function.

The question was not actually a new one. When John Edward Taylor, the founder and first editor of the *Manchester Guardian*, went round trying to raise money for his project in 1821, he found a small group of merchants and businessmen who were willing to help – not in the hope of cashing-out quickly, but because they thought Manchester needed a decent source of news. These 'respectable and moderate' figures who raised the subscription, wrote Taylor's wife, Sophie, were thinking of 'public advantage. They were willing to take risk without wishing to have any share in the profits.'

Nearly two hundred years later a Tasmanian entrepreneur with a passion for the environment, Graeme Wood, was so appalled at the media environment in Australia (especially in relation to climate change) that he offered to put up the cash for the *Guardian* to start an online edition for his country. If it made money, the *Guardian* would have to repay him. If it didn't work financially, he was happy to write it off as a philanthropic donation. Within five years the site – with support from many Australian readers – was making an operating profit. (The credit for the idea should go to the former Australian prime minister, Malcolm Turnbull.)

Or take the *Texas Tribune*, a small start-up intended to cover the nuts and bolts of public life in Texas – state house, public and higher education, healthcare, immigration, criminal justice, energy, poverty, the environment, water, transportation and so on. No frills, no celebrity, no sensation – just news about stuff that mattered. Having started in 2009 with half a dozen reporters and a cash injection from a civic-minded venture capitalist, John Thornton, it now has an editorial staff of around seventy. It relies on donations from foundations, members and philanthropists, along with sponsored events. It has around two million users a month and has registered as a 501(c)(3) non-profit, tax-exempt organisation.

The *Guardian* in America has also registered itself as a non-profit organisation in order to raise funds from individuals and foundations. The overall owner of the *Guardian*, the Scott Trust, was established in 1936 on a non-profit model which exists solely to seek to maintain the news organisation in perpetuity.

A number of big foundations working in areas such as overseas development, health, mental health, slavery and criminal justice are now supporting different channels and types of reporting, realising that they can reach large audiences and benefit from the powerful narrative and visual skills of the best journalists.

Is there a conflict of interest? Well, news organisations (and their readers and viewers) have shown they can live with native advertising *(SEE: NATIVE ADVERTISING)*. And the best newspapers have always proclaimed that Chinese walls *(SEE: CHINESE WALLS)* mean that their reporting will never, ever be influenced by any commercial revenues. So, with properly drawn-up contracts and a high degree of transparency, it has already proved possible to finance excellent and important journalism without compromising independence.

A major *FT* series towards the end of 2019 explored the growing number of companies buying into the idea of 'a purpose beyond profit'. The social enterprise and/or B Corporation movement is one way that organisations can:

- have a clear social and/or environmental mission set out in their governing documents
- reinvest the majority of their profits

- be autonomous of the state
- ~~be majority-controlled in the interests of their social mission~~
- be accountable and transparent.

The transition from conventionally-owned shareholder companies to this new breed or organisation will not be smooth – and may have to wait until the cliff-edge has been reached. But a future for news which marries a social mission with philanthropic giving is already within grasp.

PILGER, JOHN

John Pilger (b. 1939) embodies many of the classic qualities of the very best of investigative journalists: he is brave, uncompromising and tenacious. He also appears utterly secure in the armour of his own self-belief. It is an approach that has, as he put it, enabled him to 'navigate my way through the mainstream' of newspapers and broadcasters and win a slew of awards during his sixty-year career.

However, even some of his greatest fans have found him an increasingly difficult, prickly figure, shooting first and not always asking questions later.

Charlie Courtauld, a former editor of BBC's *Question Time* and a self-confessed fan – he died in 2016 – wrote about his feelings for the man in the *Independent* in 2006 when he previewed a week-long film festival of Pilger's work at the Barbican: 'I'm afraid he's compartmentalised with the late Fred Dibnah in my mind: someone I'd rather stick needles in my eyes than be stuck in a lift with – but who embodies that overused term "TV natural".'

And a TV documentary natural, he is. It is there, away from the temptations of the instant response to incidents such as the Salisbury poisonings – watch his furious rebuttal on Russia Today within hours of UK government allegations of Russian involvement – that he cuts through to ordinary people. The anger is contained by the format in a way that has brought him a long career on the commercial channel, ITV, as well as a BAFTA, Royal Television Society award and many others.

He started as a cadet at the Australian Consolidated Press. 'It was one of the strictest language courses I know,' he says. 'The aim was economy of language and accuracy. It certainly taught me to admire writing that was spare, precise and free of clichés, that didn't retreat into the passive voice and used adjectives only when absolutely necessary. I have long since slipped that leash, but those early disciplines helped shape my journalism and writing and my understanding of moving and still pictures.'

He came to London and to the *Daily Mirror*, by way of Reuters. Mike Molloy, the *Mirror*'s former editor, told the UK *Press Gazette* in 2008 that Pilger told two lies to get the job: he upped his age by a couple of years to suggest maturity, and he claimed he was a cricket fan to impress the assistant editor who was trying to put together a team and assumed an Australian would naturally be good at the game.

From that start, he has become the doyen of a certain style of uncompromising journalism. His roiling anger is palpable and grows with each passing year, using language that has certainly 'slipped the leash'.

For instance, in an article headlined 'The War On Venezuela Is Built on Lies', published on his own website in February 2019, he attacks two of his greatest enemies: America and capitalism: 'Should the CIA stooge [Juan] Guaidó and his white supremacists grab power, it will be the 68th overthrow of a sovereign government by the United States, most of them democracies. A fire sale of Venezuela's utilities and mineral wealth will surely follow, along with the theft of the country's oil, as outlined by John Bolton.'

Any counter-arguments are put in a compressed, dismissive fashion with an uptick for his heroes: 'For all the Chavistas' faults – such as allowing the Venezuelan economy to become hostage to the fortunes of oil and never seriously challenging big capital and corruption – they brought social justice and pride to millions of people and they did it with unprecedented democracy.'

His reputation is based on his ability to expose the lies and propaganda of governments and big corporations. However, his journalistic style has the power, according to his critics, to paint a misleading picture through the sin of omission.

The Coming War On China, made for ITV in 2016, departs from the conventional journalistic discipline of balance from the off: the title. It is not 'with' but 'on'. David Hutt, a Southeast Asia columnist writing for the online magazine the Diplomat in 2016, starts, once again, from the position of a fan whose decision to become a journalist was sparked by Pilger's early work. Hutt's detailed critique of the film praises and supports Pilger's analysis of the US's destruction through nuclear testing of the Marshall Islands, shown in the first forty minutes of the 113-minute film. However, he says that at the end of that section he wondered what it had to do with the subject of the film, namely the increasing tensions between the US and China. He says: '*The Coming War On China* does not engage in lies but it evades the truth so much that it is rendered invisible.'

He concedes that Pilger raises the issue of the exploitation of the poor and the Tiananmen Square massacre but briefly: 'All in all, Pilger's exploration of the modern-day problems of China lasts from the 55th minute until 66th, much of which is given over to optimistic interviews with Chinese commentators and former government officials, who downplay the crimes of the government . . . Pilger begins the documentary by saying it is "a film about the human spirit, and about the rise of an extraordinary resistance". But where is the extraordinary resistance mounted against China's foreign endeavours? Why does he not mention the resistance of the Burmese against the Myitsone Dam? Or the Lao people to stop much of the country's north being sold for cheap to Chinese businessmen? Or, for that matter, the Lao who demonstrated against their government after China decided to build dozens of dams in the country that will destroy most of the Mekong River? Or, even give one sentence over to the anti-Chinese protests in Vietnam?

'Pilger's scattershots do not cohere to a conclusion; they only seek to confirm to [sic] his narrative. His anti-Americanism blurs all. In journalism circles, one could say he is not being objective. This is not necessarily a bad thing: one enjoys a good deal of subjectivity in reporting. But Pilger takes this to the extreme.'

In this, Hutt and Pilger may find common ground because Pilger eschews objectivity and balance in robust terms. One of the Australian's major targets is the mainstream media, in particular the liberal media, and the traditional credo of objectivity. In this respect he joins a cohort that includes Noam Chomsky and Media Lens, who think that the liberal media – the BBC, Channel 4, the *New York Times* or the *Guardian*, for instance – has been far more damaging to radicalism than the right-wing media.

In an interview with Vice in August 2016 Pilger explained why he has little time for traditional journalistic conventions such as objectivity and impartiality *(SEE: IMPARTIALITY)*: 'As a young journalist going to university, I was taught, along with my colleagues, of the importance of "balance" and "objectivity", but in my reporting as an Aboriginal affairs journalist, I find this often just clouds the real picture. What is the role of objectivity in journalism – is the truth sacrificed on this sacred journalistic altar of objectivity? "Objectivity" and "impartiality" have all but lost their dictionary meanings. A lot of the time they're media propaganda terms, a kind of doublethink.

'When someone declares how impartial they are, I am immediately suspicious. It often means they report what I would call the authorised received wisdom. For example, when Tony Blair invaded Iraq, BBC reporters lined up to declare his actions "vindicated". They called that "impartial". To point out that Blair was a liar was committed journalism. It's actually Orwellian, as in "war is peace" . . .

'Too often the [academic] media courses are factories, supplying corporate fodder. Young journalists ought to be taught they are agents of people, not power.'

His choice of those he supports reflects the old adage that my enemy's enemy is my friend. This produces a mixed bag of 'friends': they include, for instance, Piers Morgan, who re-hired him for the *Mirror* in 2001, and Donald Trump.

In a February 2016 *Guardian* webchat, Pilger said Trump was 'speaking straight to ordinary Americans': although his opinions about immigration were 'gross', they were no more gross in essence than, say, David Cameron's – 'he is not planning to invade anywhere, he doesn't hate the Russians or the Chinese, he is not beholden to Israel'.

In 2017, in an article on his website, he warned that a coup against the president was under way: 'This is not because he is an odious human being, but because he has consistently made clear he does not want war with Russia. This glimpse of sanity, or simple pragmatism, is anathema to the "national security" managers who guard a system based on war, surveillance, armaments, threats and extreme capitalism.'

But he described Barack Obama, during the presidential campaign of 2008, as 'a glossy Uncle Tom who would bomb Pakistan' and said his theme was 'the renewal of America as a dominant, avaricious bully'. Columnist Sunny Hundal, writing in the *Guardian* in 2008, described that remark thus: 'For John Pilger to call Obama an "Uncle Tom" betrays an ugly contempt for those who refuse his revolutionary romanticism.'

Although Pilger finds fewer outlets for his written journalism, he continues to make attention-grabbing films, aided now by his loyal fanbase. His last two films have been successfully crowdfunded. His friends include Roger Waters, of Pink Floyd – they have a shared interest in Palestine – and Julian Assange, whom he stands by even though he forfeited his share of the bail money when the Wikileaks founder fled.

Pilger's continuing hard-core appeal is undoubted. His films are rightly critically fêted even when reviewers bemoan a level of Lear-like ranting. In an age when authenticity is a much sought after quality his 'revolutionary romanticism' brings him respect. Even if he comes in at too high a volume and with no tone or balance control, the message is unmistakable. But can it be trusted?

POLITICAL JOURNALISM

In the closing days of the miserable UK general election campaign of 2019, the political editors of the BBC and ITN simultaneously tweeted that a Labour activist had punched a ministerial adviser at Leeds General Infirmary. The hasty hospital visit had been made to discredit a *Daily Mirror* story that a four-year-old boy had been forced to lie on the floor while awaiting treatment. So the 'aide punched' claim served to distract the travelling media's attention from an NHS embarrassment and the prime minister's cavalier response when he briefly confiscated a reporter's phone containing video evidence of the child's distress.

Except the punch claim wasn't true. As footage quickly confirmed, the 'punch' was an accidental collision. In the fevered world of online micro-reporting, two highly experienced journalists had failed to double-check a familiar source misleading them, deliberately so by some accounts. Nor did most – not all – of the other reporters to whom the tidbit was then fed on the Tory campaign bus, from which the *Mirror* had already been excluded for partisan reasons.

What should a voter searching for trustworthy reporting make of this trivial incident? What of far more serious controversies, rival tax-and-spending claims, policies on homelessness or crime, when the governing party even seeks to disguise its own website as an independent fact-checker?

In one sense, the problem is as old as the printing press. Partisans place damaging information about their opponents, some of it 'fake news' whether by accident or design. They do so off the record, knowing that equally partisan media allies will help them try and get away with it in return for future favours. Shakespeare, Milton, Swift, all wrote a lot about such abuses of power. It happens in sport and City takeover battles too, always has done.

Much of the remedy lies in the readers' own hands. As with racing tips or must-buy shares, they get to learn which political journalists – news reporters, sketch writers or lofty columnists – they can trust. They should be the ones who don't slant the story out of all recognition or trim the crucial quote, people whose judgement and predictions (flamboyant or cautious) are more right than wrong, even when inconvenient to their audience. Of course, trying to be balanced, fair even, isn't what every reader wants in stridently populist times. That's what regularly gets the BBC into trouble with people who want their confirmation biases nurtured rather than challenged. The preference is more a function of temperament than of education.

What is different from scurrilous Victorian pamphleteers, odious Quintus Slide of the *People's Banner* in Trollope's novels, or the *Daily Mail's* forged Zinoviev letter in 1924, is the sheer speed of modern communications. Today's 24/7 cable TV, Facebook, Twitter, WhatsApp and the rest join forces with the data-harvesters of Cambridge Analytica and their dark-money sponsors to target voters with cynically customised and hard-to-trace messaging, bypassing quality control as profitably as doctored cocaine.

Legacy media, including terrestrial TV brands, struggles to compete with this unmediated Babel. Hence those instant tweets in Leeds. But the methodology of political news input is as much affected by new technologies as the output. Before obstacles to the reporting of

Parliament were removed in 1771, partisans like Samuel Johnson used to invent parodies for the *Gentleman's Magazine*, 'taking care that the Whig dogs did not have the best of it'.

A verbatim press gallery reporter in his youth, Charles Dickens would go on to parody politicians in his novels. But respectful gallery accounts of speeches were the dominant nineteenth-century form of political output from the mainstream press. Only gradually did background briefings by, or on behalf of, ministers keen to influence consumers of the new mass-circulation rotary presses give precedence and prestige to 'lobby correspondents'. These are the reporters with the accredited right to loiter in the Members' Lobby just outside the Commons Chamber to buttonhole MPs beneath Perpendicular Gothic windows under the gaze of long-dead titans.

How quaint and physical the memory seems when the Members' Lobby is all but deserted. Except when one of No. 10's intermittent feuds is under way, lobby correspondents still meet the PM's spokesperson twice daily – at Downing Street at eleven a.m. and in the Lobby Room in a high parliamentary tower at four. Reporters still hang around corridors to catch their best sources. Columnists, a breed more numerous and less distinguished than their Olympian forebears, still buy theirs lunch. John Major reformed what had previously been near-Masonic briefings on deep background ('the PM is believed to . . .') by making information thus obtained attributable to 'No. 10 sources'. In his openness phase, Tony Blair put briefings on the record and posted a summary on Downing Street's new-fangled website. Optimistically, he also staged monthly televised press conferences – cutting out the supposedly cynical media middlemen and (at last) women to speak directly to voters.

Such was the theory. His successors, less fluent or confident, were less keen. Besides, briefings that were all on the record were, of necessity, wholesome and usually dull. Murkier information – a colleague to be undermined as 'semi-detached' (John Biffen, according to Mrs Thatcher's spokesman Bernard Ingham), a policy gamble cautiously floated to test the waters – had, as always, to find a more discreet conduit. New technologies stepped in to help fill the breach. Emails to a select few, terse text messages or a quick session on the now-ubiquitous mobile phone left few traces. A version of what had long been known as 'the white Commonwealth' of trusties gradually re-emerged, usually including the *Telegraph* and *Mail*, the *Sun* and *Express*, sometimes the *Times*, even the *FT* and *Guardian* if Labour was in power. Rarely the provincial press.

The major radio and TV networks had to be kept sweet except during big rows, when access was curtailed in retaliation for overstepping unseen boundaries. As rivals to become the fastest source of smartphone news for most voters, even upstart websites like the HuffPost and PoliticsHome got some attention from the spin doctors – press officers with attitude. Over three decades, spinners had emerged as any government's main line of defence (sometimes attack) against the 24/7 media. They were on the public payroll but unconstrained by rules requiring civil service impartiality. Ad hoc WhatsApp groups developed to supplement official channels, as well as deeply off-the-record lobby briefings at the end of the official one – a 'huddle' or 'dark lobby'. Both developments mirrored long-established practices in the supposedly more open White House press room, where the TV cameras are quickly switched off and the named briefer magically turns into 'a senior administration official speaking on conditions of anonymity'.

But such is the scale of mistrust in an age of partisan and populist politics that by 2020 traditional White House briefings had almost ceased to exist until the coronavirus pandemic left Donald Trump and his officials no choice but to deal again with the 'fake media' they had ruthlessly denigrated. A similar Covid-19 adjustment was required in Downing Street, where Boris Johnson's Svengali, Dominic Cummings, had started to follow Trump's aggressive media marginalisation, to the point of hiring No. 10 its own photographer and TV crew, who were able to provide tame 'interviews' with no awkward questions.

The retreat from openness into open warfare and the atrophy of time-honoured rules of good conduct on both sides has included boycotts of hostile newspapers, even of flagship BBC news programmes to which ministers were instructed to give no interviews.

As with much else in Brexit-sundered Britain, it is not immediately clear whether the unavoidably shared national experience of the Covid-19 crisis – so unlike the screen-focused solitude of recent years – will restore a sense of mutual respect and forbearance between government and the political press, and between the media and anxious voters desperate for reliable guidance through the catastrophe. But, when a political leader misleads, obfuscates or even lies in the confident belief that many voters seem to prefer deception to hard truths, it shrinks the space in which media can call the powerful to account without retaliation.

'Why is this lying bastard lying to me?' is a time-honoured journalistic instinct *(SEE: LYING BASTARDS)*, but a degree of trust is also necessary. So is solid judgement, uncorrupted by the commercial imperatives of clickbait sensationalism in a shrinking market for paid news. It was ever thus, but now it is more so, in the social media frenzy and the unforgiving populism it helps to entrench. Faced with a once-unimaginable Aladdin's cave of information streams, the conscientious citizen must learn to be discriminating or risk being conscripted into the fake-news army. The multiplicity of sources allows them easily to check rival versions of events against each other: always a prudent course. Caveat emptor *(SEE: CAVEAT EMPTOR)* – let the buyer beware – as the prime minister's spokesperson and echoing newspapers never say.

POWER WITHOUT RESPONSIBILITY

The press is sometimes attacked for exercising power without responsibility. That sounds like a bad thing – and an irresponsible press can be malign in all kinds of ways – but there is another sense in which the press's lack of responsibility is its main point.

The phrase dates back to its usage by the then leader of the Conservative Party, and three-time prime minister, Stanley Baldwin: 'The newspapers attacking me are not newspapers in the ordinary sense,' Baldwin said in a speech on 17 March 1931. 'They are engines of propaganda for the constantly changing policies, desires, personal vices, personal likes and dislikes of the two men. What are their methods? Their methods are direct falsehoods, misrepresentation, half-truths, the alteration of the speaker's meaning by publishing a sentence apart from the context . . . What the proprietorship of these papers is aiming at is power, and power without responsibility – the prerogative of the harlot throughout the ages.'

As later noted by many sources, Baldwin actually 'borrowed' the phrase from his cousin, Rudyard Kipling. The 'two men' he targeted were Lord Beaverbrook (owner of the *Daily Express*) and Lord Rothermere (owner of the *Daily Mail*), neither of whom was a fan of Baldwin's.

There have been plenty of irresponsible, but great, journalists over the centuries *(SEE: ROUGH OLD TRADE)* and it's notoriously difficult to find truly independent ways of sanctioning, far less licensing, journalists. But part of the point of journalism is that it is done by people who don't have the responsibility of public office. They can think the unthinkable; say the unsayable. They add a dimension of thought and of frank speech that mainstream politics cannot match. Editors don't have to curry favour or be elected. That gives them huge freedom and is a significant privilege. We want them to be responsible in the exercise of their craft and their power. But we don't want them to have the same sort of responsibility as the people on whom they report.

PRESSTITUTES

If you work for the hated MSM (mainstream media, aka lamestream media) and saunter out into the Twittersphere you will, sooner or later, be called a presstitute. This means you have sold your soul to a corrupt calling and you should feel ashamed of yourself. It doesn't matter who you write for or what you write about. You are the worst.

PROPAGANDA MODEL

An old maxim of American journalism – which has been printed on the masthead of the *New York Times* for 124 years – holds that a paper should cover 'all the news that's fit to print'. In 1988, Edward Herman and Noam Chomsky set out to answer a question that would probe the structures of power as much as it would the media itself: who decides what's 'fit', and how *(SEE: GATEKEEPERS)*?

The resulting classic, *Manufacturing Consent: The Political Economy of the Mass Media*, laid out what the authors called a 'propaganda model' for American journalism. It traced the path of potential news to news that makes the final cut: what's allowed to be tossed onto doorsteps or, today, beamed out to cyberspace. That path, Herman and Chomsky argued, is intercepted by five 'filters' made of the money and power that has come to dominate news media in the United States. They concluded that the news, or the 'cleansed residue' of those filters, amounts to messages pre-approved by the government and major corporations – thus manufacturing the public's consent to their policies and practices through the very outlets meant to house dissent and debate.

Those five filters are:

1) **Size, ownership and profit orientation**
   The media sources that reach the largest audiences are big, for-profit businesses. Their owners are individuals or corporations who could fork over the cash to start a news outlet or buy one, and they require the capital of investors who expect them to continue generating wealth. This matters because media managers must prioritise profitability, and are constrained by the interests of owners, corporations and controlling investors with a stake in the firm. If news endangers their power or interests, it could be filtered out.

2) **The advertising licence to do business**
   News media have long depended on advertising, not sales or subscriptions, to turn a profit. This means that news outlets must make themselves attractive to advertisers by, in turn, attracting audiences who have buying power. This filter has been blamed for the steady decline of working-class newspapers, whose audiences are hardly deep-pocketed consumers. Advertisers have been said to act as a 'de facto licensing authority' determining a news outlet's success – or worse, its existence at all *(SEE: CHINESE WALLS)*.

3) **Sourcing mass media news**
   News requires sources and informants, and reporters tend to gravitate to sites from which a reliable stream of happenings flow: government agencies, police departments, corporations with household names *(SEE: SOURCES)*. These sources have the added perk of being considered reliable, precluding intensive fact-checks. Unknown or less powerful sources hoping to get their stories in the news must compete with the easier-to-report 'routine' sources,

often losing out. Media organisations themselves stand to lose access to information from governmental and corporate sources if they antagonise powerful institutions.

4) **Flak and the enforcers**

Flak is the backlash waged against news media for particular content, and can come in the form of letters, petitions, lawsuits, even proposed legislation. Costly for media outlets to respond to, flak can be and has been strategically generated: Chomsky and Herman point to the rise of corporate-sponsored thinktanks dedicated to monitoring and correcting the media, and politicians who portray themselves as media victims. Issues, position or programmes likely to be met with flak may be filtered out of the news while the enforcers consolidate their power *(SEE: ACCURACY)*.

5) **Anticommunism as a control mechanism**

At the time *Manufacturing Consent* was written, anticommunism was something of a national religion for the right-leaning political elite in the US, but Chomsky wrote in 1997 that, post-cold war, it was replaced by a fixation on terrorism. What they have in common is their role as a common enemy against which all walks of life are expected to mobilise. Views that veer too close to the enemy view are silenced in the name of security, and the mass media takes on an us versus them narrative of global events. If the war on communism – or indeed other, future taboos – is allowed to domi-nate the airwaves, other news is filtered out and the Joe McCarthys of history get their moment in the limelight *(SEE: BREXIT)*.

Does all of this amount to a conspiracy theory? In the United States, where formal censorship is largely absent and the press periodically expose corporate and government misconduct, a model based on 'propaganda' might seem heavy-handed. But it's the lack of conspiracy, Herman and Chomsky argue, that makes systematic propaganda in a democracy so sinister. Rather than a stream of oppressive directives coming from a shadowy corporate executive in a media control room, they see a slew of more innocent phenomena: 'pre-selection of right-thinking people, internalised preconceptions, and adaptation of personnel to constraints of ownership, organisation, market, and political power'. These are normal market forces, they argue. In other words, the censorship afflicting the US media is a self-censorship: entrenched, normalised, nearly undetectable (unless you're Chomsky), and a bugger to rout out.

PROPRIETORS

Sir Max Hastings enjoys hunting, fishing and shooting as much as the next editor. He is, in other words, by no means a champagne socialist or 'woke' leftie. But, after ten years of editing the *Daily Telegraph*, he had a close-up view of what it was like to work for an old-fashioned billionaire press baron and experienced first-hand what he termed 'the rich men's trade union'.

Conrad Black (b. 1944) was a very rich, very right-wing Canadian who had seized on the opportunity in 1985 to prise the *Daily Telegraph* out of the hands of the faded aristocracy who had owned it well, but whose pockets simply weren't deep enough to see the paper into the digital age. 'Those who have built large fortunes seldom lose their nervousness that some ill-wisher will find means to take their money away from them,' wrote Hastings of his former proprietor (from the safety of retirement). 'They feel an instinctive sympathy for fellow multi-millionaires, however their fortunes have been achieved. When one of the tribe falls from grace, they share the sensations of French aristocrats during the Reign of Terror, watching a laden tumbril lurch over the cobbles towards the guillotine: hairs prickle on the back of the spectators' necks.' Noam Chomsky would doubtless agree.

In the early twenty-first century someone coined 'the billionaire press' as effective shorthand for the breed of extremely wealthy individuals for whom owning a newspaper was a passport to . . . to what? For some it was a proximity to what they took to be power. Some imagined (often rightly) that the ownership of a printing press would amplify their own views and give them real power. A few – but a dwindling number over time – were simply in it for the money. A small number actually liked journalism and the company of journalists. Some appreciated the access it gave them, whether to rub shoulders with the famous or in order to advance their business interests.

Some anticipated riches in flogging off assets: swapping grandiose marble-fronted, oak-panelled newsrooms and cathedral-sized printing halls for out-of-town warehouses. The former became luxury hotels or banking HQs, the latter became content factories. A small number nursed some notion of journalism as a kind of necessary public service. Maybe more have been attracted by the prospect of a title. Buying a widget company or supermarket does not inevitably lead to the snug feeling of ermine around one's neck, a heraldic coat of arms and a seat in the House of Lords. But ownership of a newspaper seemed, in general, to go hand in hand with a veneer of nobility and the right to legislate over fellow citizens. The tradition continued right up to Lord Black of Crossharbour, who had to renounce his Canadian citizenship in order to acquire the right to legislate on behalf of British citizens without having to undergo election.

It is generally customary among the billionaires to profess no involvement in editorial decision-making. Sometimes that may even have been true. It appears as if (Lord) Jonathan Rothermere, owner of the *Daily Mail*, did not necessarily much admire the Middle-to-Little Englishness that his newspaper often embodied, but his instinct was, admirably enough, not to meddle. From all accounts Jeff Bezos, the astonishingly rich founder of Amazon, does not interfere in the editorial decisions of the *Washington Post*.

Black had no such reticence. Hastings said he used to dread the nocturnal phone calls as Black would ring up, often from the other side of the world, to give his editor the benefit of his views on the great issues of the day.

Hastings's account is a rare glimpse of how a network of extremely wealthy individuals operated in the old 'vertical' world in which information was passed down from on high. His proprietor had strong views on Europe, and the Conservative Party, and was an 'energetic supporter of the Israeli cause against that of the Palestinians'. And then there was South Africa, which had the almost miraculous good fortune of having a leader as calm and enlightened as Nelson Mandela to oversee its transition from the evils of apartheid to a black-majority society. Black had other ideas – which, in turn, came from John

Aspinall, a rakish multi-millionaire buccaneer who made his riches from running dimly lit upper-class gambling clubs in London. According to Hastings, Aspinall/Black wanted the *Telegraph* to back Chief Buthelezi, leader of South Africa's Zulus. Hastings's correspondents in the region disagreed, and while Hastings managed to avoid any dramatic change in the paper's coverage, he also 'suggested to the foreign desk that our people should tread carefully on this issue, simply to avoid wearisome exchanges of memos and telephone calls with the chairman'.

In other respects Black was a reasonably benign owner of the *Telegraph* – and it is to his credit that he appointed strong editors who would stand up to him, and gave them a decent enough period in office. The Barclay Brothers, who came later, were different. They and/or their children cashed in such assets as they could, drove the titles for profit over integrity, allowed the commercial department to hold sway over editorial decisions and relished what they imagined to be their back-channel influence with Downing Street. Editors were considered disposable: six editors in the first eleven years of owning the *Telegraph*; eight editors of the *Scotsman* in ten years.

Owning newspapers was once a licence to print money; these days the opposite is true. Yet, even as profit margins have shrivelled or disappeared altogether, the billionaires keep coming. Rupert Murdoch *(SEE: MURDOCH, RUPERT)* has had many opportunities to ditch his press ownings over the past twenty years or more, but he has doggedly held on to them. The soft pornographer Richard Desmond managed to enrich himself to the tune of nearly £400 million over seventeen years of owning the *Express* titles. He, too, denied any editorial influence over the papers, but few believed him – and he evidently rather enjoyed having himself photographed handing over a cheque for £1 million to the UKIP leader Nigel Farage at the start of the referendum campaign over Britain's future in Europe *(SEE: BREXIT)*.

Stranger still was the appearance on the British media scene of Alexander Lebedev, a former KGB officer, and his socialite son Evgeny, who snapped up the *Independent* and London *Evening Standard* titles. Why? They have probably lost money, though the financials of it all (including a part-sale of the *Independent* to Saudi interests) are cloudy. Influence? They certainly seem to have cultivated a close friendship with Boris Johnson during his time as mayor of London and as foreign secretary.

Johnson was a welcome and frequent guest at Evgeny Lebedev's restored palazzo in Perugia. While mayor of London he visited the villa four times, three of them using Lebedev's private jet. In 2018, while foreign secretary, he flew there alone for the weekend, refusing to say whether he was accompanied by any security. He was pictured at San Francesco d'Assisi airport without any bodyguards and, according to an eyewitness quoted in the *Guardian*, 'looking like he had slept in his clothes'. In 2019 Evgeny Lebedev denied that he collected dirt to compromise the future prime minister: 'I am proud to be a friend of Boris Johnson, who like most of my friends, has visited me in Umbria. And I hate to disappoint, but nothing happens there that produces "Kompromat".' In July 2020 Johnson ennobled Lebedev, giving the Russian-British citizen a seat for life in the House of Lords. Press barons were back!

The Lebedevs are simply continuing a long tradition of billionaires whose motives for becoming overlords (and they *have* all been men) of information will probably never be known. Nearly thirty years after the mysterious death of the *Mirror* owner Robert Maxwell, we still don't know much about his alleged connections with Israeli, British or Eastern European intelligence. The billionaire owner of the mining company Lonrho, Tiny Rowland, famously abused his ownership of the *Observer* to pursue dubious global political aims and smear his business rivals. Had he not died, Maxwell would almost certainly have ended up in prison, as did Conrad Black.

Going further back over time, a good many of the people who ended up as press barons were quite strikingly unpleasant characters: ruthless, unstable, megalomaniac, dishonest, self-important, bombastic, arrogant, vindictive, scurrilous, vain and hyperbolic. Several of them were also mad.

Piers Brendon's compelling 1982 study of proprietors, *The Life and Death of the Press Barons*, was a catalogue of horrors: proprietors who hired thugs to beat up rival newsboys (Chicago in the 1840s – but it was still happening in Chicago in 1910 and in the Sydney of Rupert Murdoch's childhood), barons who died in mental asylums, barons who purchased thirteen-year-old girls for £5 in order to expose alleged wrongdoing (London, 1885), barons who lived on giant soundproof yachts (Pulitzer in 1907, Scripps in the 1920s), barons who helped start wars and stirred up riots, barons who drank a gallon of whisky every day and beat up their children, barons who forced business concessions out of politicians by offering, 'Look, you can have a headline a day or a bucket of shit every day – what's it to be?'

Joseph Pulitzer (1847–1911) imagined that his *New York World* was the most important teacher and moral agent in America. He believed it should determine who should be elected president and 'should be more powerful than the President'.

And then there was William Randolph Hearst (1863–1951), who believed newspapers to be the 'greatest force in civilisation'. Not only did they 'form and express public opinion, suggest and control legislation, declare wars and punish criminals', but, as representatives of the people, they 'control the nation'. Hearst's *Chicago Tribune* journalists did a nice line in blackmail – planting a smallpox sufferer as an assistant in a department store, 'discovering' her, and then extorting advertising against threats of exposé.

Over time, proprietors advanced claims to the constitutional significance of what they did, along with pretensions to political and ethical responsibility. Lord Beaverbrook (1879–1964), though he despised Hearst's methods, had a similar notion, and set out to demonstrate 'the efficacy of the weapon of the Press: when skilfully employed at the psychological moment no politician of any party can resist it'.

In Simon Jenkins's estimation, 'it is hard to avoid the conclusion that to Beaverbrook proprietorship became access pure and simple, the thrill of involvement, the freedom to do mischief but not serious damage to public men and the power to send minions into a frenzy of activity simply by lifting the telephone'.

Lord Northcliffe (1865–1922) was a great innovator, a pungent propagandist and, by the time of his death, completely insane. His megalomania led him to back Lord Beaverbrook as prime minister. He refused to support Stanley Baldwin as prime minister 'unless I know exactly what his policy is going to be . . . and unless I am acquainted with the names of at least eight or ten of his most prominent colleagues in the next ministry' *(SEE: POWER WITHOUT RESPONSIBILITY)*.

And then we have Harold Harmsworth, the first Lord Rothermere

(1868–1940) – 'perhaps the most influential single propagandist for fascism during the wars', according to the historian Martin Pugh. He admired Mussolini ('the greatest figure of the age') and Hitler equally, visiting and corresponding with both. The anti-fascist *Daily Mail* correspondent in Germany was sidelined and the paper moved into line with its owner's avowedly anti-semitic and pro-Nazi sympathies. Rothermere also supported Britain's most prominent fascist, Oswald Mosley ('Hurrah for the Blackshirts').

Why does any of this matter? A common defence of proprietors – voiced even by people who have suffered under bad ones – is that, by being willing to pay the bills, a press baron earns a right to the megaphone. They should be free to appoint whoever they like and expect to see their voices amplified in the manner of their choosing.

That might have worked in the old vertical world, but it tests the willingness of a modern reader to place their trust in journalism. A reader approaching the second quarter of the twenty-first century is, for better or worse, a sceptical reader *(SEE: SCEPTICISM)*. They are likely to ask: who is telling me this? Why are they telling me this? Who is telling them to tell me this? Are they being paid to write this? Do they believe this stuff or are they simply obeying orders? And so on. These are reasonable questions. They go to the heart of what journalism believes about itself, never mind what it expects anyone else to believe.

Most working journalists – hazarding a wild guess – will not have read much Chomsky *(SEE: PROPAGANDA MODEL)*. But if they did, they would find nagging questions about how opinion is formed and who forms it. If part of the story is that, in Max Hastings's phrase, 'the rich man's trade union' has a disproportionate effect in the shaping of consensus – including the values which determine what is considered to be 'news' – then transparency demands that we should understand better how the whole system works. At present, you can work in or around Fleet Street for most of your life and only be allowed glimpses, which is still more than is available to the average reader.

Three things are missing from this recitation of oddballs, brutes, megalomaniacs and proto-fascists. One is that some of the billionaire press were also undoubtedly brilliant businessmen: great innovators, entrepreneurs, engineers and marketeers. The best of them weren't bean counters or driven solely by the bottom line, as are (inevitably, you might say) a good many shareholder-owned public companies. The best barons knew that good journalism required real investment – in editorial talent, as well as printing presses or sales teams or accountants. What makes a 'good' proprietor is thus a complicated question. The Hartwells, former owners of the *Telegraph*, were, by all accounts, extremely respectful of the independent role of the journalists they employed. But they simply lacked the cold-eyed business acumen to keep the show on the road once the terms and technology of trade were upended.

The second is that many of them bought into the romance of journalism, cherishing the idea and independence of newspapers, and staunchly protected and supported their editors and reporters. They built powerful institutions to defend good reporting and create an equilibrium of strength with the powers on whom they were reporting.

Finally, it omits the (shorter) list of proprietors who had no obvious ulterior motive (political, revenge, regulatory influence, social) for owning a newspaper. The Sulzbergers and Grahams – respective majority owners of the *New York Times* and *Washington Post* – were, by and large, altruistic and benevolent custodians of their titles. The same could be said of any number of family-owned city titles before the debt-fuelled age of mergers and acquisitions in the early part of the twenty-first century.

Jeff Bezos, as above, appears to exert no editorial influence over the *Washington Post* – while bringing much-needed cash and technological acumen. And then there were characters like Roy Thomson (Lord Thomson, 1894–1976), who owned many Canadian newspapers and then acquired the *Times* and *Sunday Times*.

Harold Evans's memoir, *Good Times, Bad Times*, draws a stark contrast between Thomson's stewardship of Times newspapers and the man who eventually bought the titles, Rupert Murdoch. 'Thomson's most memorable quality was an instinct for the truth . . . He could be caustic, but he did not deal in fear . . . When politicians or businessmen complained he blinked genially at them through his pebble glasses . . . He was loyal and straightforward.'

Only once did Thomson let it be known mildly which side he hoped his paper would back in a general election. On being told that Evans intended to ignore him, he took it in his stride and never mentioned it again: 'He did not expect any great weight to be attached to his political views.'

Thomson was the good – to balance against the bad and the ugly. In Evans's words, 'passing from Thomson to Murdoch was a transition from light to dark; and all of us involved were diminished by the shadows'.

As newspapers become more financially troubled, there may be fewer people queuing to be fully paid-up members of the 'rich men's trade union'. That may be no bad thing. Was it better that the ailing *Daily Express* – which once sold more than four million copies a day – was kept in some form of diminished existence for seventeen years by a billionaire former pornographer with his own particular worldview?

The Desmond *Express* maintained a level of information for an ever-dwindling number of ageing readers (fewer than 300,000 by 2020). It kept a number of journalists in paid employment at a time when thousands were being thrown out of work. It played a determined part in amplifying the pornographer's view that Brexit was a good idea for Britain. It obsessed unproductively about conspiracy theories to do with the death of Lady Di and the disappearance of Madeleine McCann. It was, for a while, a cash cow which made the pornographer even richer. It won few awards, broke few original stories, and exuded a sorry sense of clinging on to the fading brand-value of past glories. And in the end, it was folded into a publicly owned company whose share price briefly jumped at the proffered benefits of some 'cost-saving opportunities'.

The pornographer was happy with his seventeen years of earnings. And the benefit to society or journalism was . . .? Happily, there are other kinds of proprietor – not least Kay Graham, now immortalised in *The Post* by Meryl Streep – who could serve as more inspirational models to anyone tempted in future to take on the responsibility of 'owning' the news. After centuries of men 'owning the news' it would at least be welcome to have some women in that role.

PUBLIC SPHERE

When the German philosopher Jürgen Habermas defined the 'public sphere', he was credited – in the *Times* 100 Most Influential People, no less – with transforming media studies into something 'hard headed': that is, relevant to philosophy, social theory and political science.

Habermas defined the public sphere as the social realm where private people come together as a public; where they engage in rational-critical debate and collectively form what might be called 'public opinion'. Seems like an obvious feature of human societies? Habermas argued that, in Europe, it was an innovation with an origin story: it appeared in the eighteenth century as feudalism gave way to liberal democracy and the literate bourgeoisie emerged.

The public sphere is so important because, in democracies, public opinion is what allows citizens to exert control over the state, particularly when opinions crystallise into votes. A free press is – or was – crucial in its function as the public sphere's circulatory system, allowing the lifeblood of information to be exchanged without constraint amongst citizens.

But Habermas argued in 1962 that the public sphere had already met its demise. The nascent liberal democracies in eighteenth- and nineteenth-century Europe and North America saw rapid industrialisation. As their economies organised themselves in terms of consumer capitalism, citizens became primarily consumers, not political actors. The press was not immune and found itself having to cater to advertisers, donors and the politically powerful. (Two decades later, Chomsky and Herman would count these very phenomena as part of their propaganda model of contemporary mass media *(SEE: PROPAGANDA MODEL)*. The public sphere no longer had a forum free from state and corporate influences to reflect on matters of general interest – and citizen-consumers aren't interested anyway.

But has that changed? Does the internet host a new public sphere? Habermas himself, in a rare 2010 interview with the *Financial Times*, said no. He sees the web as too poorly connected – lots of fragmented forums that rarely overlap – and too messy. 'Its structure is not suited to focusing the attention of a dispersed public of citizens who form opinions simultaneously on the same topics and contributions which have been scrutinised and filtered by experts,' he said. Sociologists of the internet have suggested that information on the web feeding public discussion might actually be too filtered by experts, since search algorithms like Google's offer sources based on popularity and which often privilege established sites.

Neither of these criticisms address social media, however: Habermas, who was ninety in 2019, says he doesn't use it and 'cannot speak to [its] solidarising effect'. Does a trending hashtag sufficiently focus public discussion on a topic, and can the ability of ordinary citizens to suddenly 'go viral' chip away at the online hegemonies of the already powerful? If so, do these forums bring back citizens as political actors?

Scholars have pointed to the innovation of online political campaigns and the apparent correlation between a person's social media use and certain types of political participation. Simultaneously, they have voiced doubts about the seriousness of online debates. Can the public opinion formed on social media be taken seriously when the platforms are still dominated by other uses such as entertainment, consumerism and content sharing among (relatively contained) friend groups? And can online platforms be considered representative when there are still barriers to accessing the internet?

The jury is still out as the web grows and changes. But it might be safe to say that the internet has forged a new world of public communication, even if it's not a utopian one. It might also be just as safe to say that the snags in the web which keep it from being perfectly free and democratic look a lot like the problems which afflicted Habermas's public sphere in the analogue ages.

For example, the issue of unequal internet access – and algorithm-driven inequality – echo the arguments voiced by feminist critics of Habermas's public sphere. The bourgeois public sphere was never a unitary and uncensored space, they pointed out. Nancy Fraser's *Rethinking the Public Sphere* argued that, instead, there were 'official' public spheres marked by significant exclusions on the basis of gender, class and race, and that marginalised groups had to forge competing 'counterpublics'. Similarly, the consumerist focus of social media is nothing new: it stems from the same capitalist forces that tarnished newspapers for Habermas.

The only, rather unsurprising, conclusion is that public forums import the same barriers to democracy and equality that exist in the society around them. Media scholar Zizi Papacharissi summarises it thus: 'whether [the internet] transcends to a public sphere is not up to the technology itself'. In other words, it's up to us.

Q

QUALITY

Once, there were tabloids and broadsheets. Then — as newspapers became less easily differentiated by the physical size of the paper they were printed on — we moved to 'downmarket, mid-market and upmarket'. Failing that, there was a distinction between the 'tabloids' and the 'qualities'.

How the tabloids resented that, with its implication that journalistic worth was only to be found in a small pool of newspapers with generally small circulations. And they were right to feel offended: a great many tabloid journalists are outstandingly able at writing, pictures, layout and impact.

Nevertheless, questions about 'quality' in journalism nag away. How do you achieve it, measure it, recognise it or aspire to it? Is there a 'quality' metric *(SEE: METRICS)* that editors can invoke when all else (profits, circulation, advertising, etc.) withers away? Circulation *(SEE: CIRCULATION)* is no measure of quality; nor are clicks or eyeballs. The 'best' journalism may haemorrhage money.

Winning awards might — in some newspaper cultures — be an indicator of quality. But the gold standard of the Pulitzers is not a universal one. Whether your journalism operates in some kind of public interest, whether it is done ethically, what public purpose it serves, how 'serious', or useful, or important the subject matter is, how accurate it is — all these could add up to 'quality'.

Various attempts have been made to link quality with sustainability. The American academic Philip Meyer has spent much of his recent career trying to demonstrate that 'influence' is a more reliable business model than clicks: 'Influence is earned by trust, and the empirical evidence shows that trust depends on quality . . . the societal influence of a newspaper achieved from practicing quality journalism could be a prerequisite for financial success.'

Meyer tried reversing the argument in his book *The Vanishing Newspaper*: 'Cutbacks in content quality will, in time, erode public trust, weaken societal influence, and eventually destabilise circulation and advertising.

'So why would anyone want to cut quality? If management's policy is to deliberately harvest a company's market position, it makes sense. And pressure from owners and investors might even lead managers to do it without thinking very much about it because reducing quality has a quick effect on revenue that is instantly visible while the costs of lost quality are distant and uncertain.

'When management is myopically focused on short-term performance indicators such as quarterly or annual earnings, the harvesting strategy is understandable. If those distant costs could be made more concrete and predictable, managers and investors might make different decisions.'

But even in 2009 it was not obvious to Meyer that a conventionally-managed newspaper was capable of placing quality at the heart of what it did: 'It was an argument that might seem obvious to news-editorial people, but was not so apparent to accountants and advertisers: that product quality is necessary for sustainable profitability. It might be apparent to them now, but that horse has left the barn. The self-destruction of the traditional mass-market newspaper could be irreversible.'

Amen!

R

ROUGH OLD TRADE

The 'rough old trade' (ROT) argument about journalism seeks to forgive it. 'Don't take us too seriously,' it pleads. 'We're a rum old bunch of the good, the bad and the ugly, but we stand or fall together.'

In a sense, it's right. Delineating a good tabloid reporter from a mediocre broadsheet reporter is a pointless exercise. We're all affected by the same laws and forces of repression. Sometimes we just have to hold our nose and stand together in solidarity. Since the dawn of the printing press there have always been scoundrels and muckrakers. John Wilkes, the father of parliamentary reporting, was – to put it mildly – no saint. Nor, in the early nineteenth century, were Cobbett or Hazlitt. Get over yourself. One person's scandal is another person's sleaze. Where do you draw the line *(SEE: POWER WITHOUT RESPONSIBILITY)*?

Well, where *do* you draw the line? When the *Guardian* first started writing about phone hacking at the *News of the World*, the paper got a lot of ROT arguments thrown at it: 'Come on, none of us are choir-boys.' So the proper response was . . . what? Not to write about it? Because in this rough old trade it's better to forgive and forget?

The rough-old-traders loathe anyone getting holier than thou about what's involved in journalism. Stop washing the dirty linen in public. Stop pretending the *Guardian* or *Financial Times* or BBC are any better than the *Sun*; or the *Washington Post* than Fox News. We're all in the same line of work.

There was a certain kind of ROT memoir produced by old Fleet Street hands of a passing generation. They are chronicles of drinking, deception, fornication, guile, bugging, impersonation, betrayal and a ruthless do-anything-for-the-story gung-ho. The end – the splash in the next day's paper – justified any means. It was considered a bit humourless to deprecate either the spirit or the contents of such memoirs. 'It's a rough old trade, old boy. Now, what are you drinking?'

This argument ignored the reader, of course. It was assumed the reader would understand and, on some level, approve. They didn't imagine journalists to be angels either. But, as levels of trust in journalism plummeted, one couldn't help wondering if, actually, readers didn't like this kind of ethical swamp any more than most journalists who were required to work in it.

There are famous examples of reader boycotts: the entire city of Liverpool refused to buy the *Sun* after it published its repulsive 'THE TRUTH' headline over a bunch of lies about the 1989 Hillsborough Stadium disaster in which ninety-six football fans were killed. Then advertiser boycotts became more common. The *News of the World* was eventually felled by the toxicity of its own behaviour.

Rough old trade? In the words of the fictional reporter in the best journalism novel, Evelyn Waugh's *Scoop*: 'Up to a point, Lord Copper.'

ROYAL COVERAGE

Can you believe a word you read about the royal family? The short answer is 'probably, quite a lot of it' – but a continuing act of faith is required. Out of any beat, royal reporting is a world almost devoid of open or named sources. So, in order to believe what we're being told, we have to take it on trust that there are legions of 'aides', 'palace insiders', 'friends' and 'senior courtiers' constantly WhatsApping their favourite reporters with the latest gossip. It has been known to happen (mostly notably with the late Princess Diana and the reporter Andrew Morton). Maybe they are, maybe they aren't. We just don't know.

Britain's royal family is both the best-known and one of the most elusive institutions in the western world for journalists to cover. Its members are the objects of daily fascination and even devotion around the globe, even in countries that have no links to them or gave up their own royal families centuries ago. Yet they remain ultimately unknowable.

It is a paradox: the royal family represent an important and influential, though largely powerless, executive at the heart of the British state (and the monarch is head of state in fifteen other countries too); no monarch has vetoed legislation in three hundred years, or refused to accept a government since 1839. But access to them is only at a distance. You cannot ring them up for a private chat and they rarely give interviews, except under the most tightly controlled conditions. (When they do throw themselves open to questioning it is often a disaster, as Prince Andrew found in November 2019.) Perhaps only popes in the Vatican are so intimately inaccessible – and even they give press conferences these days.

Queen Elizabeth II, in nearly seventy years on the throne and despite meeting an estimated one million people, has never publicly expressed an opinion, still less a controversial one: a heroic forbearance. Her very lack of contentiousness is probably the reason she remains almost certainly the most popular public figure in the country today. Popular support for the monarchy, or at least her personification of it, continues to hover in all polls at between two-thirds and three-quarters.

Now, with the multiplicity of media, there is a constant chatter – the Queen even has her own Twitter account, though there is no sign that she ever uses it personally. However, newspapers remain at the heart of royal coverage, advantaged over broadcasters constrained by the actuality (pictures and sound) of television and radio, but with readerships seemingly fascinated more by the passing parade – and who can blame them? – than by relatively unchanging and serious questions about the institution's future.

It was ever thus: 'We have to be seen to be believed,' says the Queen. They can't lock themselves away as Queen Victoria tried to do following the death of Albert and lost public sympathy and support as a result. In the words of her later prime minister Lord Salisbury in the *Saturday Review*: 'Seclusion is one of the few luxuries in which Royal Personages may not indulge . . . loyalty needs a life of almost unintermitted publicity to sustain it.'

There is daily reporting and then there is inevitably also commentary and opinion – the louder the better, opinion not always having to be constrained by facts (and that applies to serious papers as much as tabloids). The royal soap opera sells papers: otherwise why does the royal family feature so regularly on the front pages? Princess Diana remained regularly on the front of the *Daily Express* for at least ten years after her death, until its then editor announced at morning conference that stories about unusual weather events should supplant her: 'The weather is the new Diana!' But even then she continued to feature.

In what remains a highly competitive national newspaper market there is a premium for the tabloid press in obtaining royal stories, with the excuse of their inherent importance, whether it is a young Prince Harry concocting an approximation of a Nazi uniform to wear to a fancy dress party or, fifteen years later, his and his wife Meghan's decision to withdraw from frontline royal duties. Even in the most trivial stories, the ramifications are endless, spreading out like ripples on a pond for several days and then breaking like a tide on the furthest shores of the Commonwealth, Europe and America.

Back to the question of how much is true and trustworthy. Again, the answer is (probably) quite a lot: with today's diverse media there is generally too much at stake to make mistakes. But we should not be blind to occasional undeclared conflicts of interests.

In 2019 the Duke and Duchess of Sussex – Harry and Meghan, as they became better known – decided to take legal actions against three of the newspaper groups most obsessed with them: the *Mirror*, the *Sun* (and the by-then-deceased *News of the World*) and Associated Newspapers, publisher of the *Mail on Sunday*. The actions were for assorted forms of invasions of privacy, including phone hacking and breach of data protection.

When, in early 2020, the couple decided to withdraw from frontline royal duties, the critics piled into them – especially in some Murdoch and Associated titles.

One of the most vehemently hostile commentators trying to rubbish their reputations was the former *Mirror* editor, Piers Morgan. But few newspapers bothered to enlighten their readers about the background legal battles. Morgan, for instance, did not find time or space to let his readers or viewers know that his name cropped up multiple times in the generic phone hacking litigation particulars of the claim in front of the Chancery Division. If Harry's phone hacking case ever got into court, Morgan might well have to answer awkward questions under oath about allegations that he knew about criminal behaviour in his newsroom. If proved, he could even end up in jail like the former *News of the World* editor Andy Coulson.

So it certainly suited Morgan to rubbish the reputation of the people who were suing his former newspaper. The same went for Murdoch titles. There were, in short, quite a lot of worried newspaper executives and former editors who had absolutely zero interest in treating the couple kindly or even-handedly.

It's called a conflict of interest. But one that – nine times out of ten – went undeclared. Readers were kept in the dark. Eventually Harry and Meghan decided enough was enough and announced in April 2020 that they would break off all communication with the tabloid press in the UK. How much it mattered, only time will tell. In a time of pandemic, both friends and critics had more important things to worry about.

In a way the royals have to share the blame for their overall coverage: their attempts at manipulation and denial have usually backfired, ever since the abdication crisis of 1936. Then, the newspaper proprietors of the day were persuaded to ignore Edward VIII's relationship with Wallis Simpson, which was being printed all over the world, almost until the last moment. It was a prime example of what was ostensibly an intimate story turning out to have huge constitutional implications. The news-papers have not made that mistake again, and nor could they in today's modern media world.

The tabloids take the royals seriously and devote money to cultivating and suborning contacts because of the commercial imperative. If the royals become boring their popularity will sink, as they occasionally appreciate *(SEE: BOREDOM)*. It is a ruthlessly symbiotic relationship on both sides: the palace press offices promote the family by supplying an endless trail of trivial information (what outfits the female royals wear on any public occasion), knowing that the coverage will be obses-sive, and the tabloids fight competitively to get their exclusives using whatever methods they can, including during the phone hacking scandal ten years ago. The metrics are irresistible. There is little hope that editors are going to dial down their coverage. It is journalism red in tooth and claw and it won't end while the royals reign.

'You cope: one does,' as the Duke of Edinburgh liked to say.

S

SCEPTICISM

It's good for both journalist and reader to be sceptical: not so good if they become cynical.

Hope for the sceptic is neither abstract nor naïve. Presented with a piece of information, the sceptic doesn't necessarily hope it's true – imagine if they were told the sea would rise to swallow their home – rather, they believe that the truth is discoverable and valuable, and assumptions deserve to be interrogated. The sceptic will seek out the evidence before accepting what they hear, and decide for themselves. It's a stance that benefits everyone: if those supplying the information, such as the press, know that those consuming the information will be sceptical, the suppliers are incentivised to articulate clearly and cite their sources. A sceptical journalist will have corroborated those sources before those citations even reach the reader. Truth is checked up and down the information supply chain.

Cynicism, on the other hand, has a hopelessness at its core. It is a feeling that no one is honest and nothing will turn out well: the truth is neither discoverable nor valuable *(SEE: FLOOD THE ZONE WITH SHIT)*. For communities who have been deceived in the past, it is certainly an understandable reaction. But here's the problem: if you believe no one is honest, then you yourself probably won't feel compelled to be honest either. And it's more than likely that a cynic won't partic- ipate in the efforts to remedy the issue about which they're cynical: it's not worth it.

For an antidote to cynicism, perhaps we could turn to God (one of them, anyway). There's a biblical story in Genesis in which Abraham strikes a bargain as he begs God not to destroy the sinful city of Sodom. He asks God to promise that if there are fifty good people, Sodom will remain standing. God agrees. What about forty-five people? Ten? God agreed on ten but, alas, ten could not be found, and you know the rest.

What if cynics could identify one, or ten, or fifty, honest journalists and politicians? Would they be persuaded to nurture enough hope to remain merely sceptical? It would be worth it.

SCIENCE

In many ways, science and news are wildly different pursuits: science is a complex, slow, incremental process in which results only make sense with caveats and context; news needs to be simple, quick, direct, free of footnotes and built around human narratives.

'Science news' might therefore seem paradoxical. How can the delicate nuances of the scientific process survive the brutal simplification required by a news editor *(SEE: CLIMATE CHANGE)*? The truth is, things often go wrong. Overblown claims, seemingly miraculous health cures or panics about new technologies are among a multitude of sins that can usually be traced back to misconstrued scientific studies, cherry-picked data or a lack of understanding of basic statistics. But it's not always like that, and there are simple ways to weed out the good from the bad.

If you ever come across a story that claims to be based on scientific research, the first thing to do is identify the original source of the core claims. Science gets into the news in a number of ways, but the ideas worth paying attention to will almost always be published in a peer-reviewed scientific journal. There are thousands of these, but the most prestigious include *Science*, *Nature* and *Cell*. In the health world, look for references to the *New England Journal of Medicine*, *The Lancet* or the *BMJ* (formerly the *British Medical Journal*).

Next, check out the authors of the study. Are they academics from reputable universities or research institutes? A quick web search of their names and affiliations will give you a list of their previous research papers and any articles about or featuring them or their work. Read around, see what kinds of opinions their work elicits from the wider community of scientists. If you want to get into even more detail about them, use Google Scholar to search through their academic literature.

Identifying sources has never been easier but accessing original research papers can be very difficult. Most scientific research sits behind punishingly expensive paywalls and the only way to get to it is through a university library or repositories such as Sci-Hub (though the legality of the latter is questionable). If all else fails, you can always email the author and ask them for a PDF – the vast majority of scientists are usually more than happy to share their work with anyone who asks.

Stories about medicine or health are the most fertile territory for confusion and misunderstanding. These topics often get the most breathless coverage because every reader has a stake and editors know they generate interest. How many times have you seen stories one month showing that drinking a glass of red wine every evening could extend your life by several years, followed the next month by a story claiming that all alcoholic drinks are categorically harmful to your health? You might read about a radical new treatment for an unpleasant brain cancer or the discovery of a new class of antibiotics that promises to kill all known drug-resistant superbugs. All of these news stories might have good scientific research to back them up, carried out by reliable scientists from quality institutions. But how do you know what to believe?

The trick here is to never put all your faith in the results of a single study. If drinking a pint of beer every day is (surprisingly) found to be as good for your health as going to the gym every day, it is not a finding that should change your behaviour if a hundred other similar studies conclude the opposite. Extraordinary claims demand extraordinary amounts of evidence. Work on the premise that if it sounds too good to be true, it probably is.

Being sceptical does not mean being dismissive, simply that you put stories in their proper context. Just because a drug works in a test tube, a nematode worm, fruit fly or rat, it is not guaranteed to work in humans. Drugs that work for one condition aren't guaranteed to work for another, as a few learned the hard way when they took drugs that they'd heard about on the news as potential cures for Covid-19.

Look for the type of study that the story is based on. In medicine, the gold standard is a double-blind randomised controlled trial, where researchers hold every factor constant across the populations in their study, except the thing they are testing (e.g. a drug or other intervention). The more people involved in the study, the better the statistics and the more meaningful (i.e. true) the results are likely to be.

Remember that correlation is not causation. If a study shows that children who grow up playing more video games end up with lower IQs as adolescents, look for an explanation of the biological mechanism for what could be going on. If there isn't one, tread cautiously.

Seeing risks put into context is particularly important. If drinking coffee seemingly increases your risk of developing stomach cancer by 50 per cent, this is only worrying if the absolute risk of that cancer is itself significant. If it only occurs naturally in one in 100 million people, a 50 per cent relative rise is probably nothing to worry about. Headlines that try to shock you with scary-sounding relative risks are a red flag that the story is a dud *(SEE: NUMBERS)*.

Perhaps the most important way to check the claims of a piece of research is to look for dissent. Other scientists – those not involved in the research being reported but whose own research area overlaps – might raise important issues with the design of the experiment or disagree with the conclusions being drawn by the authors. Look to see whether the scientists carrying out the original research have any financial or other conflicts of interests associated with what they are doing. Scientists might like to see their craft as a pure search for knowledge, but they are also humans with mortgages and research careers to think about.

Scientific thinking is not fixed; it adapts and changes over time as new evidence comes to light or better instruments are invented to test and measure us and our world. Astronomers used to think the Earth was the centre of the known universe. Before they discovered germs, doctors used to think that diseases such as cholera and plague were caused and spread by bad air. Later evidence showed that these ideas were wrong.

And that's all fine. Scientific thinking evolves and old ideas are overturned as we learn more and get closer to the real nature of the world. If that sounds a bit disappointing, then don't despair – this method of parsing the world has been hugely successful at everything from doubling human lifespans to building smartphones and rockets that have propelled humans to the moon. Science is an inherently changing, argumentative process and the ideas that we have come to think of as 'facts' are simply those that have survived repeated attempts to tear them apart.

Science news (perhaps all news) is the same. Remain sceptical *(SEE: SCEPTICISM)*, go through the checklist above and attack the claims from every angle you can. If the story remains intact, then you're probably onto something good.

SCOOP OF INTERPRETATION

A scoop of interpretation can be a thing of beauty: the bringing together of straws in the wind by a watchful journalist who binds them into the solid foundations of a good story.

Or it can be a dodgy political Sunday newspaper splash, the only virtue of which is that it is undeniable, so vague is its premise.

In the first category is the Zircon spy satellite story. Duncan Campbell, a UK-based investigative journalist specialising in intelligence matters, was commissioned by BBC Scotland in 1985 to make six *Secret Society* programmes for BBC Two. He said: 'I proposed what should be in the six slots. One was called "Zipper" to avoid the right word [Zircon] being in any papers.'

He had spotted two industry press releases issued in the late spring of 1985 about the launch of a satellite that piqued his interest. The first release came from British Aerospace and stated in part: 'The new satellite is due to be launched in 1988 and be positioned 53 degrees E as part of the growing constellation of United Kingdom military communication satellites . . .'

Two weeks later an almost identical press release came from the Society of British Aerospace Companies with one thing missing – the location of the satellite at 53 degrees E, which happened to be the longitude of the central Soviet Union (as it was then). The attempted cover-up in the later press release made him look more widely for publicly available information and build his story.

The satellite, codenamed Zircon, was the brainchild of what was the super-secret GCHQ communications centre *(SEE: NATIONAL SECURITY)*, which hitherto had to rely exclusively on US satellites for its intelligence-gathering. Zircon was meant to give the UK its own 'spy in the sky', as well as standing and independence. Campbell, however, believed that it broke an agreement between government and Parliament that military projects costing millions of pounds would come under the scrutiny of the Public Accounts Committee.

Campbell's series was due to be aired in 1986 but the BBC delayed and, after coming under pressure from a furious British government, decided to pull the Zircon episode, although it was eventually shown two years later. Campbell's success was based on the intersection of journalism where sleuth meets intelligence analyst. As he wrote in an article for the *New Statesman* in 1987 explaining the background to what had become the 'Zircon affair': 'The hasty cover-up appears to have been necessitated by the premature release of a difficult-to-explain fact – the positioning of the new satellite over the Soviet Union and Indian Ocean, not the NATO area. With no forces further east than the Gulf, there is no need for a British communications satellite there.'

It was a scoop that launched a chain of events which led to the emergence of GCHQ 'from the dark', as Campbell puts it, and even a collaboration between Campbell and GCHQ in a 2019 exhibition at the Science Museum entitled, of course, Top Secret. Unthinkable in the mid-eighties.

Attempts at scoops of interpretation do not always result in such solid journalistic achievement. Sometimes the phrase is applied pejoratively to describe the story of a journalist, often a fairly desperate one, who has extrapolated far too much from very flimsy evidence. For instance, a political correspondent might have spotted in a speech, made a couple of days before a weekend, a particularly spirited attack by a minister on an area of policy. Does this indicate a sharp change in direction for the government? Will it be announced next week at the party conference? An MP, who doesn't want to be quoted by name but considers herself a friend of the minister, says she thinks it likely. A pressure group working in that policy area thinks the same. The minister's staff refuses to comment or even 'guide' the journalist on a 'deep background' basis. In the absence of a definite 'no', the journalist files a story for the weekend, which begins: 'The government looks set to announce a major crackdown on . . .'

If there is no major takedown of the story for forty-eight hours, the journalist might consider that he or she was lucky and that such an announcement can only be a matter of time. Sometimes these stories prove entirely accurate – or not. As one news editor is alleged to have asked in a telegram to his reporter in a faraway land after a particularly blood-curdling scoop: 'Your exclusive is still exclusive. Why?'

SIDEBAR OF SHAME

The sidebar of shame (SoS) is the justified-right strip of thumbnail images and salacious celebrity headlines that is the most notorious feature of the *Daily Mail*'s web iteration, MailOnline. Though 'sidebar' accurately reflects its positioning on the site, it is arguably at the centre of the whole operation. The 'shame' element refers to the mainstay paradox: a battlefield-volume of body parts (almost always female) merged with a prudish, censorious outrage.

Sometimes the celebrities featured (and often the word 'celebrity' does a lot of heavy lifting) are attending film premieres, or fashion shows or industry parties, and are dressed up. Sexily, even. MailOnline will never not comment on this. Usually in all caps. Think of the Hollywood sign, but instead it reads: SIDEBOOB. These women are always putting on a 'display' in the manner of mannequins arranged in a shop window.

But equally, and much more troubling in terms of privacy implications, the SoS is packed with grainy paparazzi shots of famous women merely going to the shops or the gym (in MO argot: 'stepping out'). In this scenario, it must always be noted if said woman is going MAKE-UP FREE, which is often translated into looking 'tired'. Perhaps, too, a hint that daring to leave the house without lipstick or eyeliner is a sure sign of impending breakdown.

Then there are the Humbert Humbertist pieces on the daughters of celebrities. Often pre-teens whose 'leggy pins' (which: tautology) are grossly commented upon. It doesn't matter if they are fourteen years old and on their way back from school. Children are not exempt from ogling or criticism.

This disingenuous pruriency is not limited to bodies. It extends to smoking, or any other activity which might have been categorised in

South Kensington as a 'vice'. Again, it is women who bear the brunt of disapproval. Male stars might be snapped outside a club taking a neutrally termed 'fag break', but women will be 'caught' having a 'sneaky' cigarette. Often the cigarettes are 'cheeky'. Tobacco is afforded more personality than women. Another favourite is the lawyer-sidestepping phrase employed for stars smoking marijuana: 'suspicious cigarette'. (MailOnline's euphemisms are truly things of beauty: for instance, 'gal pal' for a famous woman's girlfriend. This, even if the woman in question is open about her sexuality.)

Although MailOnline uses the domain names dailymail.co.uk and dailymail.com, and is owned by Daily Mail and General Trust (DMGT), its running is – to an extent that has never been entirely clear – supposedly independent of the *Daily Mail* and *Mail on Sunday* newspapers. The digital presence is overseen by the mercurial Martin Clarke.

The *Mail*'s former editor Paul Dacre, who avoided having to use a computer if blue pencil and shouting did the trick, frequently appeared to distance himself from the digital version of his paper, perhaps rarely looking at it himself. But Clarke told the Leveson inquiry that he reported into Dacre and spoke to him 'most days of the week'.

Whilst Dacre had strong NIMBY vibes and both a small-c and capital-C conservative attitude – and certainly believed in the old-fashioned value of shame – the sidebar of shame is little more than a smorgasbord of flesh and apparent (but often banal) scandal. The online-only journalists, many of whom are young and at the beginning of their career, are encouraged to pad out picture-heavy pieces with adjectives, dissecting female bodies with all the vigour of abattoirs. Or, in one case, somehow trying to get mileage out of a singer who 'dutifully passes through airport security' and – the same singer – 'exchanging looks' with her actual husband. The verb that parades itself most often is 'flaunt'. Not a word in common everyday usage, but useful when given ten minutes to knock off an extended caption for a picture of a person you probably haven't heard of who is not wearing much.

The teams putting together these daily chronicles are required to have a mixture of skills: 'part scavenger, part sub-editor and headline writer, part reporter and picture taster, part adman, and they're often a whizz with Photoshop and video too,' wrote Adrian Addison in his book *Mail Men*. 'They're also part celebrity-magazine gossip writer; it's a vital skill to be able to spot a Kardashian in a crowd.'

The website publishes a staggering 1,500 articles and 560 videos – *a day!* – to 15 million daily readers and 10 million Snapchat users. Add in 250 million video views a month and you arrive at the most read online 'news' title in the US, UK and Australia. The constant stream of inconsequential gossip about people who don't really matter very much is, it turns out, rather addictive, with readers refreshing the home page around ninety-six times a day and then spending a long time scrolling down through the pictures and formulaic words.

One first-hand account of working on the production line – by James King on tktk.gawker.com in 2015 – recorded that a typical ten-hour shift would involve banging out four to seven articles. 'Unlike at other publications for which I've worked,' he wrote, 'writers weren't tasked with finding their own stories or calling sources. We were simply given stories written by other publications and essentially told to rewrite them. And unlike at other publications where aggregation writers are encouraged to find a unique angle or to add some information missing from an original report, the way to make a story your own at the *Mail* is to pass off someone else's work as your own.' *(SEE: CHURNALISM)*

Amusingly, the *Mail* sued over the King piece. A thirty-four-page complaint launching a $1 million action protested, without apparent irony: 'The *Mail*'s reputation, goodwill, and business have been damaged.' The suit was settled without any apology or retraction, but with Gawker (by then bankrupted by its own intrusive behaviour) agreeing to attach an 'Editor's Note' to the piece.

MailOnline has been repeatedly slammed by numerous other journalists and organisations for uncredited 'borrowings' – or straightforward plagiarism. Mostly, the website rips off other celebrity gossip. But a particularly egregious case in 2016 involved Martin Fletcher, a former foreign and associate editor of the *Times*, who financed his own trip, organised a fixer and transport, and risked his life, to report on the desecration of British war graves in Basra and Amara in Iraq.

Fletcher was writing (behind a paywall) for the *Times*. But within hours of the piece appearing, his story had been 'repackaged' and attributed to one Euan McLelland (subsequently PR manager for the Dubai boat show). It was a busy night for McLelland, whose shift had already involved writing about the importance of teaching children phonics, outrage over plans to allow a police killer outings from jail, garlic that doesn't give you bad breath, an interview with murdered soldier Lee Rigby's mother, an insight into SAS plans to attack ISIS and an update on the junior doctors' dispute. (Detective work by Liz Gerard, reported by the *Guardian*'s Roy Greenslade.)

There was a link to the *Times* way down McLelland's article, but the average reader could easily have mistaken something bashed out by a desk-bound reporter churning his way through a shift for an arduous and expensive piece of original reporting.

The fortunes of DMGT have oscillated in recent years. The share price was up 9 per cent, as of 2019, thanks to MailOnline's performance, specifically its 25 per cent annual growth in digital ad revenue, offsetting print losses felt across the industry (and for DMGT, a print ad drop of 12 per cent). This represented a comeback from the fairly disastrous preceding year when growth plummeted from 28 to 2 per cent after Facebook changed its algorithm to de-prioritise news content. But the size of the audience is still world-beatingly enormous.

A communiqué to investors in December 2018 appeared to show that Goldman Sachs had been drafted in to explore the idea of a MailOnline paywall. The question was whether people would pay for information from a site which even Wikipedia (in February 2017) regarded as untrustworthy. Wikipedia editors said at the time: 'The general themes of the support votes centred on the *Daily Mail*'s reputation for poor fact checking, sensationalism, and flat-out fabrication.' How that must have hurt in South Kensington: that a bunch of amateurs on a crowdsourced website had the nerve to outlaw proper, professional, paid journalists!

As we enter the third post-Millennium decade amidst a rapidly changing media environment, will the notorious sidebar of shame continue to flaunt its thumbnails?

The #MeToo movement, kickstarted by the exposure of Harvey Weinstein's career-long criminal lifestyle of sexual harassment, assault and misogyny, has unleashed a mainstream focus on the insidious objectification and subjugation of women (which, spoiler, isn't new). A rise in popular interest in mental health means that consumers are also questioning forms of journalism that are no more sophisticated than a combination of leering and jeering.

The *Mail* now has a new editor, Geordie Greig, who appears to have a different ambition for the digital version of his paper, not to mention for the *Mail* itself. Users of the MailOnline app are now given the option to choose 'news only', which cuts out (most) of the sidebar of shame content. Martin Clarke, though, still refers to the MO's offering, including the SoS, as 'journalism crack'.

If you were Greig, what would you do? This is not why you came into journalism. And yet the Frankenstein created by his predecessor (almost without noticing it) is throwing off cash and attracting myriad readers at a time when most other streams of revenue are vanishing. Try to migrate readers to something more serious, less . . . tacky? Convince your boss that this is slowly eating the *Mail* brand? Or, like Dacre, hold your nose and pretend it's not there?

SKIBBEREEN EAGLE

The *Skibbereen Eagle* – a small-town newspaper in Cork, Ireland – ran an editorial penned by the editor, Fred Potter, warning Czar Nicholas II on 5 September 1898 that 'the *Eagle* will still keep its eye on the Emperor of Russia and all such despotic enemies'. One hundred years later the *Irish Times* noted drily: 'The Skibbereen Eagle is no longer with us, but Russia is.' And its finger-wagging admonition of the Russian czar has become an emblem of parochial journalistic self-importance.

SLOW

Life has got faster. We are said to check our phones every twelve minutes in search of the latest, the newest, the shiniest. The fastest take all. But then came the reaction to newsrooms full of hamster-wheel reporting. One or two pioneers began to re-imagine a world in which journalists could take their time over articles. Go out of the office and meet people. Maybe read a book, phone an expert. Explore the context, examine the meaning. Analyse the trends, consider the broader significance. A bit like reporting used to be within living memory.

'Slow down, wise up' was the pithy slogan of the UK-based website

Tortoise when it launched in 2019. In his manifesto for the new organisation, the editor, former *Times* editor and BBC head of news James Harding, wrote: 'The news media, like everyone else, has been hollowed out by the internet. We produce more news than ever before; more and more, faster and faster; junk news. It's become noise. Precisely when we need to hear more, we often want to switch off. And so, in the battle for attention, the news media has sought refuge in telling people things they want to know. Instead of connecting with new audiences, news organisations have been bonding with their bases.'

A similar ambition was expressed by the Dutch news website De Correspondent: 'News mostly is about what happens today, but rarely about what happens every day . . . Put another way: we don't cover the weather, we cover the climate, informing you about how the world really works.'

One of the most successful news outlets of the modern age is the *Economist*. Its slogan – 'you've seen the news, now discover the story' – similarly implies that the surface picture that follows from breathless reporting is unreliable.

Matt Thompson, contributing editor at the *Atlantic* and a former executive at NPR, coined the phrase the 'tyranny of the recent', and predicted that, in future, we would be looking less for news than for understanding. But true understanding only reveals itself with patience and time.

SNACKING

The average reader's attention span has dramatically shrunk to a few seconds – or so an eye-catching piece of research from Microsoft in 2015 claimed. Perhaps less than a goldfish, though this may have been fake news, and a bit unfair to goldfish. But newspaper metric managers focus an unforgiving eye on how long each reader devotes to each article *(SEE: METRICS)*. In the past it was all guesswork. Now journalists are uncomfortably aware of how – with most readers, most of the time – the attention begins to wander after a few paragraphs.

The answer many editors came up with was to demand shorter stories. In 2014, Associated Press told its journalists to keep most articles between three hundred and five hundred words *(SEE: BREVITY)*.

There followed new formats that were less reliant on slabs of text. Quartz developed an app which didn't require its readers to read the news so much as chat with it: each story appeared in little chunks, like texts from a friend. More august news organisations such as the *Wall Street Journal* developed chatbot formats. CNN started providing news in personalised private messages.

The *Economist* started using Snapchat Discover in October 2016, along with the BBC and *New York Times*. Instead of longish worthy chunks of text (let's call them 'articles'), the *Economist* remade articles as easily absorbable cheat sheets. North Korea, global warming, the legalisation of drugs: they were all translated into snappy visual formats. Within a short time the newspaper was claiming it had built a significant audience of more than 7 million unique visitors, including many 14- to 24-year-olds who wouldn't have been seen dead reading a printed magazine *(SEE: YOUNG PEOPLE)*.

As smartphones became the main devices in people's lives – returned to dozens of times a day to check on updates – so session lengths shrank. By 2013 it was calculated that people might spend four minutes a day grazing on news. A new jargon developed around what was termed people's 'media repertoires': the tablet or iPad was a 'lean back' experience for more in-depth new consumption. 'Snacking' was what people did on mobile – and, increasingly, in their news viewing on television/laptop.

Academic studies found a tendency to prefer headlines to articles, immediacy over quality, impressions over solid knowledge.

The implications were chewed over. This was bad for civic engagement. Bad for the economics of news (less incentive to produce high-quality news and 'public service' content) *(SEE: QUALITY)*. A new type of news processing emerged in some newsrooms whereby the reporters produced one version of a story and editors then remade it for a variety of different platforms. It became known as 'shovelware'.

Shovelware, though an unlovely word, is doubtless with us for some time. Niche snacking platforms will continue to spring up: some of them will thrive. But mainstream legacy news providers will face the continuing problem of serving different audiences with different attention spans via different distribution channels – including laptops, tablets . . . and even print.

The more snacking displaces healthy eating, however, the bigger the implications for democracies which depend on having informed citizens.

SNOPES

Snopes.com calls itself the internet's definitive fact-checking resource. Its history pre-dates tweeted declarations of 'fake news' by two decades: it began in 1994, a year in which Yahoo.com launched under the charming moniker 'Jerry and David's Guide to the World Wide Web' and most people didn't have internet at home. Snopes was originally a site where its founders, David and Barbara Mikkelson, could publish their research on the origins and veracity of urban legends and folklore. As they later told it to the *New York Times*, this satisfied a small and devoted following . . . until the 9/11 attacks of 2001. At that point, their readers inundated the Mikkelsons with questions about alarming messages they were receiving regarding the US government's role in the attacks. Snopes covered it, and found itself expanding to respond to the ravenous public appetite for all types of checked facts. In the wild new world of viral email chains, the longstanding fact-checking efforts of newspapers and magazines were helpless. Snopes was where ordinary people could put to the test rumours circulating outside of the traditional news outlets.

By 2017, it was receiving 20 million unique visitors in one month and had hired a research team. It had become such a staple of the fact-checking world that Facebook hired it to help identify fake news on its platform. (Snopes pulled out of the partnership in early 2019, citing too much staff time spent on it.)

Snopes, however, does not call things 'fake news'. If the term once referred to a statement's inaccuracy, it now 'behaves like a rhetorical middle finger' denoting a politician's dislike of a statement regardless of its truth, writes one Snopes editor. A 2017 Gallup/Knight poll found that 51 per cent of American adults agree that accurate stories portraying politicians negatively sometimes constitute 'fake news' (28 per cent said these are 'always' fake news). Instead of fanning the flames, Snopes kicked the term out of their style guide.

A more pressing danger they have observed over the years, according to Snopes's founders, is the seductiveness of rumours. 'Rumors are a great source of comfort for people,' Barbara Mikkelson told the *NYT*. 'It's people wanting confirmation of their world view,' said David. But the answer is not to think everything is fake: indeed, David Mikkelson diagnoses 'hyper-scepticism', which might be better called cynicism, among too many Snopes readers. 'That's just as bad as being gullible in a lot of senses.'

SOCK PUPPETS

Sock puppets are members of the colourful cast of internet monsters, belonging to the same genus as trolls and catfish. Specifically, they are fake online identities intended to deceive by using a pseudonymous account to speak clandestinely through a username like a ventriloquist through a puppet. They can be used to skew public opinion ('ballot stuffing'), circumvent blocks on other accounts, target individuals ('catfishing') or infiltrate opposing groups to sow doubts ('strawmanning').

The US caught Russia's Internet Research Agency *(SEE: KREMLIN)* using sock puppets to spread pro-Trump content on social media during the 2016 US election, but how do we spot them when we don't have an intelligence agency to help? A team at the University of Maryland analysed thousands of sock puppet accounts, and offered some useful tips:

- Sock puppets rarely start new discussions: instead, they tend to comment in the same threads around the same times
- They tend to post highly controversial and sometimes abusive content: look for lots of downvotes or activity on their posts
- Check account emails or IP addresses if you can: they tend to be identical for multiple accounts
- Pay attention to writing style: they often use 'I' and 'you', generally less standard grammar, and are more combative.

Closely related to sockpuppetry is astroturfing: faked grassroots support on websites and in blog comments. Astroturfing is most usually employed by the public relations and advertising industry, and by political groups to create the illusion of widespread support for a policy, individual or product.

SOURCES

Without unofficial sources, there is no valuable journalism. Official sources are (for the most part) the easy bit. They are people paid to put information into the public domain. Some do so truthfully and straightforwardly, others not so much. Most of it is done in the open – or sort of. But unofficial sources are often crucial to truly enlightening journalism. We've heard the spin (the official version): now what's the real story?

Two different forces are at work regarding information in the twenty-first century: we might think of them as 'loose' and 'tight'.

Looseness comes from digital ubiquity: the broad ability of anyone – within the law – to say anything about anyone. Tightness is the opposite instinct: to impose a narrative on what could otherwise be chaos. The looser information becomes, the tighter the official grip. There is an explosion of PR jobs whose function is to control and filter what gets out. Increasingly, all employees – whether they're working for giant corporations or a local hospital – sign bloodcurdling NDAs and confidentiality agreements.

So, society needs people who are prepared, often at some personal risk, to talk to journalists and help them dig beneath the surface and discover the full texture of a story. What is being concealed? What's unsaid? What deserves to be known?

So far, so simple. But very little is, in fact, simple in this often hidden world of the interaction between reporter and source. Here are some basic questions:

- **How many sources** do you need in order to be sure something is true? Or (not quite the same thing) to persuade an innocent reader that something is true?
- Does the **motive of the source** matter? How much do you let the reader know about the reason someone is imparting information?

- **How open can you be** about the identity or nature of the source?
- How can you **protect the source**?

To take those in order – **how many sources**? Classically, the answer is two. You're much more likely to be right about something if you don't simply rely on one version of events. That makes sense, and it's a good general rule. But it does rather depend on a) who a source is, b) what corroborative evidence they may give you, and c) the nature of the information they're passing on.

Let's suppose the Archbishop of Canterbury (whom you know quite well) rings you to tell you he's intending to quit, and then texts you a copy of his resignation letter. The source is, you might think, a 24-karat one. You're not just going on his word: he's given you written evidence to support it. And he's telling you something about which he has direct, first-hand knowledge. Do you need a second source? Well, it's always possible he's gone mad, or is lying. But, assuming he sounds reasonably in command of his faculties, this might be a story that only needs one source.

Suppose, on the other hand, a well-placed source from within the Church of England rings with the same information. She's in a position to know. She's heard it first-hand but hasn't got anything in writing. She's always been accurate in the past. All good – but let's go for that second source, shall we?

The checking part is a bit more complicated than in the past. Once there was a kind of code of honour among, say, press officers or politicians that if you went to them to check something they would respect your exclusive. That was because you had done the decent thing and asked for confirmation and/or comment – something to be encouraged.

But not everyone plays it straight. The temptation is to get something out elsewhere first. If someone suspects you're going to write a bad story, why not take it to a friendly journalist who can shape a more sympathetic narrative? Or post something yourself on Twitter or Instagram? Why wait for news to be done to you?

Next, **what about the source's motive**? They may be leaking out of revenge or vanity, or to influence events, to stop something happening, to portray an adversary in a bad light. Or they may be giving you information to prevent a wrong, to set the record straight, because they feel they have no option but to be a whistleblower. Any experienced journalist will have dealt with hundreds, if not thousands of sources. Some of them will have very questionable motives; others will be practically saints in regard to the personal risk they are taking to put important information into the public domain.

Sometimes you may not really know the motive. Perhaps the most famous source in history was the then anonymous Deep Throat, who guided the *Washington Post*'s Bob Woodward and Carl Bernstein towards the information that would eventually destroy a US president. For years it was believed that Deep Throat was acting to save democracy. But in 2005 the former deputy head of the FBI, Mark Felt, stepped out of the shadows to reveal himself as Deep Throat – and history had to be re-written.

A number of authors claimed that Felt was, in fact, a mendacious, manipulative and opportunistic figure intended on destabilising the Acting Director, Patrick Gray, in the hope that he, Felt, would get the top job. Or maybe, it was suggested, he was simply out to spy on Nixon and selectively leak material in order to increase the FBI's control over the president.

In this revisionist version of Felt's motives, it was noted that he was later convicted (and pardoned) for illegal wiretaps and break-ins and was an admirer of widely despised former FBI chief J. Edgar Hoover. In other words, the *Washington Post* could be viewed as having allowed itself to be 'spun' by a deeply political player in facilitating the FBI's destruction of an elected president.

Does it matter? Nixon was undoubtedly a crook who deserved to be unmasked and unseated. The story Woodward and Bernstein skilfully told was, in all essential respects, true. Good results followed from someone acting with mixed motives.

A good editor and reporter should, of course, think carefully about whatever motive a source might have (insofar as that is possible). But, in the end, it is the information that counts. Is it true, is it accurate, is it important? What context can we give the readers to understand the full story? And how much is it necessary to let readers or viewers know about where the information came from, and why?

Max Frankel, executive editor of the *New York Times* at the time of the Pentagon Papers (a story overwhelmingly based on material provided by one whistleblower), later wrote: 'ALL our sources deserve to know that they are protected with us. It is, however, part of our obligation to reveal the biases and apparent purposes of the people who leak or otherwise disclose information.'

If the *NYT* had taken the Frankel principle more seriously, it might have escaped the trouble it landed itself in over the build-up to the second major war in Iraq in 2003. A subsequent May 2004 mea culpa in the paper admitted that many of the most problematic articles 'depended at least in part on information from a circle of Iraqi inform-ants, defectors and exiles bent on "regime change" in Iraq, people whose credibility has come under increasing public debate in recent weeks.' *(SEE: JUDITH MILLER)* It would have been good if the paper had been up front about that at the time.

The mea culpa also noted that one long-standing and persistent source had been identified as a prominent anti-Saddam campaigner, Ahmad Chalabi. Chalabi's motives were extremely pertinent, as the *NYT* later admitted: 'He became a favourite of hard-liners within the Bush administration and a paid broker of information from Iraqi exiles.'

Nor did a 'two source' rule help very much. When *NYT* reporters turned to governmental briefers for validation they found: 'The accounts of these exiles were often eagerly confirmed by United States officials convinced of the need to intervene in Iraq. Administration officials now acknowledge that they sometimes fell for misinformation from these exile sources. So did many news organizations – in particular, this one.'

So the Frankel principle is a well-judged one. If followed, it might even have averted a war which was to a large extent dependent on building up political and public support in advance. But is it always possible to reconcile those two sentences in the Frankel principle?

That brings us to the third question: **How open can you be** about the identity or nature of the source?

The overriding obligation of any journalist is to protect the identity of a source who wishes to remain anonymous. The more you reveal 'the biases and apparent purposes' of a whistleblower, the more you may risk helping those who want to unmask them.

In the first decades of the twenty-first century complexity layered on complexity. The great 1971 Pentagon Papers story (celebrated in Steven Spielberg's 2017 film *The Post*) dated back to a simpler age when reporters had sole access to photocopied documents in their hands. They knew where the information came from; they knew who'd given it to them. They could overwhelmingly rely on the story the documents told, regardless of why the leaker, Daniel Ellsberg, had spilled the beans.

But what happens if the intermediary is Julian Assange – not quite a source and also a publisher, editor, information anarchist, activist and hacker? In 2010 he arrived at the *Guardian*'s offices in London with a thumb drive containing more secret documents than had ever been supplied by any unofficial player in history. The original source for that story, it became apparent, was Bradley (now Chelsea) Manning, a twenty-three-year old US Army intelligence analyst. How much should editors have considered the purity of her motives? Or (as with the Pentagon Papers) was it enough just to look at the documentary evidence she had obtained? The same questions arose with Edward Snowden, who became the next most celebrated whistleblower to leak vast quantities of top secret documents, this time from the National Security Agency (NSA). No evidence has ever emerged that he was working on behalf of a foreign power, though many suggested as much. How much would it have mattered if he was?

The question acquired even more salience in 2016 when Wikileaks acquired more hacked documents and began a series of releases which appeared to some to be an attempt at destabilising the Democratic presidential candidate, Hillary Clinton. Many people felt that the disclosures looked more like information–laundering than journalism. Assange has claimed that the Russian government was not the source of the DNC and (Clinton campaign chair John) Podesta leaks. In July 2018 Special Counsel Robert Mueller indicted twelve Russian military intelligence agents alleged to be responsible for the hack. Who was telling the truth? What obligation did Assange have to identify the motives of his source, even if not naming them?

Regardless of such doubts, it was notable how many mainstream news organisations gave the material wide coverage. If the material had been sent directly to them, would they have refused even to look at documents sent to them by such a source – assuming anyone knew at the time who the source was? Regardless of the public importance of the material itself, would it have been responsible to ignore something on the grounds that it might have come from a tainted source?

Now to anonymous sources. On the face of it, anonymous sources are not much help to a reader or viewer. The most cynical of them may wonder whether a source really exists, or whether it is quite as described. It is rare for a reporter to cite 'a junior government source'. The oracle is nearly always senior.

Articles or bulletins spattered with anonymous sources are hard to evaluate. Journalism which is not believed has failed.

The New York Times has, in theory, a prohibition on certain kinds of anonymous speech. Its style guide *(SEE: STYLE)* says: 'Anonymity must not become a cloak for attacks on people . . . If pejorative remarks are worth reporting and cannot be specifically attributed they may be paraphrased or described after thorough discussion between writer and editor.

'The vivid language of direct quotation confers an unfair advantage on a speaker or writer who hides behind the newspaper, and turns of phrase are valueless to a reader who cannot assess the source.'

Anonymity can allow all involved to become lazy and unaccountable. The British lobby system of reporting *(SEE: POLITICAL JOURNALISM)* has stubbornly insisted on giving government briefers the mask of speaking unattributed. That also gives them deniability. And then there are pop-up quasi-freelance players – Bannon in the US, Cummings in the UK – who appear to be briefing all the time, but seldom in a way that allows anything to be formally traced back to them.

The reason anonymous sources persist is that – if used with integrity and care – they allow the trusting and discerning reader to learn more than if only on-the-record official sources are allowed to speak. In politics, as in virtually every other walk of life, people will often speak more honestly if they are allowed to speak anonymously. The use of non-attributed quotes can thus assist the audience towards a truer understanding than if a journalist confined him/herself to quoting the bland banalities that often characterise on-the-record quotes.

As in much else, a sceptical approach is the best. If you have reason to trust a particular newspaper – or broadcaster or reporter – then the probability is that an anonymous source will a) exist, b) be roughly as described, and c) will have used the words you read. If you start by not trusting the outlet or the writer, you may wish to be extremely suspicious about what you're being told.

And then there are newspapers, or editors, which do not deserve to be trusted. See the former editor of the *Sun*'s astonishing confession to the Leveson inquiry: 'To be frank, I didn't bother [to find out the source of stories] during my 13 years with one important exception,' Kelvin MacKenzie said. 'With this particular story I got in the news editor, the legal director, the two reporters covering it and the source himself on a Friday afternoon.

'We spent two hours going through the story and I decided that it was true and we should publish it on Monday. It caused a worldwide sensation. And four months later *The Sun* was forced to pay out a record £1m libel damages to Elton John for wholly untrue rent boy allegations. So much for checking a story. I never did it again. Basically my view was that if it sounded right it was probably right and therefore we should lob it in.'

Finally, **source protection**. People sometimes take immense risks when they talk to journalists. They may lose their job or their reputation. Some risk losing far more, even their lives. So it's not hard to see why the obligation to protect a source is the nearest experience to something sacred that most journalists will ever feel.

But it's becoming harder and harder to maintain anonymity in an age when every phone call, email, text message and physical journey can leave a permanent digital fingerprint *(SEE: SURVEILLANCE)*. Once upon a time the relationship between journalist and source was – at least in some countries – protected by both convention and law. It was not considered a good idea for the state – except in exceptional circumstances – to be able to seize papers (in the eighteenth century) or (in the twenty-first century) phone records or email metadata or browser histories.

But that idea now seems quaint. If the state can find good reason to eavesdrop on a confessional, or legislator's surgery, or medical consultation or legal conference, it will. And if it can follow a journalist around to see who they're talking to, then why not? Why not trawl through oceans of metadata to see who's been speaking to whom?

All kinds of countermeasures are imagined or trialled. Secure drop boxes for the safe depositing of secrets. End-to-end encryption for messages. Apps that train your phone to detect intrusion. Secure email keys. Reporters are turned into cryptographers. Many of these new shields would foil most hackers, if not a determinedly curious intelligence agency. But sources are undoubtedly discouraged. Why risk everything to help good information triumph over bad? The powerful gradually get a stranglehold on news.

So almost everything about sources is complicated. It's dangerous being a source. As a reader, it's difficult to understand who a source is – or even if one exists. For journalists, it's increasingly hard to be explicit about the nature or identity of sources. Meanwhile, in all this confusion and menace, charlatans prosper.

But let's hope none of that prevents sources from being sources.

SPECIALISTS

It is often said that journalists are the only people who pay attention to bylines, but who the story is written by can sometimes be as important as what it says.

For the reader, the fact that a story is by a specialist correspondent with a byline such as 'our health editor' or 'our crime correspondent' should provide some reassurance that the story is not just clickbait but is well-sourced, is worth telling, and is set in its proper context.

For the journalist, being a specialist means being able to delve deeper, spending time cultivating contacts in a particular field and setting the agenda by bringing in stories rather than simply chasing hares set by the newsdesk.

At their best a specialist journalist will have a deep knowledge of the fields they cover, a regular stream of exclusives that shape the national or international debate, and will provide the reader and viewer with the kind of authoritative context and analysis of what happens on their beat that helps make sense of the modern world.

It was notable that when, in 2019/2020, ministers in Boris Johnson's Conservative government decided not to appear on BBC news shows such as Radio 4's *Today* programme, editors often filled the gap by interviewing their specialist correspondents to provide the missing material. Their knowledge and long-term familiarity to the audience may well have made them more trusted than many a 'here today, gone tomorrow'

minister – but it didn't amount to holding the government to account.
It also takes time to dig deep into a particular field. Some of a
specialist's best sources may be people they have known for many years.
They may be high-level 'insiders' perhaps disgruntled at their successors'
approach or 'back-door' moles who may pass documents; they may
originate in watchdogs, academia or outside pressure groups. Sometimes
readers also want to share their experiences with known experts because
they recognise through their coverage that they will know what it is
they are talking about. Some seek help often in the face of official
indifference.

But many news organisations can no longer afford to devote precious
resources to reporters dedicated to covering a particular beat, especially
when specialists need time to start delivering the kind of steady stream
of exclusives that justify their cost.

Newsdesks also grow weary of being asked to run yet another instal-
ment in what seems to them to be a 'dull but important' saga of, say, the
privatisation of the probation service or the finances of the military. But
sometimes it is only by taking a story seriously over a sustained period
of time that a journalist can attract the contact who provides the evidence
that turns a policy failure into a furore. This was certainly the case in the
2018 Windrush scandal, where it took dogged and persistent coverage by
the *Guardian's* Milly Gentleman to finally ignite national outrage.

Newsroom managers are under intense pressure to provide a comprehensive and competitive news service and nowadays that means having
reporters who can process stories rapidly, often from other news sources
and with minimal checks *(SEE: CHURNALISM)*. At one extreme the
pressure on MailOnline journalists to run 750 articles a day led to an
editorial model that one ex-reporter in 2015 described as 'depending
on dishonesty, theft of copyrighted material, and sensationalism so absurd
that it crossed into fabrication'. (That's James King in 'My Year Ripping
Off the Web'.)

It is not only economic pressures in the newsroom that are leading
to specialists becoming an endangered species. Increasingly government
and commercial organisations are slamming the door on those who
take too persistent an interest in their activities. 'You know too much,'
they tell specialists who try to engage with them.

A generation ago a new specialist correspondent in the British media would be greeted by the appropriate government department with an offer of background briefings, press conferences, and interviews and contact with officials and ministers on the grounds that they would engage in a critical but grown-up exchange. Now the doors are firmly shut. Few briefings are held in Whitehall, and press offices respond to press enquiries not with an informed conversation but with a demand that all questions be put in writing on the understanding that the subsequent anodyne response will be delivered hours if not days later.

Journalists are even excluded at practitioner or academic conferences when it comes to Q&A time with participating ministers or officials, for fear that interaction may lead to unscripted news stories. Specialists increasingly find themselves bypassed, with official announcements and stories funnelled through Westminster lobby journalists who lack the time and knowledge to provide a critical reception.

It has to be said that not all specialists are paragons of virtue. Some succumb to Stockholm syndrome and become too dependent on a single source, or fail to maintain a sceptical approach to those they write about.

This is perhaps most sharply demonstrated amongst defence and security specialists. For years there was a sharp divide between those who were effectively mouthpieces of the security services in the British press and those who wrote critically about their activities and were regarded as 'hostiles' for their pains *(SEE: NATIONAL SECURITY)*.

One former editor of the *Guardian*, Peter Preston, refused to have a crime correspondent on the grounds they would spend all their time drinking with Scotland Yard detectives. When the policy changed, the *Guardian* was home to one of the finest crime reporters in the business – Duncan Campbell – whose tales of the underworld enhanced its journalism. But Preston was right to be sceptical about journalists who rely on a small pool of sources. Some education correspondents, for example, end up too close to the views of teaching unions and fail to reflect the wider interests of parents and pupils.

Specialisms have changed as society has changed. Labour correspondents used to rule the roost when Britain staggered from one industrial crisis to the next. You'd be hard pressed to find anyone with that title now. But the range of current specialisms has never been wider –

politics, science, business, home affairs, education, media, environment, ~~arts, music, fashion and even wealth can all~~ be found in the British media. Some have even helped to change society.

SPEED

When it comes to news, our internal metronome is nowadays set to Presto. We check our phones numerous times a day and expect to be kept up to the minute (if not the second) on breaking developments. Who wants to be the last to hear about that football goal, or this celebrity's death, or that governmental sacking, or that horrendous plane crash? Social media speeds everything up, with instantaneous and massive distribution of anything eye-catching or click-worthy. The notion of keeping a reader waiting until a printed newspaper dropped on their doorstep the following morning died around the turn of the century.

So pity the poor reporter, torn between wanting to get it absolutely right and the relentless pressure to get it out of the door.

Speed and accuracy do not have to be in complete tension. The great news agencies (e.g. Reuters, Bloomberg, AFP, AP, PA) pride themselves on being first with the news, but also trustworthy. 'Accuracy, as well as balance,' says Reuters' handbook of journalism, 'always takes precedence over speed.' A similar exhortation is to be found in the BBC guidelines.

But the accuracy business is now often in competition with the speed business *(SEE: ACCURACY)*. The Southeast Asian tsunami of 2004, the terrorist attacks on London in July 2005 and the multiple outrages in Paris in November 2015 were all first reported with immediacy and at scale by witnesses on the ground. Much of the reporting was accurate – but the process of verifying video clips, photos and eyewitness accounts was slow stuff. Within six hours of the 7/7 attacks in London the BBC had been sent 1,000 photographs, 20 pieces of amateur video, 4,000 texts and 20,000 emails. Today, the volume of social media after such a public event in the centre of a capital city would be overwhelming.

'The old model of broadcasting was that the editors had time to find out what is happening,' says Richard Sambrook, a former BBC head of news, quoted in a 2015 Reuters Institute paper by Reiko Saisho. 'They had time to verify and check it, and once that was sorted out then they put it out to the public. In live news you don't have time to do all of that. So effectively the audience moves alongside with the editors in real time as the information comes in.'

Social media can correct, as well as distort, mainstream newsrooms. Nearly all media, including the BBC, initially reported the 7/7 events as power failure. By 9.58 a.m. the BBC (it later concluded through subsequent analysis) had credible evidence of four bombs. Its initially erroneous reporting was soon corrected. According to Saisho, the Mumbai attack of 2008 prompted an eyewitness to send in his picture of a bus roof being blown off since it clearly demonstrated this was not an electric failure.

Stick to what you know, be explicit about what you don't know, correct immediately and prominently if you do slip up – these ought to be well-understood principles of journalism-at-speed. 'Never wrong for long' is the slyly knowing adage of rolling news. In a just world there ought to be a ready business model for people who prefer accuracy over speed *(SEE: QUALITY)*. Let's call it work in progress.

STYLE

Stylebooks set the rules by which all professional and credible news organisations operate. Regardless of your place in the editorial hierarchy – summer intern, reporter in a war zone, Nobel Prize-winning columnist – you will be subject to one unbendable rule: you must respect the stylebook.

Stylebooks dictate the layout and typography of a publication and list the spelling and grammar rules for its journalists. New words and phrases are constantly entering the language, and need to be added, along with their definitions and how they should be used.

Societal changes must also be recognised – out with fireman and policeman, in with firefighter and police officer. Out with committed suicide, a throwback to the days when killing yourself was a crime, and in with died by suicide.

Stylebooks usually come in an A–Z format. They are not a substitute for dictionaries but serve as practical language-usage guides for journalists.

Consistency in style and the absence of spelling and grammatical errors are essential to the credibility of a news organisation. One of the most common features of fake news stories is their sloppy spelling and grammar.

Editing a stylebook entails arbitrating such long-running arguments as whether there should be two spaces or just one between sentences (one space seems to have won for now). There is the low-hanging fruit, like banning the use of clichés such as 'low-hanging fruit'.

There are also rules on punctuation, capitalisation, hyphenation and just about any other kind of —ation you can think of.

George Bernard Shaw said that 'Britain and America are two nations divided by a common language', and anyone who has ever written a stylebook will agree.

So-called British and American spellings are the bane of any stylebook editor's life. Which one do you choose? If you write in British English, do you respect the American spelling of secretary of defense? If you are the *Guardian* you do, but if you are the BBC you don't – even though in the official title it is spelled 'Defense'. Then again, the *New York Times* styles the British defence secretary as 'defense secretary', so it cuts both ways.

These are the quirks of language adjudicated in stylebooks that can irritate the purists but are not going to create diplomatic incidents, unleash a torrent of online abuse or put your reporters on the ground in physical danger. But there are other style rulings that can provoke strong reactions, such as how to use a word created at the end of the Second World War.

The Polish Jewish lawyer Raphael Lemkin formed the word 'genocide' from the Greek word *genos* (race or tribe) and the Latin word *caedo* (killing) in 1944 in response to the extermination of Jews, including many of his family members, by the Nazis in the Holocaust. The United Nations subsequently adopted a convention codifying genocide as a crime in 1948.

It is a word heavy with historical, political and legal significance, and it is also a word that is widely misunderstood, including by journalists. A mass killing may qualify as a crime against humanity, but it may not fit the specific legal definition of genocide – the intentional destruction of a national, racial, ethnic or religious group. Most of the killing in Cambodia and the Balkans did not legally qualify as genocide, and whether or not the Myanmar government and military committed genocide against the Rohingya would be a matter for an international tribunal to decide. Until then, style should dictate that you use the term genocide sparingly, and preferably when quoting an official or expert.

Then there are place names. It is not a journalist's job to decide the name of a city or a country, but often the stylebook editor has to do just that. It took most western media many years to accept Myanmar as the official name of Burma, the rationale being that by doing so you were recognising an unsavoury military regime. There was a fair amount of grumbling from editors in western newsrooms about changing Bombay to Mumbai and Madras to Chennai, but eventually they had to accept that time was up for these colonial-era names.

Perhaps the most consistently difficult issue is how to use terrorist and terrorism. These words are emotive and inflammatory, and it would be difficult to explain why you would not call al-Qaida a terrorist movement. But governments often brand armed groups that have legitimate causes 'terrorist organisations', leaving the journalist to decide who is a terrorist and who is a freedom fighter.

To avoid having to make that value judgement, stylebooks will tend to recommend 'militants' or 'activists' and let the acts speak for themselves – if a suicide bomber gets on a bus and kills dozens of innocent people, does labelling him or her a 'terrorist' add anything to the story? If the government decides it was a 'terrorist' attack, then use it in quotes.

And speaking of value judgements, what should the stylebook say about calling politicians liars? The *Washington Post* calculated that President Donald Trump made more than 13,000 'false or misleading' claims in his first three years in office. British prime minister Boris Johnson was fired from his first job as a reporter for making up a quote, became notorious for his fake news coverage from Brussels, which became known as Euromyths *(SEE: BREXIT)*, and was fired from the cabinet for lying about an affair.

In the current climate of post-truth and alternative facts, the taboo of branding a public figure a liar has been broken by many mainstream media outlets, but most editors are still very reluctant to use the 'L' word. Was it an intentional falsehood – the definition of a lie – or was it a genuine error? Who are journalists to know or to judge?

The best style rule would be to prohibit calling people liars, but to require that falsehoods are surrounded with proven facts – the fact, the claim, then the fact again – and then let the readers decide. A truth sandwich, as the cognitive linguist and philosopher George Lakoff calls it.

And that leaves one last style point to decide – should it be style book, stylebook or Stylebook? We have gone with stylebook, but whichever one it is, make sure you respect it.

SUB-EDITORS

Editorial processes – what happens to a piece of copy between being writtten and being published – are (in theory at least) what helps distinguish 'professional' journalism from the rest. Crucial to the editorial production line is the role of the newspaper sub–editor (or copy editor in the US), which remained largely unchanged for decades. Typewriters disappeared, computers replaced hot metal, but the sub-editor's job stayed more or less the same. Then 'digital' happened.

On a major national newspaper, until fairly recently, a reporter would write an article, a desk editor would commission and finesse their copy, and a sub–editor would check it for correctness, clarity, sense and style. They would then liaise with designers and picture editors, cut the copy to fit, compose a grabby headline and write the rest of the page 'furniture' of subheadings, pullquotes and picture captions *(SEE: HEADLINES)*. Their day would usually begin slowly around midday, pick up speed through the afternoon, then reach a tense conclusion as first-edition deadline approached, with pre-press screaming down the phone for pages to be sent to the printers.

In the digital age, a sub–editor working for a 'legacy' publisher – one that still produces a newspaper as well as news and features for digital platforms – still acts as a gatekeeper. She or he remains the last line of defence between writer and reader. But the job is becoming more complicated. With print circulations falling, readers are now more likely to be reading an article on their phone, laptop, iPad or Kindle. They could be seeing it on Google, Facebook, Twitter or Instagram. They could be anywhere in the world.

Less than a decade ago, old lags on the subs' desk bemoaned the dark arts of writing headlines for digital: the bosses were 'killing the art of the sub-editor' and turning skilled editors into Google search-chasing automatons. Whereas not so long ago subs could rely on editorial intuition, they must now draw on audience analytics tools that tell them who's reading what and for how long, on what device and where in the world they are *(SEE: METRICS)*.

A sub-editor will add relevant body copy, links, video, graphics and explainers, and source and crop pictures. A good digital headline will include key words while remaining arresting and, when the occasion demands it, amusing. The sub will add metadata in the form of key word tags (Afghanistan, Donald Trump, Manchester United, etc.) to make the article findable.

In the modern newsroom these tasks are not always done by sub-editors. Indeed, as advertising revenues plummet and publishers seek to cut costs, 'layers' of editing have been removed and many subs done away with altogether, or the roles of commissioning editor and sub have been merged, sometimes with that of writer too. Some are experimenting with technology, looking to AI tools that will re-work or produce whole articles automatically.

Subs are an easy target for cuts. They are the unsung heroes of publishing and their contribution is often overlooked. Some notable headlines from the past would work just as well for a digital audience coming from search or social:

TITANIC SINKS, 1500 DIE

HITLER DEAD, SAY NAZIS

MAN WALKS ON THE MOON

FREDDIE STARR ATE MY HAMSTER

More problematic would be the following gems:

GOTCHA
(on the sinking of a Argentinian battleship during the Falklands war)

UP YOURS DELORS

(an attack on the EC president Jacques Delors)

ZIP ME UP BEFORE YOU GO GO
(singer George Michael arrested in flagrante)

BIN BAGGED
(on the death of Osama bin Laden)

The best headlines are still those you will click on because you just want to know the story. For that reason, 'Elvis Presley's Teeth Visit Malvern' ticks all the boxes.

SUBSIDIES

If not cover price, and if not advertising, then what?

Some journalists have always protested that they would never accept subsidies for news: it would, they say, imperil their independence. In fact, there are many hidden forms of subsidy in place in different countries already. Advertising is, of course, a form of subsidy. French news organisations get tax breaks. In many European countries there's reduced, or no, VAT (valued added tax) on newspapers. In other countries they have reduced postage rates for them.

In some Scandinavian countries governments help defray the cost of distribution or subsidise the weaker paper in local markets in order to ensure diversity of views and news. In many countries there are hidden forms of subsidy, such as governments being the major advertisers (for announcements, contracts, jobs, etc.) in newspapers. In November 2018, Canadian prime minister Justin Trudeau announced a large infusion of tax breaks – around $600 million – to support the country's news business. The BBC's Local Democracy Reporting Service (LDRS) launched in 2017 and has recruited around 150 reporters to maintain a watchdog role on local authorities: within eighteen months they had filed some 90,000 stories.

Some news organisations in the US have also applied for tax reliefs under the 501(c)(3) non-profit provisions available to, for instance, educational organisations *(SEE: PHILANTHROPY)*. And then there are billionaire subsidies. The Intercept could not have started – and may not survive – without Pierre Omidyar, the founder of eBay. Jeff Bezos, the richest person in the world after giving life to Amazon, came to the rescue of the *Washington Post*, as have assorted French businessmen to *Le Monde (SEE: PROPRIETORS)*.

There may be forms of cross-subsidy within organisations. The *Guardian* would have been a sickly animal at various points in its history without being supported by, first, the *Manchester Evening News* and then a secondhand car magazine/website, *Auto Trader*. The *Times* has occasionally relied on subventions from profitable parts of the Murdoch empire, including the red-top tabloid. The same is true of Murdoch's beloved (but loss-making) flagship title the *Australian*. The Kaplan educational business kept the *Washington Post* afloat for a while. The *FT* had some wilderness years (losses of £40 million at one stage), but was helped by a 50 per cent share in the *Economist*. There are, in other words, many forms of subsidy – hidden and apparent – already at work in a good many news organisations.

Does it matter? Well, there are clear benefits for newsrooms that would otherwise struggle, if not die. But subsidies can be withdrawn as well as granted: see, for instance, how savvy governments simply turn off the advertising tap from titles which displease them. Do they imperil independence? In theory, no more or less than any form of advertising. Journalists generally protest fiercely that they could never be bought or influenced by the people who pay for advertising. The same argument ought to apply to any form of subsidy. Readers are entitled to expect a very high degree of transparency about all sources of income.

Not everyone agrees, though. The former editor of the *Daily Mail* Paul Dacre held particular contempt for what he termed the 'subsidiariat'. 'The longer I live,' he said in a 2008 speech, 'the more I come round to the view that – in most cases – it [subsidy] ultimately perverts everything it touches. In the media, it produces a distorting prism, actually incentivising its recipients to operate in splendid isolationism, far removed from the real world that the great majority of readers and listeners have to live in.'

And, famously, James Murdoch denounced the idea of public service broadcasting in a big speech in 2009, which concluded with the ringing cry: 'The only reliable, durable, and perpetual guarantor of independence is profit.' In those far-off days he evidently could not imagine a time – barely a decade later – when the great tabloid cash cow of the family company, the *Sun*, would declare a £68 million loss amid falling print sales and the enormous cost of phone hacking claims against its parent company.

Since Murdoch made his pronouncement, however, newspaper companies around the world have begged the big tech companies to effectively subsidise the cost of their news-gathering. The 2019 UK Cairncross Review into a sustainable future for journalism came up with a number of recommendations that involved some form of subsidy. They included new tax reliefs aimed at encouraging a) payments for online news content and b) the provision of local and investigative journalism, as well as c) an extension of the LDRS, which subsidises the reporting of local councils.

But there remains a question of who should receive subsidies, and for what? Should money simply go to existing news providers? What kind of news is worth saving? It would be ridiculous to prop up showbiz gossip, for example *(SEE: SIDEBAR OF SHAME)*. If there is a public need to know what is going on in courts or council chambers, would it not be better to begin by defining the information a society or community says it needs – and then invite tenders from organisations or individuals who think they can provide it? That would create opportunities for new players rather than simply propping up the (often debt-laden) legacy companies.

The question is becoming a rather urgent one, especially after the economic devastation wreaked by Covid-19. But it also feels as if the conversation – starting with communities and what they feel they need to know – has barely begun.

SUPPRESSION FEES

Paying newspapers *not* to publish stories is not new. John Walter, the first owner of the *Times*, offered the public the opportunity to pay him not to blacken their reputations. The press historian Francis Williams recounts an episode from the late eighteenth century in which a Mrs Wells, a Drury Lane actress who bore four children by her married lover, approached Walter to suggest a deal. The married man handed a large bundle of notes to a *Times* underling, asking 'Will this be enough?' The executive, a Mr Finney, replied: 'Give me a few more and by St Patrick I'll knock out the brains of anyone in an office who dare even whisper your name.'

The celebrity publicist Max Clifford (later jailed for paedophilia offences) claimed to have 'stopped a lot more stories than I've broken'. The US *National Enquirer* kept a safe containing documents on hush-money payments and other damaging stories it suppressed as part of its cosy relationship with Donald Trump leading up to the 2016 presidential election. They were known as 'catch and kill' deals. It was reported that Trump's team had identified two women who could be bribed to keep quiet about alleged affairs. It doesn't take much imagination to see how such payments place a politician in danger of being blackmailed or subject to demands for return favours. An unscrupulous newspaper proprietor wanting a favour from a government (say, a more relaxed regulatory environment, or a particular deal waved through) could have their hand strengthened if a politician believed an editor had a safe (online, or – in the past – real) with incriminating material. There may not, in fact, be a safe or an encrypted file on a hard drive back at HQ. It is enough for a politician (or, in other scenarios, a regulator or a police chief) to believe that there might be.

When newspapers started outsourcing the surveillance of people in public life to shady private detectives and known criminals they created an atmosphere of fear in public life. The suppression fee evidently still exists in some shadier corners of journalism. But it is not hard to imagine some proprietors not wanting to be repaid in cash, but in favours.

The potential for journalism to imitate a soft form of blackmail is, alas, ever present.

SURVEILLANCE

Journalism favours transparency but sometimes depends on secrecy. Some sources need to be able to speak privately, for fear of losing their livelihoods, or even their lives *(SEE: SOURCES)*. But how does that work in an age when privacy has virtually been abolished? There was a time when the most enlightened democracies believed (sometimes through gritted teeth) in the sanctity of the journalist–source relationship. It had the same kind of status as dealings between a lawyer and client, an MP and her or his constituent, a doctor and his or her patient, a priest and a penitent.

But those days are gone. A nosy government or intelligence agency or police officer ought, in theory, to have to follow due process. But nearly all our actions now leave digital fingerprints, and it has become harder and harder for any journalist to talk to a source in a truly confidential way.

End-to-end encryption helps – but perhaps not if the spooks or the cops are determinedly involved. The camera on your laptop? The location tracking apps on your phone? Your phone itself? How difficult is it to triangulate the phones and phone masts near you in that supposedly discreet greasy spoon where you agreed to meet your hush-hush source? There is still handwriting, and there are still brown envelopes. But the easier it becomes for the snoopers, the tougher it gets for journalists and whistleblowers.

Edward Snowden did try and warn us.

T

TL;DR

It stands for too long; didn't read. It can be a criticism – 'this is too long to be worth reading' – sometimes accompanied by a two- or three-word distillation of what the writer was struggling to say. But it can also be used as a way of anticipating a shrug or yawn by including – at the top or bottom of an article or presentation – what used to be called an executive summary, but is now called tl;dr.

You can decide for yourself on the capitalisation and punctuation. It can be TLDR. Or TL;DR. Or tl;dr. Or tldr. Or . . . but already it's TL.

TOMMY ROBINSON

Tommy Robinson (b. 1982, real name Stephen Yaxley-Lennon) is a British far-right, anti-Islam activist who, as founder of the English Defence League, picked up several convictions for violence, fraud and public order offences.

News organisations have been giving a platform to Tommy Robinson on the simplistic grounds that he has a right to free speech and that they are not censors. But this argument misrepresents the issue. It is not Robinson's freedom to speak which is at stake. Journalists can refuse him a platform: he will still have that freedom (as, for example, the controversial 'media personality' Katie Hopkins has had since LBC cancelled her show and she was permanently banned from Twitter). What journalists have been giving Robinson is something else entirely, which is credibility – the status of somebody who is a source of reasonable comment and reliable information. That is a mistake because, in reality, Robinson is neither reasonable nor reliable. Journalists like to say that they can counter that by confronting him robustly. But that fails to deal with the problem. It is the mere fact that he is interviewed which gives Robinson the (unmerited) status – and the reason why he accepts regardless of how robust his interviewer promises to be.

At bottom, this is not about freedom of speech; it is about whether news organisations are trying to present facts to their readers and viewers or whether they are content to be a platform for falsehood and unreason.

TRAINING

Arguments about training for journalists often revolve around the vocational versus the academic: on-the-job versus the classroom. This in itself is often a proxy for the debate about whether journalism is a craft or a profession.

The argument has been around for a while. In 1958 Howard Strick, the executive officer for the UK's fledgling National Council for the Training of Journalists (NCTJ) explained – in a UNESCO report on journalism training worldwide – how vocational training works:

'Any new journalist inevitably undergoes vocational training when he joins a newspaper office. This may vary in extent between haphazard, fragmentary advice, suggestion and abuse and a full-scale weekly training schedule.'

Abuse? Those who have been through on-the-job journalism training in that era will recognise a certain style of pedagogic prod from a chief sub distinctly unimpressed by the way the 'junior' reporter has written the story.

Then, that junior would almost certainly not have been a graduate – although the broadsheet newspapers have always tended towards a yearly graduate intake – and would have left full-time education in their teens. However, by 2016, 86 per cent of British journalists were graduates, according to a survey by London's City University.

These days, in addition to learning traditional news-gathering techniques, trainees have to achieve a high degree of technological competence and chase fewer jobs in a fragile industry that has to compete with social media.

What in a perfect world should they be taught and what in practice are they taught?

The collapse of the industry's business model in many countries has led to significant changes in the supply of training. 'The industry has outsourced journalism training to higher education,' says Richard Sambrook, Director of the Centre for Journalism at Cardiff University – one of the UK's leading journalism schools – where courses are accredited by the NCTJ.

The fundamental practical skills haven't changed much in generations except in two crucial regards – shorthand and the technological skills needed to be a journalist in a digital age. Today's aspiring journalist needs four mandatory modules to gain an NCTJ diploma: essential journalism, essential journalism and ethics, e-portfolio for journalism (an online portfolio of ten pieces), and essential media law and regulation. Those four modules are a mix of the traditional skills of news-gathering, storytelling, interviewing and analysing data – as well as navigating ethics, law and the regulatory framework in the UK.

However, not all universities seek accreditation from the NCTJ for their undergraduate and postgraduate courses. For instance, the highly regarded City University is not accredited to the NCTJ and runs one of the most sought-after courses in the country. Here, there is a broader set of themes aimed at the role of the journalist. City's BA (Hons) course aims to 'produce critical thinkers and reflective practitioners who are skilled in multimedia and digital production' and offers 'the chance to critically reflect from an analytical perspective upon the development of contemporary local, national and international print, broadcast and digital journalism and ethical concepts such as accountability and accuracy'. The programme specification also states that it will 'encourage and develop reflection and analysis of the role of journalism and the journalist in society'.

That last is a key component of training in the US, where it has long been the case that most journalists will have undertaken a four-year bachelor's degree. According to a report by the Poynter Institute, in 2003 nearly 90 per cent of all journalists held a degree and 36 per cent of those had a journalism degree.

US trainees are likely to have been inculcated with a strong sense of the principles of objectivity *(SEE: IMPARTIALITY)* and news you can trust. In a paper written for the Reuters Institute for the Study of Journalism in 2012, Sambrook said that these values became ingrained in the character of American reporting: 'They became translated into granular practice: get both sides of the story, the right to reply, check the facts, accuracy and fairness, and news pages distinct from editorial or opinion pages. These professional norms became culturally institutionalised in American print journalism – to a far greater extent than in the UK for example – and largely remain in place to this day.'

One of the failings of most news organisations has been a lack of continuing professional development (CPD). Once journalists are on staff it has always been difficult to tear them away from their screen to attend a class – in-house or external – in case they miss a good story. It is a trait journalists will have to ditch in the future. It is also an important difference with traditional professions: doctors and lawyers are expected to maintain their professional skills throughout their careers.

So, what do you need to be a journalist now? Relentless curiosity and flexibility and adaptability are timeless values. Sambrook says aspiring journalists will also need a more entrepreneurial approach when entering the market for jobs. He believes the days of careers running smoothly on track at big organisations are largely gone and journalists now have to learn how to manage their careers not just laterally but vertically.

The skills base journalists need is expanding all the time, too. Sambrook believes that his graduates must be able to use camera phones, shoot video, understand and be active within social media, and know how to code. 'How do you maintain source confidentiality in a digital world?' he says. 'Every journalist needs to know how to work in an encrypted environment.' *(SEE: SURVEILLANCE)*

Learning to code and tell stories on social media can be learned, but would-be journalists face bigger problems than that. Perhaps the biggest is the growing tide of indifference towards the idea of journalism as a crucial part of a healthy democracy. How do you train for that?

People have also started to question the cost involved in acquiring the right paperwork to get a job in journalism. 'Should students pay $30,000 or even up to $100,000 to attend a journalism school in the United States?' asked the media commentator Frédéric Filloux in his Monday Note in February 2020. 'Is it realistic considering the starting salaries in the profession? Is teaching journalism [in] schools actually *needed*?'

Filloux calculated that, on average, a student will pay $54,000 per year to attend one of these J-schools (living expenses not included). This can act as an impediment for several reasons: 'First, journalism curriculums are less likely to attract people as they see their future financial condition – high cost of education met by low salary – degrading. Two, they are less likely to [go into] journalism as the trade mingles with multiple commercial streams: production of branded content, all forms of "corporate journalism" and the various flavors of communication, all of them hungry for genuine editorial talent.'

Filloux argued that journalism teaching was in need of profound change on two counts. 'One is bringing more expertise into the profession by making it attractive for people who have already accumulated a solid experience in a field that is particularly hard to cover (economics, science, law, medicine, you name it). Two, I don't think organizing a curriculum around one or two years makes sense anymore. In the next decades, the media market will call for numerous qualifications that no one can even fathom today.'

For the job market, the skills being taught are, in the minds of many young freelancers, largely useless if there's no job to go into, or the jobs vary greatly from what's taught in J-school (such as being taught AP style but finding work as a social media editor). For freelance reporting, training is either self-taught or the most necessary skills – how to pitch to editors, how to navigate trauma and dangerous environments, how to manage your finances – aren't deemed relevant by schools that are not adapting to the changing media landscape. With medicine and law, even though the applications of knowledge might change – for example, with the implementation of technologies that must be learned – the job market and pipelines largely remain the same, which is not the case with journalism.

T

TRANSCRIPTS

In April 2019, the British conservative philosopher Roger Scruton gave an interview to the *New Statesman*'s then joint deputy editor George Eaton. When a 900-word article based on the 54-minute interview was published online, Eaton tweeted 'a series of outrageous remarks' Scruton had supposedly made about Islamophobia, Chinese people, George Soros and anti-semitism. There was outrage: within hours Scruton had been removed from his role as chair of a government building commission. Eaton responded by posting a picture of himself drinking celebratory champagne. One more scalp.

The *New Statesman* is a left-of-centre periodical. It was not long before its right-of-centre counterpart, the *Spectator*, mysteriously managed to obtain a recording of the Scruton interview. In a cover story headlined 'The hit job' the magazine compared what Scruton had actually said with how the interview and the tweets had depicted him. The *New Statesman* initially refused to publish the transcript of the interview, but later relented. The magazine's readers' editor, Peter Wilby, subsequently criticised Eaton for his insulting social media posts, some of which he found misleading. One of them, said Wilby, suggested that Eaton had 'approached the interview as a political activist, not as a journalist'.

While all journalism is necessarily selective, continued Wilby, 'the full transcript shows that most of Scruton's comments on Muslims, Orbán and anti-Semitism were more thoughtful and nuanced than those highlighted by Eaton'. He challenged the *New Statesman* editor to consider whether a 900-word article format was sufficiently long for a wide-ranging interview with the author of more than fifty books on many diverse subjects. And he also suggested that the magazine should think about releasing full transcripts 'when the contents are complex and controversial'.

This idea was greeted with horror by some journalists. An interview, in the eyes of some, can be like a seduction or entrapment. Journalists have their techniques and guiles, and they don't want the whole world to see how they do it. At the most basic level, an interviewer may want to win the subject's confidence to begin with, to make them feel relaxed and safe. The art here is to lull them into forgetting that this will be ink-splattered headlines and text: it must feel like a cosy, private chat in an enclosed space. You may ingratiate yourself, offer little confessions of your own, laugh sycophantically. These techniques work in the room: it would be mortifying to see them in print.

'Every journalist who is not too stupid or too full of himself to notice what is going on knows that what he does is morally indefensible,' wrote the *New Yorker* journalist Janet Malcolm in her unflinching account of her own technique when writing about a convicted murderer and an author. It is a clever piece of hyperbole, but the sentence contains enough truth to have become famous.

Even straightforward interviews usually, and necessarily, involve a highly selective process of compressing a transcript of many thousands of verbatim words into a readable summary of what was said. The journalist wants to be in control – not to have a million eyes checking his or her choices against the original text.

But there are journalistic cultures and organisations which operate to different norms. It is quite typical for a German or Scandinavian journalist to offer the subject of an interview the right to see the text – either the full transcript or the proposed written text – before it's published. There are lots of reasonable reasons for not doing this (and most British journalists would regard it as anathema). Suppose you have managed to entice an interviewee into saying something that, in the cold light of day they – or their advisers or lawyers – regret? How galling to have that retrospectively excised from the record!

Equally, there are a couple of good reasons for transparency with transcripts *(SEE: TRANSPARENCY)*, and they are both to do with trust *(SEE: TRUST)*. First, a subject may be more likely to want to grant an interview if they feel they, too, have some control over it. Second, the reader may feel more likely to trust the summarised version of a conversation if they can also read the full context.

Should the interviewee have any rights to be 'in control'? Some journalists would say absolutely not: 'That's PR. We do journalism.' But 'journalism' has changed in relation to interviews. Journalists grew impatient with being stenographers, faithfully reproducing the verbatim words of their subjects. Reputations were made on producing 'psychological' interviews. 'This person may have presented themselves in this manner during my twenty minutes/hour with them,' a modern-day interviewer may think to themselves, 'but I saw through that veneer and I feel I have captured a deeper truth.'

The celebrity interviewer was born. The name in lights was not the subject but the interrogator. At its most extreme it became a form of bloodsport. Whom have they dissected this week? Have they got another scalp? Did you make them cry? Increasingly editors wanted 'stories' from interviews. Push them to say something controversial we can dress up as a row. The gotcha interview *(SEE: GOTCHA)*.

A chicken-and-egg situation developed. The more interviewers placed themselves centre-stage and presented their subjects as *they* saw them, the more interviewees clammed up or surrounded themselves with PR teams to try and obtain the best result. The PR's job was to try to identify the 'fairest' interviewer, to (where possible) limit the scope of the conversation ('she won't talk about her boyfriend/marriage/girlfriend'), to intervene if things got sticky. And, of course, the more journalists felt manipulated, the more they bridled. Trust had gone.

Once the internet was born the press lost some of its bargaining power. Of course, an interview in a newspaper still carried advantages: a large audience and (with some newspapers) a kind of badge of recognition. Equally, there were now numerous other ways of speaking directly to audiences without waiting to be mediated by someone else. So why submit yourself to intrusive questions about things you have no wish to speak about, and then find yourself subjected to faux psychoanalysis by someone with whom you've spent forty minutes of your life?

A transcript – with or without prior approval – gives some comfort to both interviewee and reader. With reliable voice recognition and transcription software improving all the time, the additional cost of providing a verbatim read-out of a conversation will become negligible. A greater willingness to release transcripts alongside major interviews might well change the interviewing style of some journalists. But it would also help the readers judge for themselves what was really said, and in what context.

Had the *New Statesman* published the full transcript of its interview with Roger Scruton alongside the much-tweeted 900-word version, we would have had a more correct and textured understanding of his views. We might still not have agreed with them, but it would have been harder to create a cartoon villain: a small contribution to a less polarised world.

TRANSPARENCY

The pandemic of false news spreading around the globe in the past ten or so years has led to the growth of quite a substantial fact-checking industry *(SEE: FACT CHECKERS)*. Over time they have developed their own code of conduct to establish the basis of agreed standards for how fact-checking should, itself, win trust. The code of principles of the International Fact-Checking Network at the Poynter Institute asks organisations to sign up to the following commitments. They are, if you like, a description of the craft of fact-checking, and might well be considered by editors trying to agree the fundamentals of the craft of journalism itself:

1) **A commitment to nonpartisanship and fairness**
   We fact-check claims using the same standard for every fact check. We do not concentrate our fact-checking on any one side. We follow the same process for every fact check and let the evidence dictate our conclusions. We do not advocate or take policy positions on the issues we fact-check.

2) **A commitment to transparency of sources**
   We want our readers to be able to verify our findings themselves. We provide all sources in enough detail that readers can replicate our work, except in cases where a source's personal security could be compromised. In such cases, we provide as much detail as possible.

3) **A commitment to transparency of funding & organization**
   We are transparent about our funding sources. If we accept funding from other organizations, we ensure that funders have no influence over the conclusions we reach in our reports. We detail the professional background of all key figures in our organization and explain our organizational structure and legal status. We clearly indicate a way for readers to communicate with us.

4) **A commitment to transparency of methodology**
   We explain the methodology we use to select, research, write, edit, publish and correct our fact checks. We encourage readers to send

us claims to fact-check and are transparent on why and how we
fact-check.

5) **A commitment to open and honest corrections**
   We publish our corrections policy and follow it scrupulously. We
   correct clearly and transparently in line with our corrections
   policy, seeking so far as possible to ensure that readers see the
   corrected version.

Should journalists themselves be more transparent about any conflicts
of interest? The UK parliament maintains a register of interests which
lobby journalists are required to fill in – but it is almost exclusively a
list of publications they write for. Only a few, including Andrew Neil,
former editor of the *Sunday Times*, declare sources of revenue from
speaking fees or consultancy. The BBC also requires its financial journalists to register their ownership of any shares, securities, unit trusts,
personal pensions or business dealings, along with consultancy work.
'Transparency is the key,' read the BBC guidelines. The test was 'would
[a journalist] or the BBC be embarrassed to read about it in the press?
If in any doubt the journalist should talk to their editor.' The US blogger
and new-media academic Jeff Jarvis keeps a register of all his business
ties, paid consultancies, angel investments and stocks (he bought into
Google in 2008 at $512. He even declares his religion ('raised Presbyterian
. . . [now] you could call me liberal').

More radical was the initiative of George Monbiot, the *Guardian*
columnist, to create his own register of interests. There he states the
value of his annual *Guardian* retainer (£60,769.72) as well all his
other gross earnings, including the rent paid by the co-operative
that leases his house (£9,480 a year). He also declares the amount
of tax he pays (£17,927 in a year in which his gross earnings were
£65,392). He lists his investments (negligible), the value of his pension
and the amount he has in savings. Each month he lists the fees he
receives for services (e.g. February 2020, £38.40 for a contribution
to the BBC).

His motive for starting this register in 2011 was the belief that an
awful lot of what presented itself as journalism could have hidden
influences. There had recently been revelations about columnists

receiving undisclosed payments (on top of the editorial fee) for favouring the clients of their paymasters.

The controversial philosopher Roger Scruton *(SEE:TRANSCRIPTS)* asked one of the world's biggest tobacco companies for a pay rise (from £4,500 to £5,500 a month) to help place pro-smoking articles in influential newspapers and magazines. The email was leaked and Scruton claimed no articles were written as a result of his hidden retainer. But, as Monbiot wrote, 'These revelations were accidental. For all we know, such deals could be commonplace. While journalists are not subject to the accountability they demand of others, their powerful position – helping to shape public opinion – is wide open to abuse.

'I believe that everyone who steps into public life should be obliged to show who is paying them, and how much. Journalists would still wield influence without responsibility. That's written into the job description. But at least we would then have some idea of whether it's the organ-grinder talking or his monkey.'

It was a bold step. There was not, it has to be said, a stampede to follow Monbiot's example. Transparency is a natural and admirable instinct in journalists when applied to others, but work in progress for ourselves.

TRIBAL EPISTEMOLOGY

> 'Where the truth or falsity of a statement depends on whether the person making it is deemed one of us or one of them.'
>
> Jonathan Freedland, the *Guardian*

TRUST

It keeps coming back to trust. The decline of trust – in journalism, but also in government and numerous institutions – is an inescapable fact of life. We are obsessed with measuring how the public think of trust. Less measured is how journalists themselves regard it.

They want to be trusted, but quite often aren't. Some don't care very much (the Millwall football chant: 'No one likes us, we don't care'.) Others do care – and can't understand why journalists linger at the bottom of any league table, along with (or even behind) politicians and secondhand car dealers. Entire two- or three-day conferences are devoted to Winning Back Trust. There must be an answer. Surely?

The irony is that journalists themselves tend, as a general rule, to trust nobody *(SEE: LYING BASTARDS)*. Of course, they will have favourite sources and confidantes. But the default setting for a reporter is scepticism. This is, broadly, a reasonable starting point for anyone *(SEE: SCEPTICISM)*. A good reporter will not accept anything is as it seems unless they can verify or test it in some way. So you could argue that journalists should expect their readers to live by similar standards – believe nothing without reasonable evidence.

In a world of information chaos a certain level of distrust is a healthy thing. It goes without saying that there's a huge amount of decent reliable journalism around, but also quite a lot that's shoddy, lazy and/ or deceitful. Only the most naïve would trust everything they watched or read, however 'mainstream'. If it's right for journalists to be sceptical, why not their audience?

British journalists, for instance, are fond of telling themselves that Britain has the best press in the world. But regular surveys find low levels of trust when Britons are asked about their faith in the media – considerably behind the US. A 2019 Eurobarometer survey of twenty-eight countries placed the British press as one of the least trusted in Europe. Only 28 per cent 'tended to trust' the written press, just above Greece and North Macedonia. The top three countries were the Netherlands (76 per cent), Sweden (70 per cent) and Finland (64 per cent).

Of course, the picture on trust becomes more complicated the more you drill down into it. People tend to trust their own favourite title, even if they don't think much of the press in general. Democrats in America trust newspapers way more than Republicans do. Older people are more trusting than younger people. Everyone is more inclined to trust news sources that reflect their own political outlook. The so-called 'informed public' trusts media a bit more than the general population. Men are a bit more trusting than women. There is a growing gap between the informed public and the mass population. And so on.

Nevertheless, there is still a huge problem with trust in the media, which remains the least-trusted institution in sixteen of the markets surveyed by Edelman. In the UK in 2019 – at the height of the shambles over Brexit – you'd think it would be hard to find a group of people less trusted than politicians (42 per cent). But no, the UK media managed to limp in behind them with a ranking similar to that found in Spain, France, Japan and Ireland.

Some of the reasons for lack of trust are not unreasonable. A Reuters Institute report in 2017 found that the main reason for mistrust was a suspicion of bias, spin and agendas: 'Simply put, a significant proportion of the public feels that powerful people are using the media to push their own political or economic interests rather than represent ordinary readers or viewers.' You can't say this is an entirely wrong view.

So here are some habits or practices that could help rebuild trust:

1. Don't expect or demand trust

It's not enough these days to say 'I work for the *FT*/the *Daily Mail*/ the *Daily Telegraph*/the *NYT*/the *East Anglian Daily Times*/the *Baltimore Sun*, so trust me.' The public may be more inclined to trust some titles more than others, but there is a general scepticism towards all media these days.

2. Show your evidence

A scientist will rarely, if ever, simply assert something. He or she will produce a concept which can be reproducibly observed. Similarly, journalists will have to get used to showing how or why they know something. Anything that allows a reader to verify for themselves what you're telling them will help. They may not bother, but it matters that you're willing to help.

3. Link

Don't simply quote from a judgment or an official report, link to it *(SEE: LINKS)*. If a reader is sufficiently interested in the story, they may want to explore the issue in more depth. Make it easy for them.

Or they may simply want to check that you've accurately summarised the original document. Again, help them do so. Or use a screenshot. Not as good as a link, which is deeper and more interactive, but a screenshot of a relevant page or document will often reinforce an assertion or argument.

4. Be transparent

Don't assume that citizens any longer (if they ever did) understand how news is gathered. Or the difference between news and comment. Or whether advertising influences news. Or how much an investigation may cost. Or what an 'editorial' is, or how it originates. Acknowledge the limits of what journalism can do (see point number eight, below). How far do you want to go in allowing your readers to know more about the backgrounds and opinions of the people who produce the news? Is there any reason not to share anxieties over your business model?

5. Be prepared to engage

Printing newspapers and distributing them was like a megaphone. A later form of mass communication (think television) was what the critic Raymond Williams described in 1958 as an 'impersonal' medium: 'much of what we call communication is, necessarily, no more in itself, than transmission; that is to say, a one-way sending. Reception and response, which complete communication, depend on other factors than the techniques.' Sixty years later we care much more about 'reception and response'. But how far are you prepared to go? Is a 'story' something which, once published, exists as a fixed artefact? Or is it something to be built on, added to, amended, brought up to date?

6. Clarify and correct quickly

We all make mistakes *(SEE: MISTAKES)* and phrase things in ways that could have been clearer. Readers will forgive a lot – but only if they see that the writer is prepared to acknowledge and remedy errors.

7. Make sure readers see their own lives reflected in your coverage

This came out of a study by the US-based 32 Percent Project, so-named because a 2016 Gallup poll in America found that just 32 per cent of those surveyed had confidence that the media would report the news 'fully, accurately and fairly'. The study found that citizens want to know that a news outlet explicitly shares the community's values, as opposed to journalists simply producing stories that arise from their own personal backgrounds. A diverse newsroom is, the researchers found, fundamental to earning trust *(SEE: GRENFELL)*.

8. Be authentic

Be comfortable in admitting what you don't know as much as what you do know. Don't over-claim – either on the importance of what you're writing ('World exclusive!') or how much you've managed to find out.

9. Avoid too many anonymous sources

There are good reasons for a source to want to keep their head down. But when anonymous sourcing becomes routine (as it increasingly does) it spells trouble. How is the reader supposed to know if information is to be trusted, if she or he can't be allowed to know where it's come from *(SEE: SOURCES)*?

10. Don't be relentlessly negative

News is about out-of-the-ordinary things. Dog bites man is, famously, not considered to be news whereas man bites dog is. But – for many readers in many communities – there's an awful lot to celebrate and cherish. A picture of a community that obsesses over the things that are not right, or are sensational, or have gone badly wrong may feel like an inaccurate representation, or a wilful distortion – and therefore not to be entirely trusted *(SEE: CONSTRUCTIVE JOURNALISM)*.

11. Separate fact from opinion

People don't necessarily mind partisan news organisations, but – according to the 2017 Reuters survey – 'it is widely disliked when it is dressed up as a news article or consistently spun in a way that distorts the truth.'

Other academics and journalists looking into the problem of trust and how to regain it will come up with a different list of potential remedies.

U

URBAN LEGENDS

You will be familiar with the genre.

- Jersey Devil: a legendary goat-like creature – possibly with wings – that lives in the Pine Barrens of South Jersey and is the namesake for the state's hockey team.
- Bloody Mary: if you chant 'Bloody Mary' (maybe Mary I, maybe Mary Queen of Scots, maybe someone else entirely) in front of a mirror thirteen times, you'll summon a vengeful ghost.
- Spider bite: a spider laid eggs in a girl's cheek, which soon erupted into hundreds of baby spiders.
- KFC: Kentucky Fried Chicken, or other fast-food chains, use mutated chickens (not to be confused with GMOs). KFC actually won a lawsuit against companies accused of spreading this rumour in 2016.
- Aerial mishap: a firefighting helicopter picked up a scuba diver by accident and dumped him on a wildfire.

With the rise of social media, the ability for urban legends to spread may be higher than ever. At least that's what two researchers at the Manchester Metropolitan University argue, pointing to recent cases such as Slender Man, which originated on an internet forum as a Photoshop challenge and later became a movie that grossed over $50 million at the box office in 2018.

Urban legends are increasingly becoming what the researchers refer to as 'false news', where the intent is to grab attention, such as the phenomenon of celebrity death hoaxes. To combat this type of online sensationalism, fact-checking websites such as Snopes *(SEE: SNOPES)* have emerged to police the dark corners of the internet (Slender Man is not real, but two twelve-year-old girls in Wisconsin did stab their classmate to supposedly appease the fictional character).

Newspapers historically played a role in spreading urban legends, especially around Halloween. In 1970, the UPI reported that a five-year-old boy died after eating Halloween candy laced with heroin. The story was picked up nationally, including by the *New York Times*. It later turned out the heroin came from his uncle, not any candy. The same story was repeated four years later, and continued into the 1990s.

In an article for the *Columbia Journalism Review*, the veteran reporter for the *New York Times* Gerald Eskenazi wrote about how urban legends were rife within newsrooms as well. He tells the story of an out-of-place *NYT* sports editor who was rumoured to have been exiled to that department because he miscaptioned a photo. When Eskenazi dug around, he discovered the entire story had been made up over the years. Similar tall tales circulate at other papers around the region, including *Newsday*, the *Long Island Press*, and the *Daily News*. People just love a good story – even fact-checkers.

V

VERIFICATION

In a horizontal world populated by a great many people who are careless about the truth – whether malignly, deliberately or accidentally – how do you work out what to believe?

'This discipline of verification,' wrote the American essayist Walter Lippmann, 'is what separates journalism from other modes of communication, such as propaganda, fiction or entertainment.'

In their 2001 book *The Elements of Journalism,* Bill Kovach and Tom Rosenstiel list what they consider to be the five key qualities of verification:

1) Never add anything that was not there
2) Never deceive the audience
3) Be as transparent as possible about your methods and motives
4) Rely on your own digital reporting
5) Exercise humility

They are good tips. But these days, it is not enough to leave it to journalists. The sheer scale of mis- and disinformation requires every individual to become better at working out right from wrong. We've all done it, but sharing bad information is not a great thing to be doing.

Some of the best verifiers in the digital space were not trained as journalists – and some of them give daily tutorials on how they set about sifting evidence from fakery.

Take a relatively trivial example. In March 2020, at the height of the Covid-19 pandemic, pictures started circulating on Twitter and elsewhere purporting to show clear water, fish and swans returning to the canals of Venice. Eliot Higgins, a citizen journalist-turned-obsessive military analyst who usually spends his days in close analysis of the weaponry being used by all sides in the Syrian conflict, found himself at home and at a loose end when his job doing data processing at a ladies' lingerie maker came to an abrupt halt.

How, then, to work out if the heartwarming pictures of nature re-asserting itself in the waters of Venice were real? Were some of the pictures actually taken in the nearby town of Burano? In a Twitter thread, Eliot proceeded to take his 105k followers through the 'pretty straightforward' steps to solving such puzzles.

He began with finding Burano on Google Maps and then, using Street View, examined all the bridges that could match the images being tweeted. In no time at all he found that one photograph hadn't been taken in Venice, but from Fondamenta degli Assassini in Burano. Then he set to work on a less obvious picture of a pair of swans, with little in the background to assist location. He had to find three buildings, painted orange, red and pink – in that order. This time he turned to Google Earth, which can show landscapes and enables searching on a larger scale than Street View.

Higgins was live-tweeting this search and, within seven minutes, the power of the crowd enabled one of his followers to find the combi-nation of buildings.

That one solved, he turned to a picture of an undistinguished bridge with fish apparently swimming under it. The difference in water colour led him to assume this might be Venice, so he now set about using 3D to glide through the canals of Venice looking for similar bridges. With the aid of his followers he soon narrowed it down (by spotting an unusual bit of ironwork) to the Ponte dei Ferali in Venice. The same programme enabled him, through historical imagery, to check the colour of the water in 2013 and 2018 and compare it with other contemporary images. Point proved.

Higgins's website, Bellingcat, has an online course teaching modern-day tools for verification which go much further. There are numerous open-source maps and satellite resources, along with endless ways of doing geolocation-based searching. There are instructions for reading, writing, removing (and manipulating) metadata for a vast number of file types

– including video. There are techniques for searching and investigating social media accounts, downloading and analysing video, checking bots and scraping a particular Twitter user's followers.

With YouTube you can perform reverse image searches of stills and find the exact uploading time. There are techniques for searching YouTube videos based on location. There are open sources for checking on flights and the position of shipping. Other open sources will help approximate the time of day using shadow direction as well as finding the weather on any particular day and in a specific location. You can analyse the links of any website and search back through archived websites.

Few everyday users of social media are going to use even a fraction of these open-source tools. But, as interesting-if-true material proliferates in every cranny of the internet, newsrooms will increasingly expect every reporter to be a dab hand at all kinds of digital verification. It should be one thing that will enable journalism to stand out from the crowd. And as the crowd gets bigger and noisier verification should come into its own, just as Lippman argued.

VICE

In the battle between traditional and new media, few outlets terrified the legacy names as much as Vice News when it launched in 2013. The insurgent's mission was to disrupt the tired methods of broadcast journalism that had been turning young audiences away from television news for years. Instead, they had their eyes on capturing the 16- to 35-year-old market. Within a year it had the BBC playing catch-up, as one executive at the corporation put it, racking up one million followers on YouTube along the way.

The Vice Media brand had been going for twenty years by the time it added a dedicated news and current affairs branch to its business, investing $50 million in the first three years of Vice News. *Vice* had started as a culture magazine in Montreal in 1994, dealing in sex, drugs and irreverence, but slowly built an online presence with subjective, first-person videos that were described as gonzo journalism for the YouTube generation.

But its early films (in particular one about people having sex with donkeys in Colombia), together with Vice's owners' youthful arrogance, would haunt the company in its efforts to become a respected news source. 'Just because you put on a fucking safari helmet and looked at some poop doesn't give you the right to insult what we do,' *New York Times* media correspondent David Carr famously dismissed Vice co-founder Shane Smith's work from Liberia in 2011. When Vice took the plunge into serious news three years after his run-in with Carr, Smith gave Politico his comeback: 'Every time the New York Times says we're shit and they're the only good ones, they just seem old and stupid and stodgy,' Smith said. 'All they can say is, "If you do differently from the way we do it then it's not real journalism."'

The venture had two facts working in its favour: At the time, broadcast news was haemorrhaging 16- to 24-year-old viewers, who were watching fewer than twenty-seven hours *a year* on TV. And while young audiences were more likely to nominate a website than TV as their most trusted source of news, newspapers were discovering it was expensive and difficult to produce video journalism online. The previous year the *Washington Post* had launched PostTV, dubbed the 'ESPN of politics' by the paper's president. Within five months it flopped.

But Vice News's early success was simpler than the factors in play around it. Defying the Alan Hansen mantra 'you can't win anything with kids', that's exactly what it did: hired young, skilled reporters and gave them opportunities to chase down and report stories from around the world. The belief was that young audiences wanted young correspondents to lead them through a story. Instead of patronising the viewer there would be a sense of joint discovery. Early reports covered South Sudan with a terrifying, heart-in-your-mouth film about the war in the world's youngest country, Russia's invasion of Ukraine in a series of more than forty dispatches called Russian Roulette, and exclusives from Syria at a time when all journalists were finding it very hard to work there.

Style played an important part in making Vice News distinctive. It was experiential journalism, showing the warts-and-all process of making TV news. Until then there had been a simple, dominant formula in which a 'voice of God' would be layered over pictures and the reporter would deliver three pieces to camera before going back to the studio.

Instead of managing-out all of the reality of being a journalist in a place, Vice News deliberately left it in there.

There was also liberation from being tied to television schedules. 'Our approach and the way we are trying to package what we do is radically different to what we see in terrestrial TV,' Kevin Sutcliffe, Vice News's then Head of News Programming (Europe), told the Edinburgh International Television Festival in 2014. 'We are trying to show a wider journalistic picture, there are different pressures on TV news shows,' he said. 'We are not trying to put things into 2 or 3 minutes. If we've got 6 minutes it runs for 6 minutes. If it is 36 minutes it runs for 36 minutes. We've found we've got engagements of 20 to 25 minutes for foreign documentaries.'

Sutcliffe had made a career doing things differently at Channel 4, where he had been deputy head of news and current affairs. As editor of the investigative documentary series *Dispatches*, he had latched on to the advantages of intimate TV journalism that built films around access rather than pre-defining what a story would be. He also knew that for Vice News to succeed it had to stake out its territory. He took aim at traditional media's struggle to represent young audiences, even describing BBC journalism as 'beige' and urging it to be more fearless.

There was a fightback. Some UK editors raised the issue of trust in Vice. 'You don't really want a kid saying "It's kicking off here, it's fucking dangerous" to tell you what is going on. You look to the trusted brands, credible reporters,' said Geoff Hill, editor of ITV News.

But this was a hard argument to maintain as Vice News continued to grow. When *The Islamic State* was published in August 2014 it racked up over 7 million views within days and broadcasters around the world queued up to syndicate the footage. The five-part world exclusive filmed inside the Syrian city of Raqqa, the self-declared capital of terror group ISIS, made no attempt to hide that filmmaker Medyan Dairieh was on a guided tour, courtesy of press officers. Alongside militants parading their armoury, doing donuts in army tanks, children explained their wish to fight and foreign recruits talked about joining the group's ranks from abroad. It remains one of the few pieces of first-hand independent journalism from inside one of the most dangerous places on earth at that time.

Not that this stopped the critics. Mary Hockaday, then the BBC's

Head of the Multimedia Newsroom, said that the BBC would not have used the video report in the way Vice did. 'It is all about the way you use this stuff,' she told the same audience in Edinburgh in 2014, adding that she would have also wanted more context and more challenge in the piece. But for Vice's original critic, David Carr, it was enough. Of his earlier judgement the journalist wrote in his *New York Times* column: 'I failed to recognize that in a world that is hostile to journalism in all its forms, where dangerous conflicts seem to jump off every other day, you can't be uppity about where your news comes from.'

VOX POPS

Vox pops have a strange, contradictory place in the culture of the British media. Canvassing the public for their opinions is often something done in the most offhand way: given to the office junior, based around the most banal questions, and never expected to deliver many insights. But at the same time, particularly in the era of populism, snatched conversations with people on the street seem ubiquitous, tacked on to each and every news item as if running an article or TV package without a sample of public opinion – 'extra views of the subject matter in hand', to quote one set of BBC guidelines – is now against the rules.

A lot of people do not like vox pops at all, as a quick skim of Twitter will prove. The torrent of anger is seemingly endless: 'I'm fed up of seeing vox pops of closet racist Dave from Blackpool and closet xenophobe Tony from Skegness.' 'Benefits of lockdown: At least the BBC aren't out on our streets gathering a never-ending selective stream of Brexity vox pops.' 'Vox pops, an absurd offshoot of reality TV, tell us nothing.'

Part of the reason for all this fury is the plain fact that a lot of vox pops are done badly. The interviewer collars people, goes straight in with a question or two about a particular subject, and tries to find a supposedly representative set of opinions: a few for, a few against, and a handful of don't-knows. The resulting material may only stretch to a couple of paragraphs, or a minute or so of screen time. The entire thing is very odd – and, for interviewees, usually rather disorientating.

But this is how the ritual of vox pops is still conducted. In the wake of the 2016 referendum on the EU, the former BBC journalist John Sweeney summed up the basic idea: 'Head straight to the main square, find the guy on a mobility scooter with a Waffen SS sticker and get his views on taking back control. Then head over to Waitrose and find some professor on their day off to put the Remain argument. Then, on the way back to the station, a mother with her kids saying: "I just want them to get on with it." Forty-five minutes tops. I could do it. But it wasn't anything to do with journalism.'

There is a different way of doing vox pops, though not enough people seem to have realised it. In an age in which the media is almost as distrusted as politicians, and people well know what the most crass vox pops look like, the key for a journalist partly lies in not playing to type and following an alternative set of rules: don't wear a suit, avoid having a camera the size of a house, forget about trying to force your interviewees into pre-ordained categories, and try and approach them with at least a modicum of humour and self-awareness.

But the most important thing is the substance of the conversations. In the real world, no one begins a conversation with someone they've never met before with a hard-edged political question: 'What do you think of Boris Johnson?' or 'Do you think we should leave the EU before Christmas?' Moreover, people's political views tend to originate in some of the deepest aspects of their lives: family, upbringing, place. To put them at their ease and get a sense of who they are, this is where the best vox pops ought to begin.

Anywhere But Westminster is a *Guardian* video series that began in 2010. The vox pops that crop up in most of its episodes are based on these ideas, which the series' creators, John Harris and John Domokos, began to grasp as they reported from places usually ignored by the media. In 2019 they wrote: 'When we spoke to people for any length of time, our questions tended not to begin with "Who are you going to vote for?" or "What do you think about Brexit?", but much more open, contextual lines of enquiry: "What's it like living here?" or "How do you feel about the future?" We did not wear suits, or carry off-puttingly cumbersome equipment, or shine lights in people's faces. If the interviewee had the time, the conversation often lasted for 10 or 15 minutes.'

The result was a run of work that alerted its viewers to the fact that politics was becoming more and more unpredictable – and that if you wanted to understand what was going on, it was best to ignore politicians and talk to voters. When doing so, a good journalist will listen not just to what people say, but how they say it, and the levels of passion, anger or disaffection that might be betrayed. They will get beyond crude questions about party politics. If a vox pop highlights something interesting, the wisest thing may not be to boil it down to a crass sentence or two, but take the number of the interviewee and arrange to talk again. For the reader or viewer, what this ends up providing ought to be much more enlightening than the words of any pundit or politician: a sense of real life, the reasons people make the choices they do, and the things that ultimately decide what kind of world we live in.

W

WOLFF, MICHAEL

In July of 2019, after Jeffrey Epstein's arrest, the journalist Vicky Ward wrote an article for the Daily Beast alleging that Michael Wolff had written a profile on Epstein for *New York Magazine* which never ran because of concerns over the fact-checking. In Ward's words, the profile 'was meant to "rehabilitate" Epstein's image and would tell of all the billionaires who still, secretly, hung out with Epstein'.

The same day, the fact-checker for Wolff's planned profile, Alex Yablon (now at the Trace), confirmed Ward's account. On Twitter, Yablon wrote that 'Wolff let Epstein dictate the the [sic] piece. He made some agreement that all fact questions would go through Epstein and only Epstein. In the piece, Wolff reported various powerful men still hung out with Epstein – but gave me no proof. I was not allowed to call them for comment.'

The lawyers for *New York Magazine* were wary about making the claims without proof or comment and, according to Yablon, Wolff's editors weren't even aware of his arrangement with Epstein. *New York Magazine* killed the story. In Yablon's words, this was 'more of a Michael Wolff story than a Jeffrey Epstein story'.

The curious anecdote, which certainly bucks traditional ideas of fact-checking and source verification, tracks with consistent criticism of Michael Wolff (b. 1953) – both his tendency to align himself too closely with powerful figures that he's ostensibly covering, and his unorthodox relationship with 'the truth'. This debate bled into the mainstream with the publication of his best-selling and salacious 2018 book *Fire and Fury: Inside the Trump White House*, but has dogged him throughout his reporting career.

After working as a journalist for two decades, Wolff founded a company eponymously named Wolff New Media, which *Wired* described as a 'Web information-packaging company'. After financial difficulties at the company, Wolff wrote about the experience in his 1998 best-selling book *Burn Rate: How I Survived the Gold Rush Years on the Internet*, which also led to his first brush with media criticism. In a review in the (also-defunct) publication *Brill's Content*, lawyer and journalist Steven Brill questioned the factuality of the book, citing thirteen characters featured in it who said that Wolff 'invented or changed quotes'. Those thirteen sources also said that they never recalled Wolff taking notes or recording their discussions. Wolff claimed to have notes backing up the interviews, but never released them.

Wolff continued to rise through the media world, winning two National Magazine Awards and working as a regular columnist for *New York Magazine* and *Vanity Fair*. He wrote on diverse subjects including a series of dispatches from the Persian Gulf in 2003 and analysis on the impending decline of media executives in his 2004 book *Autumn of the Moguls*.

He continued to face criticism from other journalists, though. In a 2004 profile of Wolff in the *New Republic*, journalist (and current *New York Times* editorial board member) Michelle Cottle details his rise to 'It Boy of New York media'. In the article, she criticises not only his indulgent and disorganised writing style, but also 'his ambition, his social climbing, his worship of status and buzz and money, his self-referentiality and solipsism'. He was not a media critic as much as someone wanting to be at the centre of his stories on power and money. In his review of Wolff's 2008 book on Rupert Murdoch, *The Man Who Owns the News*, journalist David Carr also questioned Wolff's reporting ability. In his overall positive, although cautious, review of the book, Carr wrote that it 'contains shockingly few actual quotations from Murdoch himself', despite Wolff's access, and that Wolff cares far too much about his own prose. Carr wrote that Wolff takes a different approach to journalism and that he 'has succeeded in cutting through the clutter by being far less circumspect – and sometimes more vicious – than other journalists, whom he views as archaic losers about to go the way of the Walkman.'

Although Wolff continued to burn his way through the media industry, including a short-lived tenure as editor of *Adweek* in 2010–11, his biggest mainstream success – and controversy – came with the publication of *Fire and Fury*. When the book was released, just a year after Trump took office, it set off a fervour usually reserved for a generational hit like *Harry Potter*, with *Variety* writing that 'consumers bombarded local booksellers to snag the exposé before it even made it to the shelves'. To date, it has sold more than two million copies. Sales were helped by an excerpt published before its release by Wolff's old employer *New York Magazine*, which contained details such as Steve Bannon claiming that Trump didn't trust John Bolton because of his moustache.

Wolff had unprecedented access for *Fire and Fury*, which was said to be based on two hundred interviews with Trump and his senior staff. Although Trump tweeted that Wolff never had access to the White House, Sarah Huckabee Sanders admitted that Wolff had more than a dozen 'interactions' with officials at the White House, at the request of Steve Bannon.

The White House quickly pushed back on the book, in which Bannon described Donald Trump Jr's 2016 meeting with Russians at Trump Tower as 'treasonous' and 'unpatriotic' and called Ivanka 'dumb as a brick'. Sanders said the book was 'filled with false and misleading accounts from individuals' without access to the White House (despite admitting Wolff did have access). Trump also fully distanced himself from Bannon, who had left the previous August, tweeting, 'When he was fired, he not only lost his job, he lost his mind.'

The criticism didn't only come from the White House and Trump supporters, though. *Fire and Fury* was written in an almost novelistic style, filled with pacy prose, inner thoughts and quotes. A number of factual errors came to light. The *Washington Post* reporter Mark Berman tweeted, for example, that he has never had breakfast at the Four Seasons, despite Wolff writing that he was there with Ivanka Trump. Wolff also had not done simple fact-checking, such as stating that Wilbur Ross was the labor secretary nominee as opposed to commerce. One source cited in the book, real estate investor Tom Barrack, told the *NYT*'s Maggie Haberman that 'he never said the quote attributed to him to Wolff or anyone'.

In response, numerous journalists began to express doubts about the reporting in the book. On his show in January 2018, Jake Tapper said,

'Wolff's reporting should be met with scepticism. The book is riddled with errors and rumours. And in his marketing of the book, Wolff made the unbelievable assertion that one hundred per cent of the president's family members and top advisers have concerns about his mental fitness for the job. One hundred per cent. That's simply not true.'

For *Slate*, Isaac Chotiner criticised not only Wolff's 'lazy mistakes' but his larger approach: both the issue of basing a narrative on sources known to lie to the media (going with previous criticism of Wolff's aligning too closely with powerful figures without providing context or fact-checking) and Wolff's inability to analyse politics outside of the gossipy details. Chotiner writes that Wolff is not only out of his depth, but that he 'displays all the problems with writing palace-intrigue stories about dishonest and unscrupulous people'.

Wolff is too willing to add juicy details without providing any helpful information to the reader, such as where they're coming from or how likely they are to be true *(SEE: SOURCES)*. In response, just as he did with the controversy over *Burn Rate*, Wolff defended his reporting without addressing specifics. In an interview on the Skullduggery podcast, when questioned about a factual error, Wolff said, 'Even if I was wrong, I'm not going to admit it to you.' *(SEE: TRUST)* When he continued to be confronted with inaccuracies, Wolff called the critique 'bullshit' and said the point of the book was to depict 'the emotional life of Trump world'. His latest book, *Siege: Trump Under Fire*, has received the same types of criticism, including over claims that Robert Mueller had drafted an obstruction of justice indictment against Trump that he decided not to pursue.

When the book was released in June 2019, it did not create nearly the same buzz as its predecessor. One of the causes was a deluge of Trump content since Wolff's first book hit the shelves. Then there were lingering doubts about whether Wolff's work was trustworthy. And with more reputable journalists such as Bob Woodward writing their own accounts of the Trump White House, Wolff's widely rebuked reporting style was no longer the only option.

The general consensus on Wolff in the media world seems to be that while he is certainly an engaging writer, and able to place himself close to trendy topics and subjects, he ultimately lacks the reporting rigour to back up his prose.

X

XENOPHOBIA

From the advent of the printing press, periodicals have addressed matters of difference and demography. In 1847, a *Times* leader article addressed the hot migration topic of the day. 'Ireland is pouring into the cities, and even into the villages of this island, a fetid mass of famine, naked-ness and dirt and fever,' it said.

The same story played out in the United States, where newspapers ran classifieds warning 'No Irish Need Apply' during the mid-nineteenth century. The Irish, of course, were not the only target of xenophobia, with anti-Chinese sentiment prevalent in newspapers, including racist caricatures of Chinese immigrants and conflations of crime with Chinese neighbourhoods. This continued into the 1900s, with California news-paper owner Valentine S. McClatchy spreading an anti-Japanese message during the 1920s.

After the Second World War, another dilemma: dark-skinned colonials, many of whom had been part of the war effort, came to Britain by sea. 'Thirty Thousand Colour Problems', pronounced the *Picture Post*.

Fast forward to the 1980s: a time of social upheaval and, in Brixton, public disturbances. The *Daily Mail* described one such for its readers as 'When the Black Tide Met the Thin Blue Line'.

In the United States, illegal immigration – mainly from Mexico – and terrorism became the main focus of xenophobia during the 1990s and 2000s. Between 1996 and 2015, US newspapers published far more negative articles about Muslims than any other major religion, even discounting terms such as 'terrorism' and 'extremism', with almost 70 per cent of non-terrorism-related articles mentioning Muslims deemed 'negative' by the researchers Erik Bleich and A. Maurits van der Veen. Similarly, from 2014 to 2017, 90 per cent of citations in major US newspapers attributed to the Center for Immigration Studies did not mention the extremist nature of the group.

Now consider the *Daily Mail* in 2015 and its publication of an image by its acclaimed cartoonist Mac, depicting Muslims and other refugees who might head for Britain as a horde of rats.

Skip to 2017, when the *Spectator* published what Ipso later ruled was a 'significant inaccuracy' in its claim that 'there are an estimated 32,000 Muslims eager to commit the next terror atrocity'.

The debate as to whether the media shapes or follows public opinion seems especially pertinent with regard to xenophobia. It raises questions as to the function and aspirations of print and broadcast media.

In the case of the BBC, the intention is clear. Its mission statement compels the broadcaster 'to act in the public interest, serving all audiences through the provision of impartial, high-quality and distinctive output and services which inform, educate and entertain'. But the privately run media companies face no such stricture. Some broadcasters are subject to the scrutiny of the watchdog Ofcom, but for the most part the media – and particularly the print media – operates within limits of decency and fairness they set for themselves, internally and collectively.

It can be said that there are two significant drivers. The first is the mindset of those who make decisions *(SEE: EDITORS)*. What are their views of difference, demography and diversity, and, second, to what extent do those views affect how they direct the scope and tenor of the coverage?

During his thirteen-year editorship of the *Sun*, Kelvin MacKenzie produced a newspaper regularly castigated for xenophobia. The paper was MacKenzie's voice. Subsequently he admitted what that meant for minorities. In a 2015 reflection in the *Guardian*, he wrote: 'During my 12 years as Sun editor I am sure minorities – and even majorities – were maligned. Editors think they know everything, that they have an umbilical cord to the thought processes of readers. They simply don't.' With that comment, he alluded to both drivers – his ability as a powerful editor to shape the product and his wish to do so, to align it with a perceived view of his readership. The paper's guiding spirit during his editorship was what he believed, aligned to his perception of what the readers believed.

The first is surely a function of human nature and speaks to the lack of accountability that might give an editor free rein to reflect his or her prejudices in the product, and a lack of newsroom or management diversity that might challenge those prejudices.

But the second driver should not be underestimated. Traditionally print newspapers have sought out scoops – individual news stories that attract attention and hopefully sales – but much more powerful than that in terms of commercial appeal is the brand narrative. The *Mail* seeks to reflect 'Middle England' in the hope that those who see their values reflected in its journalism will buy that product. The *Guardian* does the same. The question, then, is to what extent does an editor, believing their target audience to be to some degree xenophobic and seeking to enlist them as loyal customers with material that will elicit a response, weave xenophobia into the brand narrative?

Following the election of Donald Trump, the *New York Times* vowed to bring in more political perspectives. The paper approached this dilemma through their revamped opinion page under James Bennet, who – until he resigned in June 2020 – sought to ideologically diversify the roster of columnists and op-ed contributors with hires such as the conservative Bret Stephens. This has caused controversy, though, such as with the publication of an op-ed by Jerry Kramer, a senior research fellow at the Center for Immigration Studies, entitled 'I'm a Liberal Who Thinks Immigration Must Be Restricted'. As critics pointed out, the Center for Immigration Studies has a troubling background, with *Slate* describing it as a 'white nationalist organization'.

Beginning with Donald Trump's descent on the golden escalator and declaration about Mexicans being rapists, US outlets have been debating how to report his bombastic, xenophobic and often untrue statements. During the Covid-19 pandemic Trump frequently referenced the 'foreign virus' and 'China virus', which CNN chief White House correspondent Jim Acosta said 'smacked of xenophobia'. The justice correspondent for the *Nation*, Elie Mystal, pointed to the connection between Trump's rhetoric and a rise in hate crimes against Asians, writing, 'If the media were doing their job, this would be the story: The president of the

United States is putting lives at risk during a global pandemic by inciting violence against fellow Americans.'

Before Trump, though, xenophobic language, especially against Muslims, was prevalent in cable news. The British journalist Mehdi Hasan said, 'In many ways anti-Muslim hysteria is worse in the United States', particularly because of birther conspiracy theories against Barack Obama. Fox News features hosts such as Jeanine Pirro, who once delivered a seven-minute monologue on radical Islamists in which she stated, 'We need to kill them. We need to kill them.' In the week after the attack on *Charlie Hebdo*, Pirro's guest Steve Emerson argued that parts of France and the UK 'are totally Muslim where non-Muslims just simply don't go in'. Islamophobia, it should be noted, is not limited to Fox News: it extends to networks such as CNN and HBO too. On his popular show *Real Time*, Bill Maher attacks Islam from a liberal perspective.

In 2011, the British reporter Rich Peppiatt severed his ties with the *Daily Star* and penned a letter to Richard Desmond, then owner of *Express* newspapers. Both the *Star* and the *Express*, struggling for readers against the *Sun* and the *Mail* and apparently perceiving anti-Muslim sentiment within their target audiences, appeared to have very publicly and aggressively woven it into the brand narrative.

In his evidence to the Leveson inquiry, Peppiatt referenced a 2010 *Star* story: 'Muslim-only public loos . . . council wastes your money on hole-in-the-ground toilets'. It wasn't true. After a Press Complaints Commission inquiry, the *Star* said: 'We are pleased to make clear that the loos may be used by non-Muslims and that they were paid for by the developer.'

The *Star* said it had no anti-Muslim agenda. So how did it happen? Peppiatt told Desmond: 'Undeterred by the nuisance of truth, we omitted a few facts, plucked a couple of quotes, and suddenly anyone would think a Rochdale shopping centre had hired Osama Bin Laden to stand by the taps, handing out paper towels. I was personally tasked with writing a gloating follow-up declaring our postmodern victory in "blocking" the non-existent Islamic cisterns of evil.'

Appearing before a 2018 parliamentary select committee, Gary Jones, editor-in-chief of the *Daily* and *Sunday Express* – now owned by Reach plc, which also owns the *Mirror* – said those papers will change: 'Each and every editor has a responsibility for every single word that is published in the newspaper and yes, cumulatively, some of the headlines that have appeared in the past have created an Islamophobic sentiment, which I find uncomfortable.'

Jones is part of a changing roster of editors who have grown up in a diverse Britain and lead increasingly diverse newsrooms. They may bring different experiences to their work than their predecessors. They may in time, with more diverse instincts or more meaningful newsroom challenges, be able to avoid the lapse into xenophobia or eschew its exploitation.

In a 2017 panel on media depiction of Islam and Muslims, David Graham, a staff writer at the *Atlantic*, said, 'There are way too many people who look like me in newsrooms. They crowd out [stories on] everyday lives of Muslims in the US and abroad. It's a real blind spot.' But even then those with honest intent will confront the hard decision British editors have historically encountered: balancing the potency of xenophobia as a brand component and commercial driver with the social harm that results.

The global anger aroused by the killing of George Floyd in Minneapolis in May 2020 led to a period of intense reflection about the lack of diversity in the western media. But more than one commentator expressed scepticism about companies which had hitherto done little to promote diversity suddenly embracing the optics of being seen to say the right thing. A black square on Instagram was an inexpensive gesture.

'It is not just the tabloids,' wrote Nesrine Malik in a searing *Guardian* column published three weeks after the death of Floyd. 'From the broadsheets to the BBC, the British press has stoked racism and xenophobia, cynically exploited them for clicks and eyeballs – or hidden behind cowardly equivocation about the sacred right of racists to be heard in weekly columns. And everyone involved is still getting away with it. Editors who happily published Katie Hopkins are today cheerleading for wokeness; others are still working with people who think Black Lives Matter has "a racist agenda", and telling themselves free speech requires nothing less.'

There was a degree of soul-searching in many companies. Within weeks of Floyd's murder Anna Wintour, editor-in-chief of *Vogue*, emailed her staff, acknowledging that 'It can't be easy to be a Black employee at Vogue', and that the magazine had 'not found enough ways to elevate and give space to Black editors, writers, photographers, designers and other creators'.

Like the aftermath of Grenfell *(SEE: GRENFELL)* this was another wake-up call – there to be heard or, as so often in the past, ignored.

Y

YOUNG PEOPLE

Study after study shows that young people (typically defined as 18- to 29-year-olds, or under-35s) are increasingly glued to their screens and social media, but rarely to consume the news. As their consumption declines, so does their trust in the media: young people hold a more negative view of local TV news, broadcast TV and the journalists they read and follow than any other age group, according to the American Press Institute. The only form of news they view more positively than other age groups is social media.

Young people across the United States and the United Kingdom increasingly view traditional media as a burden, instead relying on platforms such as Reddit and Instagram to get their news. As a result, their media literacy when it comes to distinguishing opinion from news is lower than other age groups, although they are less likely to share fake news.

The Pew Research Center found that 95 per cent of American teens have access to a smartphone, with 45 per cent online 'almost constantly', mostly using YouTube, Instagram, Snapchat and Facebook. When asked to share any positive uses of social media, only 16 per cent cited greater access to news and information.

Backing these findings, the Reuters Institute and the research agency Flamingo published a report in 2019 on how young people consume the news. They tracked the smartphone behaviour of twenty participants – all under the age of thirty-five – in the United States and United Kingdom over two weeks, as well as asking a subset to keep a digital diary of the news they consumed. The smartphone was the main device for accessing the news for 69 per cent of under-35s, with TV and even computers far behind. A 2019 Ofcom study in the United Kingdom had the same conclusion, finding that those aged 16 to 24 watch on average two minutes of TV news every day, compared with thirty-three minutes for those over sixty-five. The Reuters Institute found that younger people within the age bracket were more likely to watch online videos, although everyone vastly preferred text because of control and flexibility.

News apps didn't appear in the top twenty-five apps used by any of the participants. Two participants with the BBC app both used it for less than 1 per cent of their total time spent on their phones. Instead, they were mostly consuming the news through social media. Instagram was the most popular platform, ahead of Facebook, with Twitter and Reddit as the main apps that mirror the function of traditional news.

From qualitative interviews and observation, the researchers analysed the changing attitudes of young people toward the news. In their estimation, young people don't view news as something 'you should know' but rather 'what is useful to know, what is interesting to know, and what is fun to know'. Anything beyond that 'is a chore'.

As a result, traditional channels such as broadcasters and newspapers are having trouble connecting with under-35s, who prefer a wider range of topics – such as arts, culture and LGBTQ+ issues – often told from a more global perspective. More concerningly, with the rise of free platforms and content, the overwhelming majority of young people say they won't pay for the news.

Z

ZOOMERS

From journalists on all sides of the political spectrum, Generation Z (or 'zoomers'), get a bad rep. There are three distinct tropes: cartoons (often in the *Spectator*) of students holding books with captions such as 'Hey, how do you turn this thing on?', articles based on 'Generation Z don't know how to take a joke', and just generally being confused about what a zoomer is.

Much of this content can be responded to with the oft-used Gen Z catchphrase: 'OK, boomer.'

Journalists have a fascination with these so-called digital natives who barely caught the end of VHS tapes and only just remember a world before Instagram. They also tend to get them confused with millennials, but there are key differences. Millennial is often used as a synonym for 'politically engaged youth' or 'anyone under twenty-five', but the oldest millennials are now nearing forty.

Some millennials – aka 'the generation that buys too many avocados' – now have families, ageing parents and mortgages. None of this is true of the climate-striking, meme-literate Gen Z. As young teens, zoomers saw the rise of YouTubers, influencers *(SEE: INFLUENCERS)* and online creators, all of which started to inform their choices with native advertising *(SEE: NATIVE ADVERTISING)*. Brands grew solely on Instagram, teens queued round the street to meet their favourite YouTubers, and an entirely different model was created around young consumers.

When BuzzFeed was launched in 2006 by HuffPost co-founder Jonah Peretti, it was an 'algorithm to cull stories from around the web that were showing stirrings of virality'. The concept that Peretti harnessed so effectively and which saw BuzzFeed explode into the 2010s was just this: virality. For zoomers, not all news is created equal: the content they engage with is the content that's trending. Zoomers are the least likely demographic to read a newspaper cover to cover, and are much more likely to find their news on social media or news apps, where the most-viewed content appears first.

Mainstream media are starting to cotton on: the BBC's Religion Correspondent Sophia Smith Galer – self-dubbed 'the TikTok whisperer' – uploads frequent content to the video app and also created a 'Learn the facts about Covid-19' click-through banner which appeared at the bottom of any related content.

Fake news also hits Gen Z particularly hard, but perhaps not as hard as it hits millennials, who are much more likely to use fake news hothouses such as Facebook. What's different for Gen Z is that click-worthy content, whether fake or real, reaches them only when it goes viral.

Fear of younger generations has, of course, been a reliable feature of opinion columns for years. Zoomers are used to being slammed for their 'wokeness' and for being snowflakes. But while journalists might scoff, businesses are listening in as Gen Z becomes one of the largest consumer groups in the UK. Money talks – OK, boomer?

Bibliography

All links were last accessed in September 2020.

'The 1619 Project Curriculum'. Pulitzer Center, n.d. <https://pulitzer center.org/lesson-plan-grouping/1619-project-curriculum>

'The 2019 Pulitzer Prize Winner in Explanatory Reporting: David Barstow, Susanne Craig and Russ Buettner of The New York Times'. The Pulitzer Prizes, 2019. <https://www.pulitzer.org/winners/david-barstow-susanne-craig-and-russ-buettner-new-york-times>

'About Us'. Spaceship Media. n.d. <https://spaceshipmedia.org/about/>

Abramson, Jill. *Merchants of Truth: The Business of News and the Fight for Facts*. New York: Simon & Schuster, 2019.

Adam, David. '"Climategate" review clears scientists of dishonesty over data'. *The Guardian*, 7 July 2010. <https://www.theguardian.com/environment/2010/jul/07/climategate-review-clears-scientists-dishonesty>

Adam, David. 'Confidence in climate science remains strong, poll shows'. *The Guardian*, 11 June 2010. <https://www.theguardian.com/environment/2010/jun/11/confidence-climate-science-poll>

Addison, Adrian. *Mail Men: The Unauthorized Story of the Daily Mail – The Paper That Divided and Conquered Britain*. Main edition. London: Atlantic Books, 2015.

'The Administration's View on the State of Climate Science'. House Hearing, Serial No. 111–13: Hearing before the Select Committee on Energy Independence and Global Warming, First Session, 2 December 2009. Washington, DC: US Government Printing

Office, 2010. <https://www.govinfo.gov/content/pkg/CHRG-111hhrg62520/html/CHRG-111hhrg62520.htm>

Aleaziz, Hamed. 'The Justice Department Sent Immigration Judges A White Nationalist Blog Post With Anti-Semitic Attacks'. BuzzFeed News, 23 August 2019. <https://www.buzzfeednews.com/article/hamed aleaziz/justice-department-immigration-judges-white-nationalist>

Allan, Stuart. 'Citizen Journalism and the Rise of "Mass Self-Communication": Reporting the London Bombings'. *Global Media Journal: Australian Edition*, Issue 1 Vol. 1, 2007.

Allan, Stuart. *Citizen Witnessing: Revisioning Journalism in Times of Crisis.* Cambridge, UK and Malden, MA: Polity, 2013.

Allsop, Jon. 'BuzzFeed's Trump–Cohen scoop is not dead yet'. *Columbia Journalism Review*, 22 January 2019. <https://www.cjr.org/the_media_today/buzzfeed_trump_lie_mueller.php>

Amazeen, Michelle A. and Bartosz W. Wojdynski. 'The effects of disclosure format on native advertising recognition and audience perceptions of legacy and online news publishers'. *Journalism*, 7 February 2018. <https://journals.sagepub.com/doi/abs/10.1177/1464884918754829>

'American Views: Trust, Media and Democracy'. Gallup/Knight Foundation, 2018. <https://knightfoundation.org/reports/american-views-trust-media-and-democracy/>

'Andrew Neil'. Pieces of evidence. Discover Leveson, May 2012. <https://www.discoverleveson.com/witness/Andrew_Neil/4324/?bc=9#witnessevidence>

'Award Winner: Seymour Hersh'. National Press Foundation, 2004. <https://nationalpress.org/award-winner/seymour-hersh/>

Baker, Russ. '"Scoops" and Truth at the Times'. *The Nation*, 5 June 2003. <https://www.thenation.com/article/archive/scoops-and-truth-times/>

Barbaro, Michael. 'The Lessons of 2016'. The Daily podcast, *The New York Times*, n.d. <https://www.nytimes.com/2020/01/31/podcasts/the-daily/2020-election.html>

Barlow, Nathan 'Strategies for social-ecological transformation'. *The Ecologist*, 30 October 2019. <https://theecologist.org/2019/oct/30/strategies-social-ecological-transformation>

BBC News. 'Study finds quarter of climate change tweets from bots'. 22 February 2020. <https://www.bbc.com/news/technology-51595285>

Boehlert, Eric. 'How The Iraq War Still Haunts New York Times'. Media Matters for America, 1 July 2014. <https://www.mediamatters.org/new-york-times/how-iraq-war-still-haunts-new-york-times>

Bollinger, Lee C. *Uninhibited, Robust, and Wide-Open: A Free Press for a New Century*. First edition. Oxford and New York: Oxford University Press, 2010.

Boynton, Robert S. *The New New Journalism: Conversations with America's Best Nonfiction Writers on Their Craft*. New York: Vintage, 2005.

Brainard, Curtis. 'Wanted: Climate Front-Pager'. *Columbia Journalism Review*, 7 July 2010. <https://www.cjr.org/the_observatory/wanted_climate_frontpager.php>

Brendon, Piers. *The Life and Death of the Press Barons*. London: Secker & Warburg, 1982.

Brinkley, Douglas. 'The Voice of God on TV: Walter Cronkite's 1960s'. *Newsweek*, 19 March 2012. <https://www.newsweek.com/voice-god-tv-walter-cronkites-1960s-63729>

Brisbane, Arthur S. 'Scholarly Work, Without All the Footnotes'. *The New York Times*, 2 October 2010. <https://www.nytimes.com/2010/10/03/opinion/03pubed.html>

Broder, David S. *Behind the Front Page: A Candid Look at How the News Is Made*. New York: Simon & Schuster, 2000.

Brook, Stephen. 'Duncan Campbell and David Hencke among those leaving Guardian'. *The Guardian*, 19 June 2009. <https://www.theguardian.com/media/2009/jun/19/duncan-campell-david-hencke-guardian>

Burchard, Hans von der, and Cornelius Hirsch. 'Europe's citizens back their leaders' coronavirus response, say polls'. Politico, 20 March 2020. <https://www.politico.eu/article/europes-citizens-back-their-leaders-coronavirus-response-say-polls/>

Byers, Dylan. 'The New Yorker passed on Seymour Hersh's Bin Laden story'. Politico, 11 May 2015. <https://www.politico.com/blogs/media/2015/05/the-new-yorker-passed-on-seymour-hershs-bin-laden-206933.html>

Cagé, Julia. *Saving the Media: Capitalism, Crowdfunding, and Democracy*. Cambridge, MA and London: Harvard University Press, 2016.

'The Cairncross Review: a sustainable future for journalism'. Department for Digital, Culture, Media & Sport, 12 February 2019. <https://www.

gov.uk/government/publications/the-cairncross-review-a-sustainable-future-for-journalism>

Campbell, Duncan. 'The man in the mac: a life in crime reporting'. *The Guardian*, 5 September 2009. <https://www.theguardian.com/uk/2009/sep/05/crime-reporting-duncan-campbell>

Carlisle, Sam. 'Unnecessary and Unjust: Devoted mum explains how parents are enduring cruel interrogations to prove their disabled children can claim benefits as adults'. *The Sun*, 17 August 2018. <https://www.thesun.co.uk/news/7035173/devoted-mum-explains-how-parents-are-enduring-cruel-interrogations-to-prove-their-disabled-children-can-claim-benefits-as-adults/>

Carlisle, Sam. 'Why are parents of disabled kids having to sue the Government to give them basic education?' *The Sun*, 28 June 2019. <https://www.thesun.co.uk/news/9390735/parents-disabled-kids-sue-the-government/>

Carlson, Matt. 'When news sites go native: Redefining the advertising–editorial divide in response to native advertising'. *Journalism*, 21 August 2014. <https://journals.sagepub.com/doi/10.1177/1464884914545441>

Carr, Nicholas. 'Experiments in delinkification'. Rough Type blog, 31 May 2010. <http://www.roughtype.com/?p=1378>

Carrington, Damian. 'Why the Guardian is changing the language it uses about the environment'. *The Guardian*, 17 May 2019. <https://www.theguardian.com/environment/2019/may/17/why-the-guardian-is-changing-the-language-it-uses-about-the-environment>

Christiansen, Arthur. *Headlines All My Life*. Portsmouth, NH: Heinemann, 1961.

Cillizza, Chris. 'How annotation can save journalism'. *The Washington Post*, 7 October 2015. <https://www.washingtonpost.com/news/the-fix/wp/2015/10/07/why-i-believe-annotation-is-the-future-of-journalism/>

Clarke, Cameron. 'The antidote to scale? Dutch site De Correspondent has an alternative model for web journalism – and it's paying off'. *The Drum*, 2 February 2017. <https://www.thedrum.com/news/2017/02/02/the-antidote-scale-dutch-site-de-correspondent-has-alternative-model-web-journalism>

'Code of Principles'. International Fact-Checking Network (Poynter Institute), n.d. <https://www.ifcncodeofprinciples.poynter.org/>

Codrea-Rado, Anna. 'Guardian US's award-winning interactive'. *Columbia*

Journalism Review, 27 September 2012. <https://www.cjr.org/data_points/guardian.php>

Codrea-Rado, Anna 'Must-reads of 2012: interactives'. *Columbia Journalism Review*, 27 December 2012. <https://www.cjr.org/data_points/must-reads_of_2012_interactive.php>

Cohen-Almagor, Raphael. *Speech, Media and Ethics: The Limits of Free Expression*. Basingstoke: Palgrave Macmillan, 2001.

Colhoun, Damaris. 'Bloomberg's new regime and tensions over the editorial vision'. *Columbia Journalism Review*, 30 June 2015. <https://www.cjr.org/analysis/bloomberg_news_tensions.php>

Colloff, Pamela. 'Innocence Lost'. *Texas Monthly*, October 2010. <https://features.texasmonthly.com/editorial/innocence-lost/>

Colloff, Pamela. 'The Witness'. *Texas Monthly*, September 2014. <https://www.texasmonthly.com/articles/the-witness/>

Cosgrove, Ben. 'The best job in journalism? Sorry, it's already filled by Jim Dwyer'. *Columbia Journalism Review*, 11 March 2016. <https://www.cjr.org/the_profile/jim_dwyer_new_york_times.php>

Cottle, Michelle. 'Wolff Trapped'. *The New Republic*, 30 August 2004. <https://newrepublic.com/article/67746/wolff-trapped>

Cozens, Claire. 'New York Times: we were wrong on Iraq'. *The Guardian*, 26 May 2004. <https://www.theguardian.com/media/2004/may/26/pressandpublishing.usnews>

The Daily Gazette. 'Hutton: Royal photographer receives MBE'. 16 May 2003. <https://www.gazette-news.co.uk/news/5453806.hutton-royal-photographer-receives-mbe/>

Darcy, Oliver. 'Reporter with checkered past comes back with Trump Tower Moscow bombshells for BuzzFeed'. CNN, 19 January 2019. <https://www.cnn.com/2019/01/18/media/buzzfeed-reporter-jason-leopold/index.html>

'David Barstow of *The New York Times*'. The 2009 Pulitzer Prize Winner in Investigative Reporting, n.d. <https://www.pulitzer.org/winners/david-barstow>

'David Barstow to Lead Berkeley's investigative journalism program'. Berkeley News blog, 15 July 2019. <https://news.berkeley.edu/2019/07/15/david-barstow-to-lead-berkeleys-investigative-journalism-program/>

Davies, Nick. *Flat Earth News: An award-winning reporter exposes falsehood, distortion and propaganda in the global media*. London: Vintage, 2009.

'Decision of the Complaints Committee 01032-17 Ward v The Mail on Sunday'. Independent Press Standards Organisation, 7 July 2017. <https://www.ipso.co.uk/rulings-and-resolution-statements/ruling/?id=01032-17>

'Decision of the Complaints Committee 01570-18 Ward v The Sunday Telegraph'. Independent Press Standards Organisation, 24 May 2018. <https://www.ipso.co.uk/rulings-and-resolution-statements/ruling/?id=01570-18>

Decker, Cathleen. 'Analysis: Trump's war against elites and expertise'. *Los Angeles Times*, 27 July 2017. <https://www.latimes.com/politics/la-na-pol-trump-elites-20170725-story.html>

Deutscher, Guy. 'Does Your Language Shape How You Think?' *The New York Times Magazine*, 26 August 2010. <https://www.nytimes.com/2010/08/29/magazine/29language-t.html>

'Disinformation and "Fake News": Final Report'. House of Commons Digital, Culture, Media and Sport Committee. London, 18 February 2019. <https://publications.parliament.uk/pa/cm201719/cmselect/cmcumeds/1791/179102.htm>

Dommett, Katharine and Warren Pearce. 'What do we know about public attitudes towards experts? Reviewing survey data in the United Kingdom and European Union'. *Public Understanding of Science*, 31 May 2019. <https://doi.org/10.1177/0963662519852038>

Downie Jr, Leonard and Robert G. Kaiser. *The News About the News: American Journalism in Peril*. New York: Knopf Doubleday Publishing Group, 2007.

Dubois, Elizabeth and Grant Blank. 'The echo chamber is overstated: the moderating effect of political interest and diverse media'. *Information, Communication & Society*, Vol. 21 Issue 5, 2018. <https://doi.org/10.1080/1369118X.2018.1428656>

Dugan, Emily. 'Six Months Ago, This Grandmother Was Detained And Deported. She Has Just Returned Home'. BuzzFeed News, 30 August 2017. <https://www.buzzfeed.com/emilydugan/six-months-ago-this-grandmother-was-detained-and-deported>

Dugan, Emily. 'This Leaked Report Reveals The Stark Warnings From Judges About Defendants With No Lawyer'. BuzzFeed News, 8 May 2018. <https://www.buzzfeed.com/emilydugan/the-government-tried-to-conceal-this-testimony-from-judges>

Dugan, Emily. 'This Woman Has Won Her Fight To Stay In The UK With Her British Family'. BuzzFeed News, 20 August 2018. <https://www.buzzfeed.com/emilydugan/this-woman-has-won-her-fight-to-stay-in-the-uk>

Dunn, Tom Newton and Antonella Lazzeri. 'Give me shelter: Theresa May agrees to make women's domestic violence refuges exempt from housing benefit cap'. *The Sun*, 7 September 2016. <https://www.thesun.co.uk/news/1744723/theresa-may-agrees-to-make-womens-domestic-violence-refuges-exempt-from-housing-benefit-cap/>

Dwyer, Jim. 'The True Story of How a City in Fear Brutalized the Central Park Five'. *The New York Times*, 30 May 2019 <https://www.nytimes.com/2019/05/30/arts/television/when-they-see-us-real-story.html>

Dwyer, Jim. *Subway Lives: 24 Hours in the Life of the New York City Subway*. New York: Crown Publishers, 1991.

Dwyer, Jim and Kevin Flynn. *102 Minutes: The Unforgettable Story of the Fight to Survive Inside the Twin Towers*. New York: Times Books, 2011.

Edelman. '2019 Edelman Trust Barometer Global Report'. 20 January 2019. <https://www.edelman.com/research/2019-edelman-trust-barometer>

Edelman, Maurice. *The Mirror: A Political History*. London: Hamish Hamilton, 1966.

Editorial. 'The Guardian view on climate change: a global emergency'. *The Guardian*, 8 October 2018. <https://www.theguardian.com/commentisfree/2018/oct/08/the-guardian-view-on-climate-change-a-global-emergency>

The editors. 'From the Editors; The Times and Iraq'. *The New York Times*, 26 May 2004. <https://www.nytimes.com/2004/05/26/world/from-the-editors-the-times-and-iraq.html>

Elgot, Jessica. 'Secret Boris Johnson column favoured UK remaining in EU'. *The Guardian*, 16 October 2016. <https://www.theguardian.com/politics/2016/oct/16/secret-boris-johnson-column-favoured-uk-remaining-in-eu>

Ellis, Justin. 'Q&A: The Guardian's Gabriel Dance on new tools for story and cultivating interactive journalism'. NiemanLab, 25 November 2013. <https://www.niemanlab.org/2013/11/qa-the-guardians-gabriel-dance-on-new-tools-for-story-and-cultivating-interactive-journalism/>

Embury-Dennis, Tom. 'Daily Express helped create "Islamophobic sentiment", admits newspaper's editor'. *The Independent*, 25 April 2018. <https://www.independent.co.uk/news/media/daily-express-islamophobic-sentiment-editor-gary-jones-home-affairs-select-committee-a8321026.html>

'Emily Dugan'. BuzzFeed News, n.d. <https://www.buzzfeed.com/badge/accesstojustice>

Engel, Matthew. *Tickle the Public: One Hundred Years of the Popular Press*. London: Victor Gollancz, 1996.

Epstein, Edward Jay. 'Hersh's Dark Camelot'. *The Los Angeles Times*, 28 December 1997. <http://www.edwardjayepstein.com/archived/hersh.htm>

Evans, Harold. *Good Times, Bad Times: The Explosive Inside Story of Rupert Murdoch*. London: Weidenfeld & Nicolson, 1983.

Evans, Harold. *Essential English for Journalists, Editors and Writers*. Revised edition. London: Pimlico, 2000.

Evans, Harold. *My Paper Chase: True Stories of Vanished Times*. Princeton, NJ: Little Brown & Co., 2009.

'Expert: Judith Miller'. Manhattan Institute, n.d. <https://www.manhattan-institute.org/expert/judith-miller>

Fairyington, Stephanie. 'In the era of fake news, where have all the fact-checkers gone?' *Columbia Journalism Review*, 23 February 2018. <https://www.cjr.org/business_of_news/fact-checking.php>

Farrow, Ronan and Jane Mayer. 'Senate Democrats Investigate a New Allegation of Sexual Misconduct, from Brett Kavanaugh's College Years.' *The New Yorker*, 23 September 2018. <https://www.newyorker.com/news/news-desk/senate-democrats-investigate-a-new-allegation-of-sexual-misconduct-from-the-supreme-court-nominee-brett-kavanaughs-college-years-deborah-ramirez>

Ferguson, Niall. *The Square and the Tower: Networks and Power, from the Freemasons to Facebook*. First edition. New York: Penguin Press, 2018.

The Financial Times. 'Financial Times Honoured at the 2019 British Press Awards'. 3 April 2019. <https://aboutus.ft.com/en-gb/announcements/financial-times-honoured-at-the-2019-british-press-awards/>

The Financial Times. 'FT's Madison Marriage named Business Journalist of the Year at the 2019 London Press Club Awards'. 2 May 2019. <https://aboutus.ft.com/en-gb/announcements/fts-madison-marriage-named-business-journalist-of-the-year-at-the-2019-london-press-club-awards/>

The Financial Times. 'FT's Madison Marriage wins business story of the year for Presidents Club scandal at 2019 Headline Money Awards'. 10 May 2019. <https://aboutus.ft.com/en-gb/announcements/fts-madison-marriage-wins-business-story-of-the-year-for-presidents-club-scandal-at-2019-headline-money-awards/>

Fisher, Max. 'The many problems with Seymour Hersh's Osama Bin Laden conspiracy theory'. Vox, 11 May 2015. <https://www.vox.com/2015/5/11/8584473/seymour-hersh-osama-bin-laden>

Fisher, Max. 'Seymour Hersh's bizarre new conspiracy theory about the US and Syria, explained'. Vox, 21 December 2015. <https://www.vox.com/2015/12/21/10634002/seymour-hersh-syria-joint-chiefs>

Fitzgerald, Brendan. 'Lessons on covering race and racism after Charlottesville'. *Columbia Journalism Review*, 21 September 2017. <https://www.cjr.org/united_states_project/charlottesville-racism-journalism.php>

Foer, Franklin. 'The Source of the Trouble'. *New York Magazine*, 28 May 2004. <https://nymag.com/nymetro/news/media/features/9226/>

Frankel, Max. *The Times of My Life and My Life with The Times.* New York: Random House, 1999.

Fraser, Nancy. 'Rethinking the Public Sphere: A Contribution to the Critique of Actually Existing Democracy'. *Social Text*, No. 25/26, 1990. <https://doi.org/10.2307/466240>

Frayn, Michael. *The Tin Men.* Main edition. London: Collins, 1965.

Freedland, Jonathan. 'Bush's Amazing Achievement.' *The New York Review of Books*, 14 June 2007. <https://www.nybooks.com/articles/2007/06/14/bushs-amazing-achievement/>

Freedland, Jonathan. 'The great divide of our times is not left v right, but true v false'. *The Guardian*, 20 April 2018. <https://www.theguardian.com/commentisfree/2018/apr/20/trump-us-syria-truth-tribal-robert-mueller-white-helmets-factse>

Friedman, George. 'The deeper truth about Deep Throat'. Stratfor blog, 23 December 2008. <https://mercatornet.com/the_deeper_truth_about_deep_throat/7368/>

'Gabriel J.X. Dance.' The New York Times, n.d. <https://www.nytimes.com/by/gabriel-dance>

Gerhards, Jürgen and Mike S. Schäfer. 'Is the internet a better public sphere? Comparing old and new media in the USA and Germany'.

New Media & Society, 19 January 2010. <https://doi.org/10.1177/
1461444809341444>

Gerstein, Josh. 'State Dept. to process 3,000 pages of Clinton emails before election'. Politico, 28 September 2016. <https://www.politico.com/story/2016/09/hillary-clinton-emails-state-department-228877>

Gillmor, Dan. *Mediactive*. United States: Dan Gillmor, 2010.

Gillmor, Dan. 'How One Reporter Turned to His Readers to Investigate Donald Trump'. *The Atlantic*, 21 December 2016. <https://www.theatlantic.com/politics/archive/2016/12/what-journalists-can-learn-from-david-fahrentholds-trump-coverage/511277/>

Gitlin, Todd. 'The 2004 TIME 100 – Jürgen Habermas'. *Time*, 26 April 2004. <http://content.time.com/time/specials/packages/article/0,28804,1970858_1970909_1971707,00.html>

Godin, Mélissa. 'James Murdoch Criticizes His Father's Media Empire Over Climate Crisis Denial'. *Time*, 15 January 2020. <https://time.com/5765304/rupert-murdoch-son-climate/>

Goodale, James C. 'More Than a Data Dump'. *Harper's Magazine*, April 2019. <https://harpers.org/archive/2019/04/more-than-a-data-dump-julian-assange/>

Goodale, James C. 'Pentagon Papers lawyer: The indictment of Assange is a snare and a delusion'. *The Hill*, 12 April 2019. <https://thehill.com/opinion/criminal-justice/438709-pentagon-papers-lawyer-indictment-of-assange-snare-and-delusion>

Grafton, Anthony. *The Footnote: A Curious History*. Cambridge, MA: Harvard University Press, 1997.

Granger, Jacob. 'David Leigh's survival guide to investigative journalism'. Journalism.co.uk, 31 January 2020. <https://www.journalism.co.uk/news/a-survival-guide-to-investigative-journalism-lessons-from-the-past-to-take-into-the-future/s2/a751074/>

Green, Giselle. '"What Now" for News?' HuffPost UK: The Blog. 23 February 2016. <https://www.huffingtonpost.co.uk/giselle-green/positive-news-constructive-journalism_b_9296374.html>

Greenslade, Roy. 'David Leigh, doyen of investigative journalists, steps down'. *The Guardian*, 17 April 2013. <https://www.theguardian.com/media/greenslade/2013/apr/17/investigative-journalism-theguardian>

Grove, Lloyd. 'Former NYT Reporter Judith Miller Pleads Her Shaky Case'. The Daily Beast, 14 April 2017. <https://www.thedailybeast.

com/articles/2015/04/15/former-nyt-reporter-judith-miller-pleads-her-shaky-case>

Grynbaum, Michael M. 'I, Sy: Seymour Hersh's Memoir of a Life Making the Mighty Sweat'. *The New York Times*, 3 June 2018. <https://www.nytimes.com/2018/06/03/business/media/seymour-hersh-reporter-memoir.html>

'Guidance: Financial Journalism guidance'. BBC.com, n.d. <https://www.bbc.co.uk/editorialguidelines/guidance/conflicts-of-interest/financial-journalism>

Hakim, Danny and Vivian Wang. 'Eric Schneiderman Resigns as New York Attorney General Amid Assault Claims by 4 Women'. *The New York Times*, 7 May 2018. <https://www.nytimes.com/2018/05/07/nyregion/new-york-attorney-general-eric-schneiderman-abuse.html>

Hamilton, John Maxwell. *Journalism's Roving Eye: A History of American Foreign Reporting*. Baton Rouge, LA: First edition. LSU Press, 2009.

Hannah-Jones, Nikole. '1619'. *The New York Times* podcast, 2019. <https://www.nytimes.com/2019/08/23/podcasts/1619-slavery-anniversary.html>

Hannah-Jones, Nikole. 'The 1619 Project'. *The New York Times Magazine*, 14 August 2019. <Hannah-Jones, Nikole. 'The Problem We All Live With – Part One.' This American Life podcast, 31 July 2015. <https://www.thisamericanlife.org/562/the-problem-we-all-live-with-part-one>

Harris, John. 'The experts are back in fashion as Covid-19's reality bites'. *The Guardian*, 15 March 2020. <https://www.theguardian.com/commentisfree/2020/mar/15/experts-fashion-covid-19-reality-bites-trump-johnson>

Hasan, Mehdi. 'Dear Bashar Al-Assad Apologists: Your Hero Is a War Criminal Even If He Didn't Gas Syrians'. The Intercept, 19 April 2018. <https://theintercept.com/2018/04/19/dear-bashar-al-assad-apologists-your-hero-is-a-war-criminal-even-if-he-didnt-gas-syrians/>

Hastings, Max. *Editor: An Inside Story of Newspapers*. London: Pan Macmillan, 2002.

Hendry, Sharon. 'The children dreading their summer holiday shut away inside Broadwater Farm estate'. *The Sunday Times*, 30 June 2019. <https://www.thetimes.co.uk/article/the-children-dreading-their-summer-holiday-shutaway-inside-broadwater-farm-estate-8goql9dfm>

Hendry, Sharon. '"I will never forget this": Broadwater Farm's summer of a lifetime'. *The Sunday Times*, 15 September 2019. <https://www.thetimes.co.uk/article/broadwater-farm-update-best-summer-ever-wmq5bhp3c>

Hendry, Sharon. 'My two weeks inside a pupil referral unit for excluded children'. *The Sunday Times*, 16 February 2020. <https://www.thetimes.co.uk/article/my-two-weeks-inside-a-pupil-referral-unit-for-excluded-children-pr2pwm9bh>

Hendry, Sharon, Kate Jackson and Jenna Sloan. 'Give Me Shelter: Sign our petition – Sun Campaign: We call on the Government to end a domestic violence scandal'. *The Sun*, 17 May 2015. <https://www.thesun.co.uk/archives/news/233415/give-me-shelter-sign-our-petition/>

Herman, Edward S. and Noam Chomsky. *Manufacturing Consent: The Political Economy of the Mass Media*. New York and Toronto: Pantheon Books, 1988.

Herr, Michael. *Dispatches*. Reprint edition. New York: Vintage, 1991.

Hersh, Seymour M. *The Dark Side of Camelot*. Reprint edition. New York: Back Bay Books, 1998.

Hersh, Seymour M. 'Military to Military: Seymour M. Hersh on US intelligence sharing in the Syrian war'. *London Review of Books*, 7 January 2016. <https://www.lrb.co.uk/the-paper/v38/n01/seymour-m.-hersh/military-to-military>

Hersh, Seymour M. *Reporter: A Memoir*. First edition. New York: Knopf, 2018.

Hickman, Leo. 'Exclusive: BBC issues internal guidance on how to report climate change'. Carbon Brief, 7 September 2018. <https://www.carbonbrief.org/exclusive-bbc-issues-internal-guidance-on-how-to-report-climate-change>

Hodgkinson, Liz. *Ladies of the Street*. Brighton: Revel Barker, 2008.

Hosenball, Mark. 'The JFK-Marilyn Hoax'. *Newsweek*, 5 October 1997. <https://www.newsweek.com/jfk-marilyn-hoax-174044>

Huberman, Bond. '"Fake News": Why Snopes Prefers Not to Say It Anymore'. Snopes, 9 July 2019. <https://www.snopes.com/2019/07/09/fake-news-why-snopes-prefers-not-to-say-it-anymore/>

Hutt, David. 'The Trouble With John Pilger's *The Coming War on China*'. The Diplomat, 23 December 2016. <https://thediplomat.com/2016/12/the-trouble-with-john-pilgers-the-coming-war-on-china/>

Illing, Sean. '"Flood the zone with shit": How misinformation over-whelmed our democracy'. Vox, 6 February 2020. <https://www.vox.com/policy-and-politics/2020/1/16/20991816/impeachment-trial-trump-bannon-misinformation>

Ingelhart, Louis Edward. *Press and Speech Freedoms in the World, from Antiquity until 1998: A Chronology.* Westport, CT: Greenwood Press, 1998.

'Israel and the Palestinians'. BBC Academy, 19 September 2017. <https://www.bbc.co.uk/academy/en/articles/art20130702112133696>

Ivanova, Irina. 'As Australia burns, it's Murdoch versus Murdoch on climate change'. 17 January 2020. <https://www.cbsnews.com/news/james-murdoch-accuses-father-rupert-of-climate-change-denial-as-australia-burns/>

'Jamelle Bouie'. *The New York Times*, n.d. <https://www.nytimes.com/column/jamelle-bouie>

'James Poniewozik'. *The New York Times*, n.d. <https://www.nytimes.com/by/james-poniewozik>

'Jane Mayer'. *The New Yorker*, n.d. <https://www.newyorker.com/contributors/jane-mayer>

Janeway, Michael. *Republic of Denial: Press, Politics, and Public Life*. New Haven, CT: Yale University Press, 1999.

Jarvis, Jeff. 'About Me & Disclosures'. BuzzMachine, 4 July 2005. <https://buzzmachine.com/about/>

Jones, Tom. 'Times' David Barstow ties record for most Pulitzers'. Poynter, 15 April 2019. <https://www.poynter.org/reporting-editing/2019/davidbarstowpulitzer/>

'J-School Grads Awarded 4 of 14 Pulitzer Prizes'. *Columbia University Record*, Vol. 20 No. 26, 28 April 1995. <http://www.columbia.edu/cu/record/archives/vol20/vol20_iss26/record2026.18.html>

Kamm, Oliver. 'Big voice, too many false notes'. *The Times*, 20 September 2006. <https://www.thetimes.co.uk/article/big-voice-too-many-false-notes-g2k2zqqxlhg>

'Kelvin MacKenzie'. Statement and pieces of evidence. Discover Leveson, January 2012. <https://www.discoverleveson.com/witness/Kelvin_MacKenzie/3968/?bc=10>

Klein, Julia M. 'Judith Miller tells her side of *The Story*'. *Columbia Journalism Review*, 22 April 2015. <https://www.cjr.org/analysis/miller_review.php>

Koliska, Michael and Karin Assmann. 'Lügenpresse: The lying press and German journalists' responses to a stigma'. *Journalism*, 11 December 2019. <https://journals.sagepub.com/doi/abs/10.1177/1464884919894088?journalCode=>

Kovach, Bill and Tom Rosenstiel. *The Elements of Journalism: What Newspeople Should Know and the Public Should Expect*. Revised and updated edition. New York: Three Rivers Press, 2014.

Lamb, Larry. *Sunrise*. London: Macmillan, 1989.

Langmuir, Molly. 'What's Next For *New Yorker* Reporter Jane Mayer?' *Elle*, 27 February 2019. <https://www.elle.com/culture/a26537529/jane-mayer-new-yorker-interview-kavanaugh/>

Leigh, David. 'Secrets of the Masters: "Be Prepared To Be Disliked"'. International Consortium of Investigative Journalists blog, 18 December 2012. <https://www.icij.org/blog/2012/12/be-prepared-be-disliked/>

Leigh, David and Garry Blight. 'Offshore secrets: UK property purchases – interactive map'. *The Guardian*, 26 November 2012. <http://www.theguardian.com/uk/interactive/2012/nov/26/offshore-secrets-uk-property-purchases-interactive-map>

Leiserowitz, A., E. Maibach, C. Roser-Renouf, N. Smith and E. Dawson. 'Climategate, Public Opinion, and the Loss of Trust'. *American Behavioral Scientist*, 13 September 2012. <https://climatecommunication.yale.edu/publications/climategate-public-opinion-and-the-loss-of-trust/>

Lemon, Jason. 'Over 70% of Americans Prefer a National Quarantine as Trump Eyes Lifting Restrictions by Easter, Poll Shows'. *Newsweek*, 25 March 2020. <https://www.newsweek.com/over-70-americans-prefer-national-quarantine-trump-eyes-lifting-restrictions-easter-pollshows-1494174>

Leopold, Jason, Emma Loop, Zoe Tillman, Anthony Cormier and Ellie Hall. 'The Mueller Report's Secret Memos'. BuzzFeed News, 2 November 2019. <https://www.buzzfeednews.com/article/jasonleopold/mueller-report-secret-memos-1>

Lippmann, Walter. *Public Opinion*. Reissue edition. New York: Free Press, 1997.

Liptak, Adam. 'Reporter Jailed After Refusing to Name Source'. *The New York Times*, 7 July 2005. <https://www.nytimes.com/2005/07/07/politics/reporter-jailed-after-refusing-to-name-source.html>

Loader, Brian D. and Dan Mercea. 'Networking Democracy?' *Information,*

Communication & Society, Vol. 14 Issue 6, August 2011. <https://doi.org/10.1080/1369118X.2011.592648>

Lutzke, Lauren, Caitlin Drummond, Paul Slovic and Joseph Árvai. 'Priming critical thinking: Simple interventions limit the influence of fake news about climate change on Facebook'. *Global Environmental Change*, Vol. 58, September 2019. <https://doi.org/10.1016/j.gloenvcha.2019.101964>

MacKenzie, Kelvin. 'I've changed. I now believe Britain needs migrants'. *The Guardian*, 24 March 2015. <https://www.theguardian.com/commentisfree/2015/mar/24/britain-needs-migrants-sun-editor-kelvin-mackenzie>

Mackie, Kyle S. '"Your story is in the textbooks. Ours isn't." Buffalo schools adopt The 1619 Project'. Buffalo: WBFO-NPR, 17 January 2020. <https://news.wbfo.org/post/your-story-textbooks-ours-isn-t-buffalo-schools-adopt-1619-project>

MacMath, Terence Handley. 'Interview: Emily Dugan, journalist'. *Church Times*, 18 September 2015. <https://www.churchtimes.co.uk/articles/2015/18-september/features/interviews/interview-emily-dugan-journalist>

'Maggie Haberman'. Longform podcast, #254, 26 July 2017. <https://longform.org/posts/longform-podcast-254-maggie-haberman>

Maier, Scott R. 'Accuracy Matters: A Cross-Market Assessment of Newspaper Error and Credibility'. *Journalism & Mass Communication Quarterly*, Vol. 82 Issue 3, September 2005. <https://doi.org/10.1177/107769900508200304>

Mair, John, Tor Clark and Neil Fowler (eds). *Brexit, Trump and the Media*. Bury St Edmunds: Abramis, 2017.

Maity, Suman Kalyan, Aishik Chakraborty, Pawan Goyal and Animesh Mukherjee. 'Detection of Sockpuppets in Social Media'. *CSCW '17 Companion*, February 2017. <https://doi.org/10.1145/3022198.3026360>

Marriage, Madison. 'Men Only: Inside the charity fundraiser where hostesses are put on show'. *The Financial Times*, 23 January 2018. <https://www.ft.com/content/075d679e-0033-11e8-9650-9c0ad2d7c5b5>

Marriage, Madison. 'Madison Marriage: "The Presidents Club Dinner Was Grotesque"'. *Marie Claire*, 7 March 2018. <https://www.marie-claire.co.uk/life/work/madison-marriage-presidents-club-583371>

Marriage, Madison. 'Presidents Club trustees criticised by UK charity regulator'. *The Financial Times*, 12 July 2018. <https://www.ft.com/content/d17623b6-85cd-11e8-96dd-fa565ec55929>

Marriage, Madison and Lizzie Cernik. 'FT investigation: The darker side of a British tech baron'. *The Financial Times*, 23 October 2019. <https://www.ft.com/content/afffb542-f577-11e9-b018-3ef8794b17c6>

Marriage, Madison and Matthew Garrahan. 'Martin Sorrell's downfall: Why the ad king left WPP'. *The Financial Times*, 11 June 2018. <https://www.ft.com/content/617147b4-6cda-11e8-852d-d8b934ff5ffa>

Martin, Iain. 'One word in defence of Andrea Leadsom'. Reaction, 9 July 2016. <https://reaction.life/one-word-defence-andrea-leadsom/>

Martinson, Jane. 'How Metro became the most read paper in Britain'. *Prospect*, 20 August 2018. <https://www.prospectmagazine.co.uk/magazine/how-metro-became-the-most-read-paper-in-britain>

Massing, Michael. 'Now They Tell Us'. *The New York Review of Books*, 26 February 2004. <https://www.nybooks.com/articles/2004/02/26/now-they-tell-us/>

Massing, Michael. 'Breaking News: Seymour Hersh and the ambiguities of investigative reporting'. *The Nation*, 27 September 2018. <https://www.thenation.com/article/archive/seymour-hersh-reporter/>

Mayhew, Freddy. 'Times titles win big at Society of Editors' Press Awards'. *Press Gazette*, 3 April 2019. https://www.pressgazette.co.uk/times-titles-win-big-at-society-of-editors-press-awards/.

Mayhew, Freddy. 'Buzzfeed's Emily Dugan wins Private Eye Paul Foot Award 2019 for reports exposing 'broken legal system'' *Press Gazette*, 19 June 2019. <https://www.pressgazette.co.uk/buzzfeeds-emily-dugan-wins-private-eye-paul-foot-award-2019-for-reports-exposing-broken-legal-system/>

McDermott, Terry. 'Review: Judith Miller's "The Story: A Reporter's Journey"'. *The New York Times*, 7 April 2015. <https://www.nytimes.com/2015/04/08/books/review-judith-millers-the-story-a-reporters-journey.html>

McGill, Andrew. 'U.S. Media's Real Elitism Problem'. *The Atlantic*, 19 November 2016. <https://www.theatlantic.com/politics/archive/2016/11/fixing-americas-nearsighted-press-corps/508088/>

McKibben, Bill. 'Is covering climate change going to be ultimate test of the value of journalism?' presented at the 'Journalism is Dead: Long Live Journalism' conference, Denver, Colorado, 3 April 2013. <http://newshare.com/jtm-denver/mckibben.pdf>

McQuire, Amy. 'John Pilger on "Utopia", Objectivity, and the State of

Australian Indigenous Affairs'.Vice, 26 August 2014. <https://www.vice.com/en_us/article/vdpxva/john-pilger-on-utopia-%0Aobjectivity-and-the-state-of-australian-indigenous-affairs>

Meares, Joel. 'Q&A: Politico's Maggie Haberman'. *Columbia Journalism Review,* 2 September 2010. <https://www.cjr.org/campaign_desk/q_a_politicos_maggie_haberman.php>

Media Lens. 'Advertising Makes A Mockery Of Press Freedom'. 19 October 2001. <https://www.medialens.org/2001/advertising-makes-a-mockery-of-press-freedom/>

Meyer, Philip. *The Vanishing Newspaper: Saving Journalism in the Information Age.* Columbia, MO: University of Missouri Press, 2004.

Miller, Judith. 'A Nation Challenged: The Letter; Fear Hits Newsroom In a Cloud of Powder'. *The New York Times,* 14 October 2001. <https://www.nytimes.com/2001/10/14/us/a-nation-challenged-the-letter-fear-hits-newsroom-in-a-cloud-of-powder.html>

Miller, Judith. 'The Iraq War and Stubborn Myths'. *The Wall Street Journal,* 3 April 2015. <https://www.wsj.com/articles/the-iraq-war-and-stubborn-myths-1428087215>

Mina, An Xiao. 'The Death of Consensus, Not the Death of Truth'. NiemanLab Predictions for Journalism 2019, December 2018. <https://www.niemanlab.org/2018/12/the-death-of-consensus-not-the-death-of-truth/>

Mitchell, Bill. 'Journalists Are More Likely to Be College Graduates'. Poynter, 6 April 2003. <https://www.poynter.org/archive/2003/journalists-are-more-likely-to-be-college-graduates/>

Molyneux, Logan. 'Mobile News Consumption'. *Digital Journalism,* Vol. 6 Issue 5, 2018. <https://doi.org/10.1080/21670811.2017.1334567>

Monbiot, George. 'Registry of Interests'. Monbiot.com, n.d. <https://www.monbiot.com/registry-of-interests/>

Monck, Adrian with Mike Hanley. *Can You Trust the Media?* London: Icon Books, 2008.

Montanaro, Domenico. 'Poll: Americans Don't Trust What They're Hearing From Trump On Coronavirus'. NPR Special Series: The Coronvirus Crisis, 17 March 2020. <https://www.npr.org/2020/03/17/816680033/poll-americans-dont-trust-what-they-re-hearing-from-trump-on-coronavirus>

Morello, Lauren. '"Climategate" Scientist Admits "Awful E-Mails," but

Peers Say IPCC Conclusions Remain Sound'. *The New York Times*, 2 March 2010. <https://archive.nytimes.com/www.nytimes.com/cwire/2010/03/02/02climatewire-climategate-scientist-admits-awful-e-mails-b-66224.html?pagewanted=1>

Mullin, Chris. 'We'll All Be Murdered in Our Beds: The Shocking History of Crime Reporting in Britain by Duncan Campbell – review'. *The Observer*, 23 May 2016. <https://www.theguardian.com/books/2016/may/23/all-be-murdered-beds-shocking-history-crime-reporting-britain-duncan-campbell-review>

Murgia, Madhumita. 'How data brokers sell your identity'. TEDxExeter, April 2017. <https://www.ted.com/talks/madhumita_murgia_how_data_brokers_sell_your_identity>

Murphy, James E. 'The New Journalism: A Critical Perspective. Journalism Monographs, No. 34'. *Association for Education in Journalism*, May 1974.

The New York Times. '1992 Pulitzer Prize Winners and Their Works in Journalism and the Arts'. 8 April 1992. <https://www.nytimes.com/1992/04/08/nyregion/1992-pulitzer-prize-winners-and-their-works-in-journalism-and-the-arts.html>

The New York Times. 'Best Sellers: November 4, 2001'. 4 November 2001. <https://www.nytimes.com/2001/11/04/books/best-sellers-november-4-2001.html>

Newman, Nic and Richard Fletcher. 'Bias, Bullshit and Lies: Audience Perspectives on Low Trust in the Media'. Digital News Project: Reuters Institute for the Study of Journalism, 2017. <https://reutersinstitute.politics.ox.ac.uk/our-research/bias-bullshit-and-lies-audience-perspectives-low-trust-media>

Nielsen, Rasmus Kleis and Lucas Graves. '"News you don't believe": Audience perspectives on fake news'. Reuters Institute for the Study of Journalism, October 2017. <https://reutersinstitute.politics.ox.ac.uk/our-research/news-you-dont-believe-audience-perspectives-fake-news>

Norris, Michele and Melissa Block. 'Former Death Row Inmate Freed In Texas'. *All Things Considered*, NPR, 28 October 2010. <https://www.npr.org/templates/story/story.php?storyId=130895436>

Oborne, Peter. 'Why I have resigned from the Telegraph'. OpenDemocracy, 17 February 2015. <https://www.opendemocracy.net/en/opendemocracyuk/why-i-have-resigned-from-telegraph/>

O'Neill, Sean. 'Sean O'Neill on the problems with his cancer treatment'.

The Times, 12 May 2018. <https://www.thetimes.co.uk/article/sean-oneill-on-the-problems-with-his-cancer-treatment-70535qvxv>

O'Neill, Sean 'NHS scraps restrictions on life-changing leukaemia drug ibrutinib'. *The Times*, 10 August 2018. <https://www.thetimes.co.uk/article/nhs-scraps-restrictions-on-life-changing-leukaemia-drug-ibrutinib-r20z3mx3j>

O'Neill, Sean. 'Aid charities urged to join scheme that vets sex predators'. *The Times*, 25 February 2020. <https://www.thetimes.co.uk/article/aid-charities-urged-to-join-scheme-that-vets-sex-predators-pmv83fp2r>

Ooker. 'What is the difference between "skeptical" and "cynical"?' StackExchange: English Language & Usage (blog). <https://english.stackexchange.com/posts/293559/revisions>

The Orwell Foundation. '2019 Exposing Britain's Social Evils Prize Short List'. OrwellFoundation.com, 2019. <https://www.orwellfoundation.com/investigative/madison-marriage/>

Orwell, George. *The Collected Essays, Journalism and Letters of George Orwell, Volume 4: In Front of Your Nose 1945–1950*. Harmondsworth: Penguin, 1970.

Osborne, Martin. '5 reasons why a Green New Deal and Universal Basic Income go hand in hand'. Bright Green (blog), 10 October 2019. <http://bright-green.org/2019/10/10/5-reasons-why-a-green-new-deal-and-basic-income-go-hand-in-hand/>

Papacharissi, Zizi. 'The virtual sphere: The internet as a public sphere'. *New Media & Society*, 1 February 2002. <https://doi.org/10.1177/14614440222226244>

Pappu, Sridhar. 'Off the Record'. Observer, 28 April 2003. <https://observer.com/2003/04/off-the-record-35/>

Parrella, Gilda C. 'Consensus-Building Journalism: An Immodest Proposal'. Nieman Reports, 9 September 2011. <https://niemanreports.org/articles/consensus-building-journalism-an-immodest-proposal/>

Payne, Sebastian. 'How Leave won: behind the scenes in the battle for Brexit'. *The Financial Times*, 11 November 2016. <https://www.ft.com/content/18211880-a5e1-11e6-8b69-02899e8bd9d1>

Pearce, Fred. '"Climategate" was "a game-changer" in science reporting, say climatologists'. *The Guardian*, 4 July 2010. <https://www.theguardian.com/environment/2010/jul/04/climatechange-hacked-emails-muir-russell>

Peppiatt, Richard. 'Richard Peppiatt's letter to Daily Star proprietor Richard Desmond'. *The Guardian*, 4 March 2011. <https://www.theguardian.com/media/2011/mar/04/daily-star-reporter-letter-full>

Phil Williamson. 'Two views of ocean acidification – which is fatally flawed?' Marine Biological Association, 2016. <https://www.mba.ac.uk/two-views-ocean-acidification-which-fatally-flawed>

Philp, Catherine and Richard Spencer. 'Critics leap on reporter Robert Fisk's failure to find signs of gas attack'. *The Times*, 18 April 2018. <https://www.thetimes.co.uk/article/critics-leap-on-reporter-robert-fisk-s-failure-to-find-signs-of-gas-attack-fx7f3fs2r>

Pickard, Victor. 'Take the profit motive out of news'. *The Guardian*, 23 July 2009. <https://www.theguardian.com/commentisfree/cifamerica/2009/jul/23/newspapers-internet-adverstising>

Pilger, John. 'War by media and the triumph of propaganda'. JohnPilger. Com, 5 December 2014. <http://johnpilger.com/articles/war-by-media-and-the-triumph-of-propaganda>

Plunkett, John. 'BBC names David Shukman as first science editor'. *The Guardian*, 16 January 2012. <https://www.theguardian.com/media/2012/jan/16/bbc-david-shukman-science-editor>

Pomerantsev, Peter. *This Is Not Propaganda: Adventures in the War Against Reality*. London: Faber & Faber, 2019.

Pompeo, Joe. 'Is Trump-Whisperer Maggie Haberman Changing *The New York Times*?' *Vanity Fair*, 5 October 2017. <https://www.vanityfair.com/news/2017/10/is-trump-whisperer-maggie-haberman-changing-the-new-york-times>

Poniewozik, James. 'Roger Ailes Fused TV With Politics, Changing Both'. *The New York Times*, 21 July 2016. <https://www.nytimes.com/2016/07/22/arts/television/roger-ailes-out-fox-news.html>

Ponsford, Dominic. 'Metro Editor Ted Young warns of 'lemming-like rush' to digital away from newspapers'. *Press Gazette*, 10 October 2017. <https://www.pressgazette.co.uk/metro-editor-ted-young-warns-of-lemming-like-rush-to-digital-away-from-newspapers/>

Press Gazette. 'Rachel Sylvester of The Times "thrilled to be vindicated" at British Journalism Awards after Leadsom "gutter journalism" jibe'. 9 December 2016. <https://www.awards.pressgazette.co.uk/2016/12/09/rachel-sylvester-of-the-times-thrilled-to-be-vindicated-at-british-journalism-awards-after-leadsom-gutter-journalism-jibe/>

Price, Lance. *Where Power Lies: Prime Ministers v the Media*. London: Simon & Schuster, 2010.

Pugh, Martin. *'Hurrah for the Blackshirts!': Fascists and Fascism in Britain Between the Wars*. London: Pimlico, 2005.

Purnell, Sonia. *Just Boris: A Tale of Blond Ambition - A Biography of Boris Johnson*. London: Aurum Press, 2012.

Rafsky, Sara. 'In government-media fight, Argentine journalism suffers'. Committee to Protect Journalists, 27 September 2012. <https://cpj.org/reports/2012/09/amid-government-media-fight-argentine-journalism-suffers.php>

Rafsky, Sara. 'Media Mecca or News Desert? Covering local news in New York City'. *Columbia Journalism Review*, 7 January 2020. <https://www.cjr.org/tow_center_reports/local-news-deserts.php/>

Randall, Mike. *The Funny Side of the Street*. First edition. London: Bloomsbury, 1988.

Readfearn, Graham. 'Rupert Murdoch says "there are no climate change deniers around" News Corp'. *The Guardian*, 21 November 2019. <https://www.theguardian.com/media/2019/nov/21/news-corps-rupert-murdoch-says-there-are-no-climate-change-deniers-around-here>

Rheingold, Howard. 'Crap Detection 101'. *San Francisco Chronicle*, 30 June 2009. <http://blog.sfgate.com/rheingold/2009/06/30/crap-detection-101/>

'Robert Fisk Makes Things Up'. Harry's Place blog, 23 March 2012. <http://hurryupharry.org/2012/03/23/robert-fisk-makes-things-up/>

Roberts, David. 'Donald Trump and the rise of tribal epistemology'. Vox, 19 May 2017. <https://www.vox.com/policy-and-politics/2017/3/22/14762030/donald-trump-tribal-epistemology>

Roberts, David. 'America is facing an epistemic crisis'. Vox, 2 November 2017. <https://www.vox.com/policy-and-politics/2017/11/2/16588964/america-epistemic-crisis>

Rodriguez, Ashley. 'How a single deal with a decidedly unhip tech company built the Vice media behemoth'. Quartz, 8 September 2016. <https://qz.com/776628/shane-smith-how-a-single-native-advertising-deal-with-intel-intc-built-the-vice-media-behemoth/>

Rosen, Jay. 'The View from Nowhere: Questions and Answers'. PressThink blog, 10 November 2010. <https://pressthink.org/2010/11/the-view-from-nowhere-questions-and-answers/>

Rosen, Jay. 'Prospects for the American press under Trump, part two'. PressThink blog, 30 December 2016. <https://pressthink.org/2016/12/prospects-american-press-trump-part-two/>

Rosen, Jay. 'Responsible parties at the New York Times explain to the country what went wrong with Times journalism in the election of 2016. Part Two.'. *PressThink* (blog). 5 February 2020. <https://pressthink.org/2020/02/responsible-parties-at-the-new-york-times-explain-to-the-country-what-went-wrong-with-times-journalism-in-the-election-of-2016-part-two/>

Rosen, Jay. 'The Citizens Agenda in Campaign Coverage'. *PressThink* blog, 15 August 2010. <http://archive.pressthink.org/>

Rosin, Hanna. 'Hello, My Name Is Stephen Glass, and I'm Sorry'. *The New Republic*, 11 November 2014. <https://newrepublic.com/article/120145/stephen-glass-new-republic-scandal-still-haunts-his-law-career>

Rusbridger, Alan. 'Down among the press lords'. *London Review of Books*, 3 March 1983. <https://www.lrb.co.uk/the-paper/v05/n04/alan-rusbridger/down-among-the-press-lords>

Rusbridger, Alan. 'Seymour M. Hersh – the Journalist as Lone Wolf'. *The New York Times*, 13 June 2018. <https://www.nytimes.com/2018/06/13/books/review/seymour-m-hersh-reporter.html>

'Russ Buettner'. *The New York Times*, n.d. <https://www.nytimes.com/by/russ-buettner>

Saisho, Reiko. 'Speed vs Accuracy in Time of Crisis'. Journalist Fellows' Papers, Reuters Institute for the Study of Journalism, 2015. <https://reutersinstitute.politics.ox.ac.uk/our-research/speed-vs-accuracy-time-crisis>

Schmid-Petri, Hannah, Silke Adam, Ivo Schmucki and Thomas Häussler. 'A changing climate of skepticism: The factors shaping climate change coverage in the US press'. *Public Understanding of Science*, Vol. 26 Issue 4, 9 November 2015. <https://doi.org/10.1177/0963662515612276>

Schmidt, Christine. 'Can 5,000 strangers have a productive Facebook dialogue? Spaceship Media is about to try'. NiemanLab, 7 December 2017. <https://www.niemanlab.org/2017/12/can-5000-strangers-have-a-productive-facebook-dialogue-spaceship-media-is-about-to-try/>

Schudson, Michael. *Why Democracies Need an Unlovable Press*. Cambridge, UK and Malden, MA: Polity Press, 2008.

Segura, Melissa. 'A Chicago Cop Is Accused Of Framing 51 People For

Murder. Now, The Fight For Justice'. BuzzFeed News, 4 April 2017. <https://www.buzzfeednews.com/article/melissasegura/detective-guevaras-witnesses>

Segura, Melissa and Mike Hayes. 'Murder Convictions Overturned, Two Men Are Immediately Seized By ICE'. BuzzFeed News, 22 December 2017. <https://www.buzzfeednews.com/article/mikehayes/prosecutors-tossed-their-murder-convictions-so-ice-seized>

Serwer, Adam. 'The Fight Over the 1619 Project Is Not About the Facts'. *The Atlantic*, 23 December 2019. <https://www.theatlantic.com/ideas/archive/2019/12/historians-clash-1619-project/604093/>

Shafer, Jack. 'How the byline beast was born'. Reuters blog, 6 July 2012. <http://blogs.reuters.com/jackshafer/2012/07/06/how-the-byline-beast-was-born/>

Shafer, Jack. 'The Real Problem with Judith Miller'. Politico Magazine, 10 April 2015. <https://www.politico.com/magazine/story/2015/04/judy-miller-book-nytimes-116869.html>

Shipman, Tim. 'Cabinet coup to ditch Theresa May for emergency PM'. *The Sunday Times*, 24 March 2019. <https://www.thetimes.co.uk/article/cabinet-coup-to-ditch-theresa-may-for-emergency-pm-t7xndp0x2>

Shirky, Clay. *Here Comes Everybody: How Change Happens When People Come Together*. New York: Penguin, 2009.

Shirky, Clay. 'Newspapers and Thinking the Unthinkable.' *Risk Management*, Vol. 56 Issue 4, May 2009. <https://go.gale.com/ps/anonymous?id=GALE%7CA200184027&sid=googleScholar&v=2.1&it=r&linkaccess=abs&issn=00355593&p=AONE&sw=w>

Shorten, Kristin. 'Looking through a royal lens with Arthur Edwards'. News.Com.Au, 12 April 2014. <https://www.news.com.au/entertainment/celebrity-life/looking-through-a-royal-lens-with-arthur-edwards/news-story/7e20cc778f384f5ff001ca6de5b7191d#.vln70>

Silverman, Craig. *Regret the Error: How Media Mistakes Pollute the Press and Imperil Free Speech*. New York: Union Square Press, 2007.

Small, Mike. 'IPCC Report: British Press Focus on Snog over Smog as Scientists Warn of Climate Crisis'. DeSmog UK, 9 October 2018. <https://www.desmog.co.uk/2018/10/09/comment-media-responses-ipcc-are-part-problem>

Smith, Anthony. *The Politics of Information: Problems of Policy in Modern Media*. London: Macmillan, 1978.

Smith, Ben. 'How We Characterized Michael Cohen's Testimony'. BuzzFeed News, 18 April 2019. <https://www.buzzfeednews.com/article/bensmith/how-we-characterized-michael-cohens-testimony>

Smith, Ben. 'Rupert Murdoch Put His Son in Charge of Fox. It Was a Dangerous Mistake'. *The New York Times*, 22 March 2020. <https://www.nytimes.com/2020/03/22/business/coronavirus-fox-news-lachlan-murdoch.html>

Snow, Jon. 'The Best and Worst of Times'. MacTaggart Lecture presented at the Edinburgh TV Festival, 23 August 2017. <https://www.channel4.com/news/by/jon-snow/blogs/mactaggart-lecture-edinburgh-2017>

Solomos, John. *Race and Racism in Britain*. Third edition. Basingstoke: Palgrave Macmillan, 2003.

Sparrow, Andrew. 'Running the Guardian's politics blog: "We've never had so many readers"' *The Guardian*, 20 July 2019. <https://www.theguardian.com/politics/blog/2019/jul/20/politics-live-blog-andrew-sparrow>

Stelter, Brian. 'Debunkers of Fictions Sift the Net'. *The New York Times*, 4 April 2010. <https://www.nytimes.com/2010/04/05/technology/05snopes.html>

Stelter, Brian. 'How the shocking hot mic tape of Donald Trump was exposed'. Money.CNN.com, 7 October 2016. <https://money.cnn.com/2016/10/07/media/access-hollywood-donald-trump-tape/index.html>

Stoppard, Tom. *Night and Day*. Reprint edition. New York: Black Cat, 2018.

Stray, Jonathan. 'Why link out? Four journalistic purposes of the noble hyperlink'. NiemanLab, 8 June 2010. <https://www.niemanlab.org/2010/06/why-link-out-four-journalistic-purposes-of-the-noble-hyperlink/>

Suciu, Peter. 'More Americans Are Getting Their News From Social Media'. *Forbes*, 11 October 2019. <https://www.forbes.com/sites/petersuciu/2019/10/11/more-americans-are-getting-their-news-from-social-media/#3cd7038a3e17>

Suellentrop, Chris. 'Sy Hersh Says It's Okay to Lie (Just Not in Print)'. *New York Magazine*, 8 April 2005. <https://nymag.com/nymetro/news/people/features/11719/>

Sultan, Kamal. 'News Associates Presents JournoFest 2019: In Conversation with the Times Chief Reporter Sean O'Neill'. News Associates, 15

April 2019. <https://newsassociates.co.uk/news-associates-presents-journofest-2019-in-conversation-with-the-times-chief-reporter-sean-oneill/>

'Susanne Craig'. *The New York Times*, n.d. <https://www.nytimes.com/by/susanne-craig>

Terkel, Amanda. 'Fox News Hires Disgraced Reporter Judith Miller'. ThinkProgress, 20 October 2008. <https://archive.thinkprogress.org/fox-news-hires-disgraced-reporter-judith-miller-dfe2fbba2b95/>

Tetlock, Philip E. *Expert Political Judgment: How Good Is It? How Can We Know?* Revised edition. Princeton, NJ: Princeton University Press, 2013.

Thielman, Sam. 'Despite backlash, Jason Leopold stands by his story'. *Columbia Journalism Review*, 20 February 2019. <https://www.cjr.org/tow_center/jason-leopold-buzzfeed-cohen.php>

Thompson, Mark. *Enough Said: What's Gone Wrong with the Language of Politics?* New York: The Bodley Head, 2016.

Thurman, Neil, Alessio Cornia and Jessica Kunert. 'Journalists in the UK'. Reuters Institute for the Study of Journalism, 2016. <https://reutersinstitute.politics.ox.ac.uk/our-research/journalists-uk>

Tiku, Nitasha. 'Julian Assange Picks a Media Fight With the *Guardian*'. *New York Magazine*, 21 December 2010. <https://nymag.com/intelligencer/2010/12/julian_assange_picks_a_media.html>

The Times. 'The Times view on the press under coronavirus'. 4 April 2020. <https://www.thetimes.co.uk/article/the-times-view-on-the-press-under-coronavirus-7cvfk36vl>

Timm, Trevor. 'The media's reaction to Seymour Hersh's bin Laden scoop has been disgraceful'. *Columbia Journalism Review*, 15 May 2015. <https://www.cjr.org/analysis/seymour_hersh_osama_bin_laden.php>

Tobitt, Charlotte. '"Cancer battle freed me up to work on Oxfam scoop and stumble into NHS drugs story", says Times reporter Sean O'Neill'. *Press Gazette*, 20 August 2018. <https://www.pressgazette.co.uk/cancer-battle-freed-me-up-to-work-on-oxfam-scoop-and-stumble-into-nhs-drugs-story-says-times-reporter-sean-oneill/>

Tokmetzis, Dimitri. 'Help wanted for security industry investigation'. The Correspondent, 3 April 2016. <https://thecorrespondent.com/4274/help-wanted-for-security-industry-investigation/208130978-b312e43c>

Turnbull, Malcolm. *A Bigger Picture*. London: Hardie Grant, 2020.

Turvill, William. 'Investigative journalist David Leigh retires after 30 years with The Guardian'. *Press Gazette*, 15 April 2013. <https://www.pressgazette.co.uk/investigative-journalist-david-leigh-retires-after-30-years-guardian/>

Uberti, David. 'The future of the #SlatePitch in Trump's world'. *Columbia Journalism Review*, 16 January 2019. <https://www.cjr.org/analysis/slate-magazine-podcast-trump-staff-departures.php>

University of Sheffield. 'No evidence that public have "had enough of experts" study finds'. Phys.Org blog, 3 June 2019. <https://phys.org/news/2019-06-evidence-experts.html>

Vashi, Sonam. 'Between immigration authorities and the people they target'. *Columbia Journalism Review*, 22 August 2019. <https://www.cjr.org/united_states_project/atlanta-immigration-ice-viral-guevara.php>

Venkataramanan, Madhumita. 'Madhumita Venkataramanan: My identity for sale'. *Wired*, 30 October 2014. <https://www.wired.co.uk/article/my-identity-for-sale>

Vernon, Pete. 'Dancing around the word "Racist" in coverage of Trump'. *Columbia Journalism Review*, 25 September 2017. <https://www.cjr.org/politics/trump-racism.php>

Vernon, Pete. 'Lie? Falsehood? What to call the president's words'. *Columbia Journalism Review*, 29 May 2018. <https://www.cjr.org/the_media_today/trump-lie-falsehood.php>

Victor, Daniel. 'New York Times Will Offer Employee Buyouts and Eliminate Public Editor Role'. *The New York Times*, 31 May 2017. <https://www.nytimes.com/2017/05/31/business/media/new-york-times-buyouts.html>

Villanueva, Kristine. 'Q&A: Hamed Aleaziz on the Connection between the DOJ and a White Nationalist Blog'. Center for Public Integrity blog, 6 September 2019. <https://publicintegrity.org/inside-publici/watchdog-q-a/qa-hamed-aleaziz-on-the-connection-between-the-doj-and-a-white-nationalist-blog/>

Vinsel, Lee and Benjamin C. Waterhouse. 'One upside of the pandemic? Americans are listening to experts again'. *The Washington Post*, 6 April 2020. <https://www.washingtonpost.com/outlook/2020/04/06/one-upside-pandemic-americans-are-listening-experts-again/>

Waldman, Scott. 'Facebook fact checker has ties to news outlet that promotes climate doubt'. *Science.Magazine*, 25 April 2019. <https://

www.sciencemag.org/news/2019/04/facebook-fact-checker-has-ties-news-outlet-promotes-climate-doubt>

Waldrop, Theresa, Dave Alsup and Eliott C. McLaughlin. 'Fearing coronavirus, Arizona man dies after taking a form of chloroquine used to treat aquariums'. CNN, 25 March 2020. <https://www.cnn.com/2020/03/23/health/arizona-coronavirus-chloroquine-death/index.html>

Walker, Hunter. 'Sarah Palin defends Donald Trump: "WTH, LAMESTREAM MEDIA!"'. *Business Insider*, 28 August 2015. <https://www.businessinsider.com/sarah-palin-defends-donald-trump-on-bible-question-2015-8>

Walker, James. 'Ministry of Justice staff called Buzzfeed UK reporter "bitch" and "crazy" in internal messages after leaked report story'. *Press Gazette*, 7 January 2019 <https://www.pressgazette.co.uk/ministry-of-justice-staff-called-buzzfeed-uk-reporter-bitch-and-crazy-in-internal-messages-after-leaked-report-story/>

Ward, Bob. 'Fundamental flaw in Press watchdog's complaints process helps newspapers to promote climate change denial'. LSE Grantham Research Institute on Climate Change and the Environment blog, 24 January 2019. <http://www.lse.ac.uk/GranthamInstitute/news/fundamental-flaw-in-press-watchdogs-complaints-process-helps-newspapers-to-promote-climate-change-denial/>

Ward, Bob. '"The Mail on Sunday" admits publishing more fake news about climate change'. LSE Grantham Research Institute on Climate Change and the Environment blog, 22 April 2018. <http://www.lse.ac.uk/GranthamInstitute/news/the-mail-on-sunday-admits-publishing-more-fake-news-about-climate-change/>

Wardle, Claire. 'Fake news. It's complicated'. First Draft, 16 February 2017. <https://medium.com/1st-draft/fake-news-its-complicated-d0f773766c79>

Wardle, Claire and Hossein Derakhshan. 'Information disorder: Toward an interdisciplinary framework for research and policy making'. Council of Europe, 2017. <https://edoc.coe.int/en/media/7495-information-disorder-toward-an-interdisciplinary-framework-for-research-and-policy-making.html>

Warren, James. 'Bloomberg gets its first Pulitzer'. Poynter, 20 April 2015. <https://www.poynter.org/reporting-editing/2015/bloomberg-gets-its-first-pulitzer/>

Waterhouse, Keith. *Waterhouse on Newspaper Style.* Third revised edition. Brighton: Revel Barker, 2010.

Waugh, Evelyn. *Scoop.* London: Chapman & Hall, 1938.

Wemple, Erik. 2015. 'Maggie Haberman leaves huge hole at Politico, moves to New York Times'. *The Washington Post,* 9 January 2015. <https://www.washingtonpost.com/blogs/erik-wemple/wp/2015/01/09/maggie-haberman-leaves-huge-hole-at-politico-moves-to-new-york-times/>

Wilhite, David. 'Susanne Craig provides a look into The New York Times' Trump tax exposé – SABEW 19'. Society for Advancing Business Editing and Writing blog, 19 May 2019. <https://sabew.org/2019/05/susanne-craig-provides-a-look-into-the-new-york-times-trump-tax-expose/>

Williams, Francis. *Dangerous Estate: The Anatomy of Newspapers.* First edition. London: Longmans, Green, 1957.

Williams, Martin. 'Two Guardian journalists win Orwell prize for journalism'. *The Guardian,* 21 May 2014. <https://www.theguardian.com/books/2014/may/21/guardian-journalists-jonathan-freedland-ghaith-abdul-ahad-win-orwell-prize-journalism>

Williams, Raymond. *Culture and Society, 1780–1950.* London: Chatto and Windus, 1958.

Winder, Robert. *Bloody Foreigners: The Story of Immigration to Britain.* London: Hachette, 2004.

Wittenberg, Dick. 'New to the Netherlands'. The Correspondent, n.d. <https://us6.campaign-archive.com/?u=8afce7db3ef-b3457925a48c26&id=5f04d706fb>

Wojdynski, Bartosz W. 'The Deceptiveness of Sponsored News Articles: How Readers Recognize and Perceive Native Advertising'. *American Behavioral Scientist, Vol.* 60 Issue 12, 2016. <https://doi.org/10.1177/0002764216660140>

Wolfe, Tom. *The New Journalism.* Reprints edition. London: Picador, 1990.

Wolff, Michael. *Fire and Fury: Inside the Trump White House.* First edition. New York: Henry Holt and Co., 2018.

Wynne, Brian. 'Creating Public Alienation: Expert Cultures of Risk and Ethics on GMOs'. *Science as Culture,* Vol. 10 No. 4, 2001. <https://www.tandfonline.com/doi/abs/10.1080/09505430120093586>

Acknowledgements

I'd like to thank Simon Thorogood at Canongate, for his quiet wisdom and patience; Alex Wade, for his legal mine-clearing skills; Lorraine McCann, for hawk-eyed editing; Anna Frame, for spreading the word; and my agent, Rebecca Carter.